D0553811

. . . mankind participated in this process of change and transformation, and all the other living beings upon earth, but also those which are divine, and by Zeus, even the four elements, which are changed and transformed upwards and downwards, as earth becomes water, and water, air, and air again is transformed into ether; and there is the same kind of transformation downwards. If a man endeavors to incline his mind to these things, and to persuade himself to accept of his own accord what needs must befall him, he will have a very reasonable and Mousikos (harmonious) life.

Epictetus

TRANS

A Memoir by Eleanor King

FORMA

The Humphrey-Weidman Era

TIONS

Library - St. Joseph's College
222 Clinton Avenue
Brooklyn, N. Y. 11205

Our thanks to the following for permission to reprint from articles and/or reviews which originally appeared in their publications: *The Daily World* (for reviews from *The Daily Worker*), *Dance Magazine*, *Dance News*, *Mademoiselle*, *The New York Times*, *The New Yorker*, *Variety*. Thanks also to Tom Borek for permission to quote from his article "On Doris Humphrey" from *Dance Scope*, Spring/Summer 1973; to John Houseman for permission to quote from his autobiography *Run-through*, Random House, 1972; to Mrs. Carlton Humphrey Palmer for permission to quote from *Theatrical Dancing in America*, Bernard Ackerman, 1945; to Arturo Vivant for permission to quote the lines from Lauro de Bosis's *Icaro*, translated by Ruth Draper, Oxford University Press, 1933; to Samuel French Inc. for the use of the excerpts from *The School for Husbands* by Arthur Guiterman and Lawrence Langner, 1933; to Prentice-Hall, Inc. for permission to quote from *Variety Music Cavalcade*, by Julius Mattfeld, 1971; and to Random House for permission to quote from Margaret Lloyd's *Borzoi Book of Modern Dance*, Alfred A. Knopf, Inc., 1949. Material from *The New York Times* © 1928/29/30/31/32/33/34/35 by The New York Times Company. Reprinted by permission.

Special thanks are offered to Barbara Morgan and Thomas Bouchard for permission to use their photographs.

Copyright © 1978 by Eleanor King

All rights reserved. No part of this book may be reproduced or utilized in any form or by any means, electronic or mechanical, including photocopying or recording, or by any information storage and retrieval system, without permission in writing from the Publisher.

ISBN 0-87127-100-1

Library of Congress Catalog Card Number 76-44682

Printed in the United States of America

Dance Horizons, 1801 East 26th Street, Brooklyn, N.Y. 11229

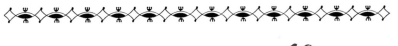

106693

CONTENTS

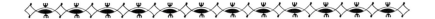

ILLUSTRATIONS

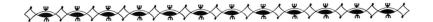

FOREWORD

MEMORY (that fickle girl), undated scrapbooks and letters provide the basis for this recording of the early days of the American modern dance by a dancer who experienced them.

The good will and untiring assistance of Genevieve Oswald, Curator of the Dance Collection at the Lincoln Center Museum and Library of the Performing Arts in New York, with the dedicated assistance of Andrew Wentink, Librarian in charge of the Humphrey Collection, made it possible for me to peruse Doris Humphrey's letters. For permission to quote from the source, I am profoundly grateful.

Reading Doris Humphrey's letters to her parents was an overwhelming experience. That she managed to create, in spite of the financial wants that plagued her, was a miracle of will. She lived for the art of the dance which she helped to establish in America.

Reliance on quotations from the press seems a justifiable indulgence in the case of John Martin, whose perceptive, insightful support in the columns of *The New York Times* created and educated an audience for the new forms. He was as much a creator as the artists about whom he wrote. Lists of program titles of dances from the thirties may seem an indulgence also, but even the titles reveal the import of what dancers were concerned about, their reason for taking the stage.

To support personal recollections I have attempted to reach colleagues of the early Humphrey-Weidman period. Selections from their comments shed further light on the experiences. For sharing reminiscences I am profoundly grateful to Louise Allen, Leon Arkus, George Bockman, Emily Hahn, Perkins Harnley, Letitia Ide, Gertrude Kurath, Ada Korvin-Kroukovsky, Paul Love, Hyla Rubin Samrock, Helen Savery Hungerford and Ernestine Stodelle Chamberlain.

Madeleine Gutman's generous letters about Mikhail Mordkin, with her permission to quote from them, is another debt I am happy to acknowledge.

The episodes concerning Ruth St. Denis are reprinted courtesy of *Dance Magazine*, February 1976, from an article entitled "Other Ruths." The chronology of the political, musical, and dramatic events of the times are from Julius Mattfeld's *Variety Music Calvacade, 1620– 1961*, Prentice-Hall, 3rd edition.

The Kabuki theatre in Japan has a traditional *Kojo* ceremony, which presents members of a professional dynastic family seated formally in a row on the stage. One by one, they pay their respects to their predecessors, pronouncing each name and defining the art which has made that name unique.

I proclaim Doris Humphrey and Charles Weidman, my teachers; Pauline Lawrence, genius behind the throne; and José Limón, fellow-dancer—four creators who shaped our American dance. To the memory of their gifts I offer these pages.

Santa Fe, 1976   Eleanor King

The gods have not returned. "They have never left us."
They have not returned.

Ezra Pound

Evelyn Feitelbaum, Cleo Atheneos, Sylvia Manning, Rose Yasgour, Celia Rausch in Air for the G String.

CHAPTER ONE: 1928

All Beginnings Are Difficult

THE CURTAIN was about to go up on the first concert of Doris Humphrey, Charles Weidman and pupils of the Denishawn School. The date was March 24, 1928. We were trying out at the Brooklyn Little Theatre, before a New York opening. Most of the dancers in the company had been dancing for years, like the leaders, but this was my first professional dance performance. I felt seasick.

We were called on stage for a few words of inspiration and encouragement from Doris. Then everyone cleared, except Celia Rausch, Rose (later Paula) Yasgour, Cleo Atheneos, Evelyn Fields, and Sylvia Manning, who had the honor of opening with Bach's *Air for the G String*. Grouped together down front, they stood with their backs to the audience. The curtain rose, the violins in the orchestra pit sounded, the dancers glided upstage, long silk trains unfolding behind them. With lifted chests and opened arms, they rose like waves, extending, bowing, greeting each other in Gothic curves and arches. We watched from the wings the prayerful aspiration designed by Miss Humphrey for Fra Angelican angels, as they invoked spiritual blessings with quiet simplicity and flowing lines.

Next, in a short red Greek tunic Doris danced, solo, the delightful triplets of a Bach gigue, hopping on one foot while her arms made arabesques about her body, a tour-de-force of quick rhythmic grace.

A rush to the dressing room for a final check while the set of six-paneled tall screens and a platform of steps were put in place on the stage. A reassuring glance at the dressing table with sprigs of

1

fresh iris attached to pairs of velvet-thonged Japanese slippers—a present from Doris to each of the ensemble. Then a return to the stage. Heart pounding, I took my place, end girl at the right side of a line of eight dancers, right arm raised, the other arm connecting at shoulder level to the chain we made, for the first movement of Grieg's *Piano Concerto in A Minor*. The stage lights came on, mercifully blinding me as the curtains lifted on a black void, a vast emptiness which we were about to fill with our dancing. The neophyte felt her soul x-rayed, transparent, exposed to the world.

Doris, in her black silk tunic, was lying face down, concealed in a red silk banner. On the opening chords (played by Louis Horst, with Pauline Lawrence at the second piano in the pit) she shot up in front of the group, all in cello-colored tunics. Doris was dancing the piano solo role; we represented the orchestral themes. Before her commanding gestures, our wall separated, withdrawing to the side, leaving the center free.

Doris moved into the space stating a theme of power, as if testing a bow for strength with strong oppositional pulls of her arms and deep successions through the body; then she enticed a group of five dancers on the raised platform at the rear to join her now capricious motions. Leaping from the platform, they joined the other two sides, which in one mass now leapt up then sank in a stage-wide successional fall to the floor. Lyrically threading in and out of the group, the soloist gradually drew thirteen dancers together, but as she advanced with stronger force, they sank back, resisting, unwilling to follow. With a passionate running leap onto the platform, the leader continued to exhort her followers. Circling the stage and seizing the red banner on the arpeggios, she whipped it so that it crackled through the air. Then, dropping the banner, she whirled with increasing intensity til the faltering cadence closed and she sank in exhaustion onto the steps.

With the orchestral theme the group stirred as if the vital image influenced their dreaming. Surging back and forth, they gathered momentum, rising to meet their leader, now restored and waiting. In a final triumphant run of the stage, strong, free, they stretched out their arms and stood in two lines, heads in profile. In front of them on her knees, back to the audience, arms open, Doris faced the once resistant ensemble, now in unanimity with her.

"What are you crying about?" asked Evelyn, standing near me in the line. "I'm not crying—the lights make my eyes water," I sniffed. But Ronnie Johannson, the visiting Swedish dancer, seeing the dress rehearsal of the *Concerto* in Alys Bentley's Carnegie Hall Studio, had wept real tears at this "inspired instance of music visualization, in which the music seemed to hover over the dancers as the gods hovered over the actors in the tragedies of the ancient Greeks," as John Martin later wrote.

While hot and panting, we changed in the dressing room. Meanwhile Charles, on stage in a huge piece of canvas tenting, danced his impressionistic *Cathédrale engloutie,* followed by Doris dancing a Debussy waltz. Charles's delightful pantomime comedy trio, *Minstrels,* with John Glenn, Eugene LeSieur, and himself, had the audience laughing. Ending the first half of the program, Doris danced *Papillons* (Rosenthal).

A few months before, for the beginning students of my Denishawn class, Doris, in the chartreuse chiffon costume with accordion-pleated sleeves, had danced *Papillons* for us. In the dressing room I had lingered afterward to stammer, "O, Miss Humphrey, that was so beautiful." Miss Humphrey did not seem pleased. She tossed her auburn curls and said impatiently, "So you like my pretty dances." Of course I did. What did I know about dance? Weren't dances

Doris Humphrey and Group in Grieg Concerto. *Photo by Vandamm.*

supposed to be pretty? To me, a beginner, every dance was a mysteriously put together masterpiece making a charmed whole. I could not say what part was more breathtaking than another; all of it seemed miraculous. How did people learn to move like that, to remember so many changes of balance and articulations of the body?

After intermission, the group gathered on stage for another premiere: *Color Harmony*. Unlike the previous dances, which had been inspired or influenced by music, *Color Harmony* was breaking new ground, for the movement had been composed first and the music by Clifford Vaughan written afterward. A special tingle of excitement went with this performance, for here we were carrying dance experience to a new level.

Doris's concept was an abstract movement statement of the Helmholtz theory of light, depicting three primary colors—red, green, purple—first separately, then in combination, with conflicting colors emerging. White, symbol of intelligence, appears to clarify the confusion and chaos, leading them on to blended strands of harmony. Thanks to this theme, Doris had invited me, a very green young pupil but fortuitously tall enough for a Purple, to join the concert group.

In our various color groups, costumed in short tunics with long-sleeves, wearing matching Greek-style turbans, legs and feet bare as in *Concerto*, we waited for the composer, Clifford Vaughan, to settle himself at the piano.

The dark Reds, huddled on the floor, began their warm, sensuous, earthbound, circular movements. The sharp, percussive Scarlets, so many flames, a red ribbon spiraling up one arm, darted and flashed about to syncopated rhythms, activating the dark Reds. They combined in a whirling pool of motion, ending in a tight spiral around the Scarlet leader.

The Greens, with pliant successions through the body, like Spring herself, stepped softly from stage left to right. The majestic Purples walked straight-backed or knelt, as Leja Gorska, the Violet soloist, wove through the ranks, aspiring, stretched up on her toes. (Leja, the beautiful Czech dancer, was the sister of an even more famous beauty, Desha, who danced in Paris revues, and modeled for Harriet Frishmuth's sculptured bronze figurines, which could be seen in Gorham's windows on Fifth Avenue.)

The second section was more dynamic, the colors rushing, mingling, clashing. On collision, long, tinted silk scarves shot into the air. More and more confusion, dim out to black; we lie prostrate on the floor. A single white spot comes on. Robert Gorham of the body like a Greek god, wearing a silver breechcloth, appears slowly moving

Charles Weidman with the Humphrey Group in Color Harmony.

center, to separate the colors. In reverse order from purple to red to green to lavender, we reach up to the white figure at the top of a flight of steps, a connected spiral band.

Six more numbers, lighter in weight: Charles's *Pierrot* (Scott); Doris's *Pavane for the Sleeping Beauty* and *The Fairy Garden* (Ravel); Sylvia and Evelyn in Beethoven's *Bagatelle,* full of question-and-answer runs and skips; Charles's *Juggler* (to Borodin's *Scherzo*)—which brought down the house; finally Doris's and Charles's romantic duet in the Scriabin *Pathetic Study*.

This long evening of dance, for all it broke new ground with the first abstract ballet in America, contained traditional Denishawn attitudes and influences—veils, music visualization, pretty posing. But Doris's music visualizations were beyond any other dancer's. To Mary F. Watkins of the *New York Herald Tribune,* it was "the most supreme reflection of sound in movement which we ever remember. As for the simple essentials of rhythm and tempo, these are the Denishawn A,B,C's, learned and mastered in the cradle. Their discipline is so faultless that it is inconspicuous. The training has reached the ultimate ideal of apparent spontaneity."

"It's all so new to me," said Father (an M.I.T. engineer-draftsman, designer, inventor) back home in the Stratford Road apartment in Brooklyn where we lived. "I think it was very good, but I don't understand it enough to be able to discuss it." "Oh dear," said Mother, who belonged to the D.A.R., "why must you dance barefoot? You get your feet so dirty."

Sunday night three weeks later we repeated the same program in New York at the John Golden Theatre. Doris added her new solo *Banshee,* which Henry Cowell, the composer, played by plucking the back strings of the piano, producing hair-raising effects. Hiding behind a box shape, Doris emerged in a spooky light, occasionally stretching a white arm into view, or we saw a flash of leg, or her veiled mouth open wide, as if screaming and wailing. It was eerie, fantastically imaginative.

In *The New York Times,* John Martin pronounced that "To all intents and purposes the performance opened a new chapter in American dancing . . . revealing for the first time in this country the type of ensemble dance which has swept over Europe in the past few years . . . the general tendency toward mass movement has here found its expression at the hands of an authoritative and creatively minded artist."

The following Friday, April 20, seventeen students of Denishawn appeared at Washington Irving High School in sixteen dances. Sylvia Manning, Evelyn Fields, Rose Yasgour, and Gertrude Shurr shared their solo talents with lesser dancers in *Floods of Spring* (Rachmaninoff); *Choeur Danse* (Stchbalcheff); Debussy's *First and Second Arabesques*; Beethoven's *Sonata Pathetique*; and Couperin's *Rondeau*; as well as in exotic Mexican, Singalese, Japanese, East Indian, and Algerian dances. As an absolute beginner, I appeared with seven girls in Poulenc's *Adagietto,* the simplest dance of all, choreographed by Hazel Krans.

The typical Denishawn student had danced from the time she was a child. She had been taught everything there was to know about dance technique, from "barefoot ballet"—Shawn's barre work without toe slippers—to all the exotic forms of the world, especially the Far East. I had not caught up with this background of "classics" in my first year of evening classes at Denishawn, because Doris was teaching creatively, and it would be years later until I did.

How I envied the other girls with their perfect balance and their strong agile legs capable of high extensions; how quickly they picked up new measures and phrases, how quickly their bodies did what was required. In class, Doris would stop the group, saying, "Now let Eleanor do it." Cheeks flaming with pride and joy, I would do it alone. Then Doris would add, "Now, Evelyn, please." After Evelyn, Doris would say, "Evelyn's way was right." Self-conscious agonies and doubts filled my mind. Did I belong among these divinities who always did everything perfectly? Had I any right to stand on the stage with them? Would I be able to dance, ever? Yet to be dancing at all, however ineptly, was blissful.

The first encouragement came from Charles. One day in class he spoke of Geraldine Farrar, what a magnificent artist she was. "All great artists have it here," he said, pointing to his chest. "You have to have a chest. Now there's Eleanor. She has a chest." Charles was often teasing; this was a beneficial tease. After that class I walked on air toward New York's glamorous intersection at 57th Street and Fifth Avenue, feeling the thrill of possibility, of youthful hope at that moment of being on top of the wonderful city which was New York. If I had a chest to start with—no doubt from adolescent summers spent swimming and diving—perhaps some of the other essentials would come later.

The day Doris asked me if I would be a Purple in the new *Color Harmony* ballet was a great day, but just how portentous I could not even guess. A new form of dance was being created, and everything was for the first time. Along with *Color Harmony* I found myself included in the Grieg *Concerto* with the same group. How carefully we rehearsed and prepared for the spring debut!

One day we traveled by subway to 225th Street in the Bronx, to Denishawn House, so that Doris could take a more objective look at what we were doing. A three-story Hollywood-style stucco palazzo, it was well-designed for its purpose, with its huge studio floor space, high ceilings, and living quarters on balconies upstairs. Pauline Lawrence showed us through the empty place, for Ruth St. Denis and Ted Shawn were on the road with the Zeigfield Follies earning money to pay for this new structure. There was a burst of laughter when we came to Shawn's room, for on the bed reposed a pillow, a large green satin frog. "Teddie-bumps' pet froggie," explained Pauline. After rehearsal Pauline served refreshments to us on individual Japanese lacquered trays. Everything in the house was from some part of the Orient, except for huge mural-size paintings or photos of the American dance leaders.

For me the rehearsal had been another of those embarrassing times. Once Doris stopped the music and came to my side of the group. "Eleanor isn't doing this right. It's this way, put your leg here, first, then fall." On the way back to Manhattan, I found myself sitting next to Doris, and was grateful that the noisy screeching subway made conversation impossible, for I could think of nothing to say. Trivial chitchat with this goddess was absurd. Besides, she might say, "What makes you think you can dance?"

For the dress rehearsal we had moved down the hall to Studio 67 in Carnegie Hall. It was exciting to be in the studio where Isadora danced when Ethelbert Nevin played for her. The studio, long blue curtains at the back, was much bigger than the place rented by Denishawn that year. We threw ourselves into the *Concerto* with Ronnie Johannson looking on. At the end, she embraced Doris, wiping tears from her eyes.

There was general euphoria in the air. Fifteen nations had signed the Kellogg-Briand Pact, agreeing to settle international difficulties by peaceful means. Ordinary people were beginning to dabble in the stock market hoping to get rich quick. With Walter Damrosch conducting, the new NBC Symphony started weekly concerts on radio. George Gershwin's symphonic tone-poem *An American in Paris* was an immediate hit. We were singing "Short'nin' Bread," Cole Porter's "Let's Do It," "Diga Diga Doo," "That's My Weakness Now," "There's a Rainbow Round My Shoulder," and "Button Up Your Overcoat." Among the plays on Broadway that ran for more than two hundred performances were *The Road to Rome* with Jane Cowl, *Diamond Lil* with Mae West (whom Charles particularly admired), *Holiday* with Ann Harding, and *The Age of Innocence*. Most impressive of all was the Theatre Guild's production of Eugene O'Neill's *Strange Interlude* with Lynn Fontanne and Earl Larimore. The O'Neill play lasted five hours (for Americans an unconscionable time to sit still), necessitating a dinner break. Nevertheless, it was so innovative, with its four characters' monologues revealing their Freudian subconscious, that the play moved to the John Golden Theatre and had a long run.

We were scheduled to have group pictures taken of the *Concerto* and *Color Harmony* on a "dark Sunday" when there was no performance at that theatre. Not long before, I attended a performance of *Strange Interlude* which had a surprise in it when one of the actors blew his lines. After the dinner interlude, the audience sleepy and not too alert, Mr. Larimore suddenly came to that unforgivable moment, a dead halt. He waited for help but the other characters were sunk in their inner monologues and could not toss him the line. He made several attempts, going back to the beginning of the long speech, coming to a stop at the same block each time. He looked into the wings and snapped his fingers in vain. Finally he called out "Prompter" in stentorian tone. We heard rushing footsteps, pages turning, murmurs, and the play went on.

The Sunday came when we were to have our pictures taken. Going on stage for the space rehearsal before the pictures, I looked into the prompter's box. Where the play script should have been, I noticed a copy of James Joyce's *Ulysses*, wrapped in brown paper. *Ulysses* was on the banned list in the United States, but the copies surreptitiously carried about were easily identified by the unique bulk of the book.

After the Brooklyn tryout and the New York artistic success of the John Golden Theatre debut, we had one more appearance. Performing for the American Women's Association in the Grand Ballroom of the Pennsylvania Hotel, and assisted for the last time by "Dancers from the Denishawn School," Doris Humphrey danced the *Air for the G String*, the Beethoven *Bagatelle* with Evelyn and Sylvia, and the first movement of the Grieg *Concerto*.

Shortly after, Doris called a meeting of the group in the Denishawn Studio at Carnegie Hall. The time had come when we would individually have to make a decision about our careers, she told us. If we chose to remain with Denishawn we would always be assured of jobs—and "be able to wear fur coats." She, Charles Weidman, and Pauline Lawrence were leaving Denishawn to continue to create new modern dances. All they could offer us was plenty of hard work and an unknown future.

The reasons they were leaving Denishawn after a ten-year association were many. Doris had been summoned to appear before the board members of Greater Denishawn at the new house to listen to the new policies, outlined by Ruth St. Denis. The first time she had ever heard either director express racial prejudice, she was shocked to hear Miss Ruth propose, as the first item on the agenda, that the number of Jewish students be limited to ten percent of the whole. As in most New York studios, the majority of the students were Jewish. Doris wondered about the many talented young Jewish girls already in the school and what was to become of them.

Then Ted Shawn spoke about another policy which Denishawn intended to effect, with respect to morals. It had come to his attention that various "affairs" had been going on from time to time. Such things were questionable, if not downright immoral, as they did not result in marriage. A committee was to be established to hear the evidence in such cases. Permission to continue in Denishawn might be granted, or marriage would be advised. If the advice were ignored, the guilty parties would be dismissed at once. Doris thought this preposterous, private lives not being the concern of any board.

Doris and Charles had a third reason for leaving: the financial necessity of sending out another Follies road company to help with the payments on the excessively large mortgage on the school. Shawn was calling on Doris and Charles to do their share by touring next year. Doris, thinking of her exciting new experiments in movement and her hopes of composing in a new style, told him she did not think she could do that. Artistically she had been shocked to see how much the Denishawn dances had deteriorated on the road, how the tempi became ever faster, and Miss Ruth's skirts rose ever higher.

Miss Ruth's reaction was to burst into tears and ramble incoherently that she had always been respectable, unlike Isadora Duncan, who ran all over Europe having babies by different men. And Shawn, coming to her defense, turned to Doris and asked, "Do you mean to say that Jesus Christ was any the less great because he addressed the common people?" Doris replied, "No. But you're not Jesus Christ." Shawn then replied, "But I am. I *am* the Jesus Christ of the dance."

After further talk about loyalty, obligation and devotion to ideals, Shawn asked Doris whether or not she would go into the Follies for a season to do her share for Greater Denishawn. Doris replied that she would not—some other way would have to be found. Accusing her of disloyalty and lack of responsibility and ability to sacrifice, Shawn called for a voice vote as to whether Doris was to remain a member in good standing. She was thereupon voted out of the Denishawn fold.

Chauvinism, interference in people's private lives, and being asked to go on tour for monetary reasons were causes enough, but essentially Doris could not bring herself to settle for artistic standards which she considered unworthy of Denishawn, compromising her own standards into the bargain. She had already been told that her new approaches and experiments were unnecessary. Denishawn had already "thought of everything"; it was perfect the way it was. More important to her than any organization was the dance itself—the art she served, with Charles's and Pauline's help, and with those of us who felt the same way. She could not abandon the new direction she had taken.

At first incredulous at the reactionary attitudes of Miss Ruth and Shawn, then increasingly indignant, the group unamimously agreed to follow the young pioneers. Only two defected later, one who married, and another who went over to the "enemy." For me, so new to the world of dance, this was a situation without conflict. The only dance artists I had seen were Pavlova on her farewell tour, then the Denishawns on their return from the Orient. Indifferent to the leaders of Denishawn, I had been fascinated by the young Humphrey and Weidman. Though registered as a student at Miss Ruth's & Ted's prestigious school, I somehow never conceived of myself as a Denishawn dancer, being a student of Doris, Charles, and Hazel Krans. Never having met Miss Ruth or Ted personally, at this point I had no desire to make their acquaintance.

The "unholy three"—Doris, Charles, and Pauline—would find a studio of their own. Classes and rehearsals would continue there. Doris had been declared "disloyal to Denishawn," and the word "loyalty" forever after had a bitter connotation for her. She was obeying inevitably the essential greater loyalty to her own creative gifts.

That summer Emily Hahn, a Denishawn friend, offered me a job at a children's camp in Southampton where she was head counselor. My duties were to help her in daily planning and to teach dance, drama, swimming, diving, canoeing, lifesaving. I would live with three problem children in a tent and occasionally chaperone riding trips. I found the organized camp life with noisy children and endless responsibilities tedious, though I loved being outdoors and being able to go surf bathing in the Atlantic. While the children rode their ponies, the Irish grooms—who were always a little tipsy—brought Irish hunters from the Southampton Riding and Hunt Club for me. I

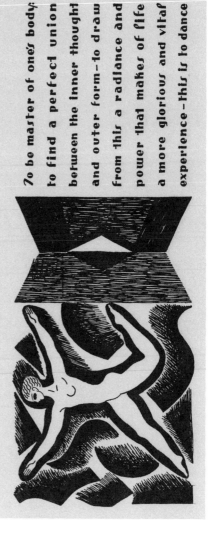

DORIS HUMPHREY
CHARLES WEIDMAN
INSTRUCTION IN THE
ART of the DANCE

NINE EAST FIFTY NINTH

To be master of one's body,
to find a perfect union
between the inner thought
and outer form—to draw
from this a radiance and
power that makes of life
a more glorious and vital
experience—this is to dance

Buk Ulrich's design for the brochure for the Humphrey–Weidman School.

knew just enough to hang on with my knees, and would sail, astonished, over fences. The great beasts' smooth canters and stretched-out galloping rhythms were so intoxicating that, dismounted, I would continue to prance and gallop on my own two legs.

It was a great relief to return to the city; to open the new Humphrey-Weidman announcement, a black and white folder with a Buk Ulrich drawing of a dancer on the cover, credo inside: "To find the outer form for the inner need. To be master of one's body: to find a perfect union between the inner thought and outer form—to draw from this a radiance and power that makes of life a more glorious experience—this is to dance."

Eagerly I approached the 9 East 59th Street address and took the elevator, passing the Dalcroze School on the way, to the fifth floor. The oblong studio had high ceilings, a skylight, parquet floor and walls painted gray. It was spacious and elegant. Between the 59th Street windows, two tall iron candelabra balanced a Buk Ulrich oil painting. A Japanese gold and silver folding screen marked off the dressing room area from the studio. Beyond was a small living room with two couches covered in blue, Rockwell Kent drawings on the wall; behind it a smaller room for Doris. Down the hall was a costume room for Pauline. A combined kitchen-bathroom with old-fashioned conveniences allowed them to eat and live there. Once the iceman with his chunk of ice arrived as Doris was having a bath in the kitchen tub. Pauline pulled the tub's wooden lid over her until he filled the icebox and went away.

Rehearsals and the classes I could take were scheduled for evenings. Earning a living was a primary problem. I was twenty-two, fourth of six children, and still living at home, where "all for one and one for all" meant that the three girls helped to put the three boys through school. Out of the money I earned on boring clerical jobs I contributed to the family and was able to pay for my lessons. My clothes were remodeled dresses or occasional castoffs from sisters or well-off friends. I worked at Lord and Taylor's for one day and at Schraffts as a hostess for one week. For one dreadfully long year I stamped bills "paid" for the telephone company; then was an office assistant for a newspaper representative. At the time of the Denishawn break I worked in the promotion department of *The Star* magazine. These dreary ways of earning a living catapulted me into each dance class with supercharged energy to make up for the humdrum eight hours of toil. Salvation, "making of life that more glorious and vital experience," was achieved through the dance.

Cleo cleverly practiced her pliés in turned-out position as she stood from nine to five in front of the filing cabinets of a huge insurance company. Some of the group members modeled.

One day Rose (Paula) Yasgour gave me a list of sculptors for whom she posed. The pay was only one dollar an hour but artists were interesting to work for; you were part of a creative process, you learned about form as you watched. Perspiring greatly, I undressed for the eyes of Mario Korbel, whose bronze "Three Graces" long stood in the Metropolitan Museum's foyer, and for Edward McCarten, sculptor of the classical pediment atop Grand Central Terminal. Korbel exclaimed at my "tors"; McCarten squinted at my legs; neither wanted a model. But Grace Helen Talbot at 1 Fifth Avenue needed me, and for several years she paid me a weekly salary whether she worked or not.

This was morning work, and taxing, but in the charming atmosphere of the red-brick, white-trimmed Rhinelander apartments, reminiscent of Henry James's old Washington Square. Talbot's top-floor studio apartment faced Macdougal Alley. Green-eyed, red-haired Talbot sculpted with slender fingers or took measurements with long calipers, then marked the proportions with blue chalk on my skin. Every twenty minutes I rested, then revolved to face another direction, giving us both a different perspective, so it was not altogether static. As she worked in plastalene, modeled about an armature, we had long friendly discussions about art, life, books, music, dancing. She followed the Humphrey concerts with enthusiasm. Her teacher, Harriet Frishmuth, was one of the few American women artists then earning $50,000 a year. Grace Helen followed the same path, making the representational garden sculptures that were so much in demand.

The rotogravure section of the Sunday *Times* published a photograph of the first work I posed for—a half-life-size figure of a girl with a Russian wolfhound. Since "all the news that's fit to print" did not include front face or profiles of nudes, the backview appeared. One whimsical Talbot composition was a nymph riding backward on an ass, whispering a funny story—from the *Golden Ass*—into one of its bent-back ears. This necessitated a trip to the Bronx Zoo, where I pulled up grass and fed the animal while she sketched it.

After completing a fountain figure of a girl sitting with one leg dangling, holding a shell in her hands, Talbot began a standing figure, this time with arms raised, holding the shell over her head. To this she added a putto figure at the base clinging to the girl's legs. For the model a healthy baby selected by her own physician was duly

Plaster cast for Grace Helen Talbot's bronze sculpture of Eleanor King.
Photo by Louis H. Dryer.

brought to the studio. The toddler, daughter of a city fireman, was too young to pose and had to be kept happy. This involved one or other of the parents, the French maid, Coco the poodle, Grace Helen or myself.

Just before the plaster cast was to leave for Gorham's Bronze Factory Talbot had second thoughts, and in the interest of variety she changed the sex of the putto to male. When the completed bronze was returned from the factory, the parents came to the viewing party. The proud papa, in seventh heaven at the idea of seeing his darling immortalized in bronze, circled the now transformed image and said nothing, but the back of his neck and ears turned red.

Posing for painters was far more difficult. Talbot sent me to the painter Jane Freeman in one of the tower studios of Carnegie Hall. Freeman's indoor-outdoor subject was a study of the New York skyline seen from her window, with a nude figure lying on a couch in the foreground. Quite cross, Miss Freeman asked me not to move my diaphragm at all because every time I breathed the shadows on the cushions changed. Another time Talbot sent me to Orland Campbell's Macdougal Alley studio to model for his restoration of the seventeenth century nymph fading from the foreground of a Poussain landscape, which the Metropolitan Museum wished restored. Another time Miss Frishmuth was about to complete a statue but wasn't satisfied with the smile on the face. Talbot recommended me. Miss Frishmuth modeled from dozens of dancers—one for legs, one for arms, one for bosom, one for hands—and was dreadfully businesslike. "Pose, please!" she commanded. In ghastly silence I grimaced for thirty minutes at a time without one word of encouragement from her, an agonizing experience.

One sculptress I posed for—as José did later—was tiny, incandescent Joan Hartley, whose work was abstract. She taught Archipenko's abstract principles to her class of students; Her ideas were always big—a floor-to-ceiling Joan of Arc, one elongated flame, dominated her studio.

At the studio, classes were increasingly stimulating. Emily Hahn, who started at Denishawn in 1926, the year before me, recalls that at that time every class began with slow controlled ballet movement, followed by dances in Balinese, East Indian, Spanish or Japanese style. She loved the dances "though the finger movement where the fingers had to bend far backward were painfully difficult and the neck movements from side to side were not easy to do." But by 1927, the year I started, the teaching method changed. Gone were the slow controlled ballet warmups. Instead, Doris beat a gong or sometimes a drum and we were led through a different type of movement. "All movement begins in the center and moves out through the finger tips," Doris taught. Sometimes we had music, sometimes no sound other than the rhythmic beat of the movements. These started out as small confined movements that gradually spread out, maintaining a beat that became more involved as the movement enlarged.

There was an immediate intelligence about Doris's conceptions; she had thought everything through before we took a step. Unlike ballet masters calling step sequences in French with never a word of expressive value, Doris's meaning was crystal clear. As with most innovative artists, the idea came first, then the technique to implement it. So after the *Water Study* was accomplished, she developed sideward succession studies to MacDowell's *Sea Pieces,* and forward and backward successions to gong and drum. We learned Schumann's *Grillen,* a strongly rhythmic group dance from Denishawn, and the more modern *Work* and *Play* etudes to music of Krenek, stark and simple. She taught us her solo *Quasi-Waltz* of Scriabin, lyrical and flowing.

As she put behind her the romantic softness of Denishawn, she became interested in exploiting the design elements of oppositions and parallels. In class with partners we composed alternating measures of flight and pursuit, moving, then holding still, to the second prelude of Bach's *Well-Tempered Clavier.* We danced more and more to percussion, and learned opposition studies, seated, walking and running. Asymmetry became a provocative new harmony resolved in the imagination; isolation studies taught us to move with succinctness in every part. As we diligently practiced successions of motion, we acquired more control with staccato gestures, first with one leg, then the torso alone, the head, a single arm, making each part sharp which had been flowing and smooth. Soon Doris pulled Cleo Atheneos and me from the back row to places in the front where she "could see better what we were doing."

Cleo, a striking beauty with a Greek profile, flashing eyes, and dark hair, was a spirited dancer with a strong dramatic flair. Cleo and I particularly loved working with Charles's class too, where he gave us strong dramatic twists and thrusts from his *Savonarola,* necessitating a quick backbend drop to the knees. And the insouciant patterns of his Scarlatti dances were delightful.

When José Limón walked into the 59th Street studio (1929) to take classes, he was as startled and awed by modern dance as we were by his appearance.[1] Except for Charles's sometimes supporting

Denishawn dancers, John Glenn and Eugene LeSieur, José entered a dance world composed largely of women. Part Spanish, part Yaqui Indian, the untamed lion from Mexico was six feet tall, with small deepset eyes, high cheekbones and a life-enhancing presence. Sophisticated—yet at the same time primitive, he had an outward manner that was courteous and dignified, but his speech was surprisingly racy. In class we took care to keep out of the way of the volcanic Limón energy, raw as it was, for at the beginning José had very little balance and no control; he was all over the place.

At first sight Charles said, "He'll never be a dancer." Soon Doris perceived the diamond under the rough exterior and declared, "This boy is creative; he will be a dancer." Sitting next to me on the floor watching the principals rehearse before a concert, José kept up a running comment which revealed his new irrevocable calling. "Isn't it marvelous? Where do their ideas come from? I want to learn to move like that. How do you find such movements? How do they remember what they are going to do next?"

Like a Newfoundland puppy, José exuded affection for his new family of dancers. We would be greeted with great bear hugs and kisses, yet always the intense dark eyes seemed focused at the same time on some far distant planet.

The atmosphere of the studio was spartan, the working lives of the dancers a constant round of classes and rehearsals, with no time for anything but work in progress. One day Doris received as a gift, or perhaps bought for herself, a Fortuny Greek pleated robe of apricot satin, so fine the whole could be coiled up in a flower box the size of a bunch of violets. She had been invited to a big party, and she tried it on for us to admire. It suited her auburn hair and classic qualities perfectly. At the party, Pauline told us later, Doris remembered being introduced to a Miss Millay, afterward sharing a taxi with the same person on the way downtown. America's leading poetess and America's leading creative dancer sat side by side riding down Fifth Avenue, neither one speaking a word. The next day, too late, Doris realized it was Edna St. Vincent Millay.

Perhaps Miss Millay had been on the wrong side of Doris, who was deaf in one ear. This could be a blessing in certain circumstances, such as trying to sleep on noisy train trips, but undoubtedly this limitation was one of the isolating factors in Doris's circumscribed life. She was isolated by her genius, her hearing defect and her dedication to the art she served. When she seemed unresponsive, it may have been that she did not hear what was said. It was Pauline who told of the affliction; Doris never mentioned it.

Library - St. Joseph's College
222 Clinton Avenue
Brooklyn, N. Y. 11205

The first Christmas party in the studio was celebrated with an auction. Hundreds of beans had been scattered over the studio and we had a limited time to find as many as possible. These were then used as currency when Charles, the auctioneer, offered mysteriously named and wrapped Oriental packages for which we bid. I saved my beans for a "Chinese whatsis"—a cloisonné jar with a dragon winding around its sides. The group presented Doris with a formal dark blue afternoon dress. She lived in a brown tweed suit which had a short shoulder cape trimmed with fox. We saw her only in leotards or that suit. No one remembers seeing her ever wear the blue dress. Doris gave blue woolen sweaters to the group, welcome warmth for evening rehearsals. Charles gave little books. He had decided I looked like Ouspenskaya, so on the flyleaf of my copy of Ladd's *With Eyes of the Past* he wrote: "To the slippery saucy Slav!" Before the party ended we had a contest making instant sculptures out of chewing gum and toothpicks.

Doris corralled the group for special occasions when Dane Rudhyar and Henry Cowell were invited to the studio to play for us. Once Mary Wood Hinman, Doris's beloved teacher from Chicago, came to New York to watch and praise the continuing advance of her gifted pupil, and we saw the bond linking one great teacher to another. Doris endeavored to train our bodies, feed our minds, make us into artists.

The year before, on September 14, 1927, in France, Isadora Duncan had stood up in an open car and called out to her friends: "Je vais à la gloire!" The car started and the long red scarf she was wearing became entangled in the back wheel of the car. Two swift revolutions of the wheel and she was dead, her neck broken. She had indeed gone to glory. Now a collection of her writings on dance, along with other writings about her, had been published in *The Art of the Dance*. One day Doris called us into the little studio living room. We gathered around her on the couch and the floor while she read to us with satisfaction, in her husky voice, Shaemas O'Sheel's tribute to the greatest woman artist since Sappho. Then she went on to read to us some of the high points of Isadora's philosophy of dance. Neither Doris, nor Pauline, nor Charles, nor any of us had ever seen Isadora dance. Like a comet she had blazed across the sky, a portent of what was to come, and her existence and vision were to inspire us all. However, there was one dissident voice about Isadora: Ted Shawn, puritanically shocked at Isadora's concept of freedom in love affairs, and with his chauvinism outraged at her enthusiastic espousal of the Russian Revolution, had declared that her biography *My Life* was the

CHAPTER TWO: 1929

Something Never Seen Before

ART AND ECONOMICS have always been strange bedfellows, progress in one having little to do with progress in the other.

Despite economic disaster as the twenties came to a close, for the dance 1929 was a year of astonishing artistic growth. Doris's next ensemble choreography strode so far ahead of *Color Harmony* of the year before, that the once revolutionary work looked pale in comparison to the new abstractions. We worked in the studio that fall and winter on the musicless *Water Study*, and the nearly musicless *Life of the Bee*, for spring showing at the Guild Theatre.

Water Study remains today the most satisfying of all Humphrey works to perform. Anyone viewing it can recognize the experience contained in this poetic image of water as truthfully conceived, a masterpiece of flowing motion, full of lightness and grandeur. In the succession patterns which determine the flow, every inch of the exhilarated body moves, as the repeated successions pass from the toes through the knees, hips, and spine to the crown of the head.

Making the dance an independent art happened gradually. In the Denishawn repertory a *Tragica Sonata*, originally choreographed by Doris to MacDowell's music of the same title, was structurally and rhythmically such a strong composition that it was equally effective when divorced from the music, so it was successfully billed and presented as a dance without music. With *Color Harmony*, the composer had been called in after the movements were set, the music supporting or following what had already been created in movement. Now the silent pulses of *Water Study*, having nothing to do with regular beats or measures, were built on simple breath rhythm, physically analogous to the rise and fall, the crest suspension and trough, of wave motion itself.

Eleven dancers, asymmetrically spaced across the stage, began on their knees, bodies bowed, heads down. At first, when we were learning the dance, Doris walked along the line humming the length of the opening wave rhythm as she went, until we had memorized the space-time intervals between impulsive lift and fall. The single wave theme graduated from floor to standing level, where opposed sides would dive in relays, run together, leap in the air and fall back. As one mass we rushed together across the space, the front group somersaulting low, the back group, arms held high, leaping up to fall and slide between the tumbling bodies. Unified, we rushed from one corner of the stage diagonally to its opposite, dropping fast with flowing speed, lifting up against gravity with heavy weighted arms. As the intensity diminished, we ran with light chopping hand motions above our heads, until one set, hands linked, made a half circle of the stage, breaking apart with quick isolated jumps in the air. These diminshed, with the last and smallest girl, into a curvetting spiral fall. The other front set slowly shifted at horizontal level, falling from one side to the other.

We traveled slowly, swaying from side to side, back to our original places, shifting to kneel again in profile, the rocking rhythm reduced as we lowered our hips onto our heels, the wave successions now moving through extended arms forward and back. A cadence of single arm circles, progressing from front to back, began quickly, backs arched and heads relaxed backward, weight resting on the forearms, then slowly came to rest. Then the back row began the dissolving wave. Each in turn lifted the back, slid forward on one hand, then the other, and *Water Study* sank into stillness, the way it began.

On the wall of the dressing space Doris posted reading lists on dance; one list, from Barnard College, she may have been asked to draw up for its physical education department. History and philosophy were included. I remember Vuillier's *La Danse*; Havelock Ellis's *The Dance of Life*; Virginia Woolf's *A Room of One's Own*; Nietzsche; Gordon Craig; Adolphe Appia. Maeterlinck's *Life of the Bee* was a reading assignment.

In *Water Study* we had been impersonal components of water— "the more impersonal, the more abstract, the greater the work." Now in *Bee*, we were animal-insect impersonal shapes again: worker bees, the drones in a hive, moving on high arched feet, heels always lifted

Doris Humphrey and Group in Life of the Bee. *Photo by Soichi Sunami.*

from the ground, with turned-out bent knees, arms angled like wings. Instead of curves, acute angles of the body; the breathing, violently expelled from the thorax, almost percussive in effect.

The drones' opening dance warms the hive in anticipation of the birth of the queen. Cleo, whose distinguished role this was, lies on her back, her bent-back legs folded outward, arms crossed on her chest. The background was humming sounds—produced by Pauline and Olga Frye off stage. To supplement this, the drones also hummed in overlapping phrases to maintain a steady tone. To this background sound the workers sharply open and close their arms (wings), rising from contracted positions, stepping over one another, legs sharply articulated in staccato beats. Beating full-scale wings, we circle and swarm about Cleo, then close in, bees standing on other bees in a semicircular pyramid, heads tilted downward. Three workers attend the pupa in a kind of ritual pointing of one arm, as if withdrawing a sheath or membrane. Then the pupa, supported high in the air by the group (still on the balls of the feet, heels lifted high), has her forelegs opened out and is carefully set down on her toes. The workers withdraw, making a protective wall around her. The struggle of the pupa to metamorphose into a new queen bee is dramatic and beautiful, again a matter of breath rhythm. With short sharp thoracic breathing, she straightens her body and arms, unsteadily balances on delicate feet, collapses forward. Again. And again— except that the third struggle to gain equilibrium succeeds. Now she jumps assertively on both feet, arms out, and is ready. Slowly she begins a wavelike rise and fall investigation of the hive.

Suddenly at a piercing new sound—Pauline breathing through a tissue-paper-wrapped comb—the insects freeze. Poised on the top of a short flight of steps stands the old queen (Doris), come to take possession of the hive. The law of the hive: only one queen may rule. Doris holds her right arm high, thumb extended. Three menacing wrist circles, then she brings both hands across her face, elbows out, making a half-mask so that only the eyes show. Extending her right arm to the side, her hand vibrates. The left knee flicks in, then out. She lunges with ferocity toward the new rival, accenting her chin sideward, each accent a provocative insult. Alarmed, the worker bees slant away, drawing their arms inward. In the far left corner they lower their bodies to the floor, weight on the hands, elbows out, to watch the dramatic duel for supremacy.

The young queen jerks her head toward her enemy, left arm extended, hand vibrating. The queens defy each other with chin thrusts and quivering arms, then come together, circling, foreheads touching. They break apart with forward and backward rushes. The young queen backs down to her knees, the old queen stepping over her. Again and again they tangle until the younger sinks down, belly up. Arching back triumphantly, the old queen raises her stinger hand high, then plunges it toward the other's abdomen. After a few convulsive lifts, the young queen drops into stillness.

Some of the drones quickly roll the body of the dead queen out of sight while the rest flail around aimlessly. The victorious queen slowly advances to the center, recovering from battle stress. She gives a handclap signal, and begins fanning her wings with strenuous deep breathing. One by one the workers fall in behind her. Wings beating more and more strongly, they circle in a pattern of spirals and, in a golden exit, swarm after her up the stairs and out.

Cleo's costume was a long wraparound sheath of black-banded gold tissue; Doris wore black velvet, a metallic lining to the split skirt. The worker bees wore short tunics of silver with long sleeves. We all had black mouths, slanted eyebrows and close-fitting black velvet toques. The queens' larger headdresses were banded with gold.

Quite opposite to the earthy gravitational flow of *Water Study*, creatures of air sustaining the turned-out bent-knee position balanced high on the balls of the feet, the *Bees* required strength of back and lungs. Far more demanding, it was less gratifying than *Water Study*.

*Ernestine Henoch, Paula Yasgour, Eleanor King, Dorothy Lathrop, Doris Humphrey
at Fire Island. Photo by Soichi Sunami.*

Having succeeded so well on the musicless dance path, Doris began another group composition in the same direction, called *Air Study*. Generally her conceptions were clearly visualized from beginning to end before she began to work with the company. *Air Study* started as a procession of cloud forms moving slowly across the stage. She selected me to cross the floor with arms curved high, "a small single white cloud," which slowly expanded. The rest followed in small groups that merged into one big Dragon Cloud. But that was as far as the work progressed. Listed on the Guild Theatre program, *Air Study* appeared in print with a purple cancellation stamp, the one abandoned work I recall of Doris's productivity. To say goodbye to my first tiny solo bit was disappointing. Actually this sketch, probably bogging down because it was too representational and not abstract enough to start with, was not wasted. The opening processional of the *Drama of Motion,* which came later and succeeded brilliantly, used the same general structure of slowly changing shapes. *Air Study* may have been the germ for it.

Determined to move away from her pretty dances at all costs, Doris composed an unaccompanied solo for herself, *Speed,* performed almost in one spot. A technically accomplished abstraction, it pleased nobody; it was too abstract. In a white leotard, with an unfortunate wig of white hair—neither metallic nor streamlined enough—her arms and legs worked piston-like, and the balances were breathtaking. But *Speed* was a masculine image, lacking all the nuances and grace which were Doris's by nature. Successfully though it was in extending her vocabulary, it violated her essentially lyrical qualities.

In our century all the arts have lived by repudiating their immediate past, and like all innovators, the modern dance leaders devoted themselves to that which was new. Ballet classicism, East or West, were now anathema, outmoded forms which could contribute nothing to the creative forms being produced. Our masters, who had had all this classicism in their backgrounds, now soared beyond it, dragging us with them. My teachers were so involved with forging a new language of motion never tried before, it did not occur to them to recommend some ballet discipline as good for my untutored legs. All efforts were bent on evolving and perfecting the new group choreography. My particular anatomical instrument was capable of elevation and I was good at jumping; but if high leg extensions with turn-out were beyond me, this defect had its compensations. Since I didn't work at a barre every day with a ballet teacher, there was nothing to keep me from trying to compose. Technically I knew little, but my mind was not bound by technique.

The Metropolitan Museum's collection of medieval French ivory figurines enchanted me. After studying them I managed to memorize a sequence of postures, standing very much in one place, to the adagio of a Beethoven quartet. Why Beethoven? I didn't know any better. One afternoon I showed this to Doris. At the end she said, "You need a long costume for that," and left the room. Since she said nothing whatever about the movement, I felt an implication that perhaps it wasn't really a dance. It didn't, I suddenly realized, go anywhere. Was it worth a costume?

I was crushed, but only temporarily. Justine Douglas and I concocted a duet to one of Debussy's amorphous light pieces. Justine was tall, with black hair, blue eyes, and a very white skin. A relative of Leon Kroll, the painter, she had sat for some of his work. A year later, young, beautiful, pale Justine would be dead of leukemia.

At that stage, as a beginning choreographer, duets were easier than the solo form: you had twice as much to work with—four legs, four arms, two bodies! Charles remarked later that my first dances were perfectly awful. Evidently what Justine and I did was literally the music, for this time Doris's comment was dismaying but excellent advice: "You like music too much. You should learn to compose without it." In my second year of dance, what did I know of movement? How could anyone except Doris or Charles initiate movements without the stimulus of music in the first place? This would remain mysterious to me for a long time. Among the sixteen girls in the group, with their Denishawn academic background, composing was not their forte at all; it was the last thing most of them wanted to do.

One day the Dalcroze school sent up a young pianist to accompany class. John Colman delighted us all with his improvisations. He was an entrancing fifteen, incredibly thin-chested, slender and wiry, a musical prodigy with faunlike ears and a wonderful sense of humor. We became friends and were soon, with Cleo, exchanging lessons. We taught him what we knew of Humphrey's techniques; he taught us Dalcroze eurythmics. A shock of brown hair falling in his eyes, shouting with laughter, he gave us the fun and games of Dalcroze concentration: clapping beats, walking one rhythm while moving the arms in another, performing one measure while listening to the next, learning to appreciate dynamic changes. John's improvisations could make sticks and stones move. I gained a new sense of musicality, a sense of freedom and power in movement, and the ability to improvise. It was heady and releasing in a way that classes with Doris could not be. She was training us to become dancers of her dances.

John's friends, Gladys Lee (the Dalcroze secretary) and Sylvia

Saunders, loved to sight-read madrigals, catches, and glees, as well as to sight-sing through Gilbert and Sullivan scores. It was always fun to go to their East 52nd Street apartment, where John would conduct, play and sing. Gladys, from Virginia, made perfect Southern spoonbread and was an elegant cook. Later, at her house one evening, Thomas Wolfe, author of *Look Homeward Angel*, came to dinner. A huge, oversized boyish figure of a man, just returned from Germany, he was excited by the images of Nazism he had experienced at the time of the 1936 Berlin Olympics. Nazism was something we were reading about in the papers from time to time. Wolfe, who had actually seen its manifestations clearly evidenced in Berlin, was deeply troubled by them. The Italian form of fascism was to touch my life later and here I must digress to tell how this happened.

My childhood summers had been spent in the family cottage at Mount Gretna, Pennsylvania. Dad had bought the cottage from Miss Ella Reizenstein. One day when I was eleven she came walking by, leaning on her cane, to ask me to come and play with her young niece, Jane Herrmann, from New York. Jane, a sophisticated city child, was two years younger, but she had great zest and humor and we became great friends, a closeness which lasted through adolescence. I spent my teen summers with the Herrmann family at their summer camp on Long Lake in Belgrade, Maine; visited Jane in New York, was hired as her companion-tutor, and was in some ways almost an adopted daughter of her family. One of Jane's uncles was Julius Rosenwald; her grandmother Hammerslough was connected with the Goldman-Sachs family. Jane's mother, Elsa, a brilliant executive in the matriarchal tradition, served on the board of the Henry Street Settlement. When Jane went to boarding school, Mrs. Herrmann sent me to Philadelphia to visit her homesick daughter.

The Herrmann family was a cultural education for me. The intense family feeling, the passion for life, the involvement with good causes, were stimulating. The long golden summers living close to nature in the beauty of Maine's lakes and forests, reading books aloud, helped to balance the stresses of adolescence. Best of all were tickets to concerts and theatre in New York, and meeting some of the movers and shakers of the world, such as Count Tolstoi, son of the novelist, when he visited at Henry Street. It was Jane, later majoring in art history in Florence, who first became acquainted with young Italian poets.

One night in 1929 Jane invited me to dinner when one of the guests was the extraordinary Lauro de Bosis, then lecturing at the Casa Italiana. Lauro was the son of a Roman poet, a distinguished translator of Shelley; his mother, an American of New England stock. When he learned I was a dancer, he immediately said that I must be choreographer for production of his new translations, just completed, of Sophocles' *Oedipus Rex* and *Antigone*. I certainly had no qualifications for choreographing anything, and Lauro had never seen me dance. When he naively offered me the copy of his text, I just as naively accepted it. We journeyed up to the Casa Italiana one day and he showed me the setting where *Oedipus* would be performed.

I was fascinated with the young man's radiant personality: my first genuine poet. And none of my admiration was dimmed by Jane's declaring that Lauro was so devoted to Ruth Draper that once, when the great monologist was sailing for Europe, he went to the ship to say goodby and remained aboard for the whole Atlantic crossing because he couldn't bear to say it. That made him all the more romantic in my eyes. And if Ruth Draper was old enough to be his mother, it somehow seemed suitable; I adored Ruth Draper too.

Fortunately for me, the alarming prospect of having to create the movement for such a great classic—I don't think I had yet seen a Greek play—was to come later. In the meantime Lauro was going back to Rome. When he returned the next year, we would work together on the Casa Italiana production.

Events were to alter this rosy plan as neither of us could have guessed. I never heard from Lauro again. In 1933 Ruth Draper published his last letter, *The Story of My Death*, together with the Italian text of his verse-drama, *Icaro*, and her translation. I was to find in that dance-drama the vehicle I was searching for, and four years later to choreograph choruses of it as a memorial to the act with which De Bosis gave his life for his ideal of freedom. He was the airman who flew over Rome at sunset one day in 1931, scattering anti-fascist leaflets. Whether he disappeared into the sea like Icarus or was brought down on Italian soil, nobody knows for sure. He had set out with just enough gas to reach Rome, and the Italian Air Corps pursued him from the city.

Charles Laskey now appeared at the studio, adding another man to the group working with Charles Weidman. A boxing instructor with a physical education degree, he was a natural for Weidman's new George Bellows-etching-come-to-life of *Ringside*, which pitted John Glenn against Laskey. Winthrop Sargeant wrote the score for this. Although Laskey didn't stay more than a year, he was the one who initiated the organization which later became "The Little Group."

One day Ernestine, José, and I took the ferry to Staten Island and spent an afternoon at Charles Laskey's home, dreaming aloud about a dance group of our own. Laskey surprised us. In addition to muscles, he had long lists of titles and themes for future dance compositions. True, masculine themes repeated themselves—Mars, Dance of War, Hercules, Combat—but he also included *Dance of the Planets* (Holst), which we could be enthusiastic about. José, still in the learning-right-from-left coordination stage, had already caught creative fever. Ernestine Henoch (Stodelle) had a pretty face, fine eyes, and long arms and legs. She was one of the striking girls from Doris's new Understudy Group. The other was Letitia Ide, who was tallest of all and had a perfect bone structure. Letitia, the magnificent Greek goddess, came into The Little Group later.

After the Staten Island meeting, Charles, José, Ernestine, Cleo, and I held a luncheon meeting at Sardi's, agreeing to work together on solos, duos, trios, quartets and quintets, and, when ready, to present them in concert form. Where, when, how did not concern us immediately. More important was getting dances made. While we remained apprentices with the major artists, whose activities were steadily increasing, our progress would necessarily be slow. But we would be fulfilling instructions to create, while learning our craft, experimenting in The Little Group.

Though Laskey was the actual starter, he never accomplished one of that series of titles with us. He began to work for Balanchine, progressed to supporting first Tilly Losch then Vera Zorina in Balanchine's *Errante* (1933), but thereafter dropped from sight in the dance world. When Cleo later became too involved as a teacher to continue, Letitia came in, completing the quartet with Ernestine, José, and myself.

My experience of theatre was meager. I had become acquainted with drama at the age of five when *Uncle Tom's Cabin*, surely touring its last stand, came to Middletown, Pennsylvania, my home town. The company advertised the show with a daytime brass-band parade and real bloodhounds on a leash. That night Dad took the family to see the play. The death scene of little Eva, with Uncle Tom at her bedside, reduced me to tears. I was not more astounded by the tableau with little Eva at the top of a ladder, a white sheet tastefully draped to suggest wings about her, than by the quick change which brought little Eva directly from heaven to the aisles of the theatre at intermission, where she offered peanuts for sale. How odious was Simon Legree with his whip! How breathtaking Eliza crossing the papier-mâché ice-floes! It was all glorious. I was stage struck from then on.

A few years later the local Mothers Congress, of which my beloved Aunt Marion was president, engaged the Rogers Production Company to stage a revue for charity. Almost everybody in town took part. My debut on the boards was as one of a group of children, each encased in a square block costume with a different letter on each side. As we shifted about, we spelled out different themes. This *Yama Yama* production was probably adapted from a Broadway musical. The next year another revue was staged. For this I graduated to a long skirt with panniers and a white wig, for a minuet. I felt perfectly at home in the larger than life atmosphere of the stage, and liked it better than anything.

After America entered World War I, a chum wrote a play that we performed as a benefit. The plot had to do with bravery, cowardice and enlistment. John Becker, aged twelve, played the cruel father whose words to his daughter were, "Harry Waters indeed! Dorothy Lane, you must be crazy!" I spoke a few lines while patriotically knitting a white washcloth for some poor soldier. Dances of the nations embellished this benefit. Cast as a Dutch girl dancing in clumsy wooden shoes, I didn't care much for this dance experience.

About this time, aged twelve, I was a guest of Jane Herrmann's at Mount Gretna, early in the season before all the summer people had arrived. Children entertained themselves all day long in the pre-electronic age, so Jane and I decided to give a performance. Together we wrote a play; we divided the parts between us; I danced between the acts. To show how villainous I could be in the villain's role, I put a cigarette between my lips. Not knowing how to talk around the cigarette, I ended that part of my performance picking bits of tobacco out of my mouth. And later, to the phonograph recording of Geraldine Farrar singing *the* aria from *Madame Butterfly,* I danced with so much feeling that the upper part of my costume—consisting of the red silk scarf from my middyblouse—slipped from my flat chest down to my waist. The audience of Jane's mother and aunt and a visiting uncle feigned indifference while I turned my back and pulled the scarf up again. The audience applauded heartily. Jane's mother thought I had talent and imagination.

I was twelve when Mother took me to a Harrisburg Orpheum matinee to see Walter Hampden's production of *The Merchant of Venice.* At one point Shylock, played by Hampden, stepped down to the footlights to lecture the noisy, inattentive gallery audience on its rude behavior. He threatened that he would never come to Harrisburg again if they did not stop. They calmed down; the play went on. Perhaps once or twice a year we saw vaudeville at Keith's Orpheum in Harrisburg or in Philadelphia. Vaudeville's short comic turns, tumbling, singing, dancing, and he-and-she skits were amusing. Vernon and Irene Castle, dancing elegantly, were a great attraction, and so was Julian Eltinge, the "female impersonator" who was thought to be a marvelous mime.

An impressionable child, I was overwhelmed later when I heard the Philadelphia Orchestra with that veritable god of music and light, young Leopold Stokowski, conducting. Experiencing the world of symphonic utterance for the first time, I felt that here was Elysium.

Father thought opportunities were too limited for his children in Middletown, so, when I was sixteen, we moved to Brooklyn. Trying to pass the Regents Examinations at Erasmus Hall High School kept me so busy that I could not join the dance, drama or poetry clubs, which interested me. But on the outside I was taking in New York theatre.

The generous Jane Cowl, who had herself attended Erasmus, offered gold, silver, and bronze medals to high school students for essays on her production of *Romeo and Juliet*. The top three winners in every high school in the city were presented the prizes personally one afternoon on the stage of the Henry Miller Theatre. My essay won a gold medal. When it came to my turn, she began to autograph a photograph for me. I asked her if I could have two, one for my friend Jane, who had taken me to see the play. "Oh greedy, greedy!" she cried happily. Years later, when Jane Cowl and Helen Hayes were starring in *Twelfth Night*, I went backstage and asked the doorman to show Miss Cowl the medal. Her dressing room door immediately flew open and she held out both hands. "Oh, you must promise to keep it forever!" she exclaimed. Then she looked at me closely and said, "What do you do? You look as if you could do anything."

Shortly after we moved to New York, Anna Pavlova appeared on a farewell tour at the Manhattan Opera House. From high in the balcony I watched my first vision of dance as theatre art. This had a seal of perfection about it. It never occurred to me that this was something I, a sixteen year old, could do too. Pavlova, in an empire gown and poke bonnet of yellow silk, holding her train with one hand, a long walking stick in the other, crossing the stage in a gavotte, was delectable. A long ballet with scenery—courtiers standing about, princes in white perukes, a gypsy—made a strong visual impression. But after *The Swan* I went home, to write: "She moved / and moving lived / the Swan's own life. / And so she moved / that my heart bled to see / the Swan die so / Silently."

With no money to go to college, after high school I clerked in a business office of the telephone company and rehearsed at night with the Beverly Players, an amateur group in Brooklyn, in the chorus of *The Trojan Women.* This experience revealed to me that though I loved the theatre I had no technique for it. To remedy this I took evening classes at Clare Tree Major's School of the Theatre, in the Princess Theatre building (later Labor Stage) on 40th Street.

My first dance teacher was Priscilla Robineau, who taught movement for actors. A gifted, attractive young person, to strengthen a weak back, she had originally studied dance with Adolph Bolm, then she had studied mime with Yvette Guilbert in Paris. She had a Maurice Chevalier grin, and her mime was captivating. (Charles Weidman was her partner in a New York concert later.) We followed her Diana-like figure—hair trimmed in a boyish bob—around the pillars in the theatre basement lobby and over the pink-flowered brown carpet, learning to run-run-leap with Duncanesque arms to Chopin waltzes. And we tie-dyed and weighted our own circular gauze skirts for a Gopi-Nautch dance (no doubt borrowed from Denishawn) and imitated Robineau's gestures, clutching after our own shadows, daggers to the heart, to stagger, fall, and die to Beethoven's *Pathetique Sonata.*

Upstairs Isabel Merson taught Shakespeare; her sister taught diction. These marvelous British ladies with straight backs and tremendous voices enunciated Shakespeare à la Sarah Siddons. Hamlet's advice to the players, the Ghost's lines, Lady Macbeth's sleepwalking, Juliet's "gallop apace" scene—on these we were drilled to do exactly what teacher did. Somehow acting seemed bound up with restrictions—the set pieces, the lines, the prescribed motion— whereas dance was pure wordless joy of motion, not tying up but releasing the emotions to beautiful music. Robineau was far more inspiring than diction and Shakespeare. I dropped the acting lessons and continued with dance.

At the end of the spring term, Robineau called Celia McLaughlin and me aside after class to tell us that she hoped we would become professional dancers. Later I was to appreciate her rare generosity of spirit. She went on to say, "You must study at Denishawn. They can do more for you than I can. And don't take any substitutes; be sure you have Ruth St. Denis."

When I flew on wings into the family living room and repeated Robineau's words, Father put down his book and Mother looked up from her magazine, staring at me in astonishment, completely taken aback. The prospect of having their daughter become a dancer was alarming to them. How did dancers make a living? They said little, but I sensed their dismay. No matter; in elation, Celia and I celebrated by dancing early on May Day morning in Prospect Park on the green. We threw off our coats and shoes, and in short pastel tunics we skipped, ran and waltzed on the grass, with one surprised policeman looking on.

Celia, a Spanish major, did not intend to become a professional dancer; she wanted to be a teacher. Together we heard Raquel Meller's delightful program, Celia translating the songs for me. Then Celia attended Anna Duncan's recital at the Guild Theatre and showed me the program. It contained an advertisement for the Theatre Guild School, which was offering scholarships. The name of the director was Hamilton MacFadden.

"Hamilton MacFadden, how extraordinary!" I exclaimed. "Do you know him?" Celia asked. "Well, yes and no." I had clerked for a few weeks before Christmas at Brentano's bookstore—not, as I had wished, with fascinating books, but merely in the stationery department. However, one day a young man came in, ordered more boxes of stationery sent to more ladies than any other customer had done, then leaned across the counter to ask, "Are you interested in theatre?" "Why, of course! How did you know?" was my instant reply. "Here is my card," said he. I glanced at the Harvard Club address. "If I can ever help you in any way, just let me know."

"Celia, I am going to interview him at the Guild. Maybe I can get a scholarship there." I did go for the interview and did get a scholarship. It lasted three months, when I was eased out of the school. The directors had concluded that I had something in me, but they weren't sure what. MacFadden thought it was comedy. Of course I preferred tragic roles, and was disappointed. "But anyone can play tragedy, it just depends on feeling. Comedy is much more difficult," he said. "Comedy requires brains and timing." Louise Gifford, who taught movement, thought I was "clever." But the consensus was not strong enough for me to be among the twenty surviving graduates the following June, out of the original five hundred applicants.

In 1927 and 1928 the American theatre was at its alltime high of productivity. If many of the plays were in the *Up in Mabel's Room* category of sheer floss, it was possible to see—as I did—*The Royal Family*, based on the Barrymores; Walter Huston in *The Barker* and *Desire Under the Elms*; Leslie Howard in *Escape*, *The Little Clay Cart*, and *Craig's Wife*; Walter Hampden in *Caponsacchi*; Holbrook Blinn in *The Play's the Thing*; Ruth Draper in her inimitable monologues; Max Reinhardt's *Jedermann* with Moissi; Alla Nazimova in *The Cherry Orchard*; Eva Le Gallienne's *Peter Pan*; Winthrop Ames's prestigious

Iolanthe; Jane Cowl in *The Road to Rome;* Helen Hayes in *What Every Woman Knows;* Lynn Fontanne in *Strange Interlude;* and Alfred Lunt in *Marco Millions,* and as Mosca the fly in *Volpone.*

The Theatre Guild was also at the peak of its career with the finest acting company in decades. It had a successful repertory system, with seven hits in New York and *Marco Millions, Volpone* and *Porgy* touring the leading cities of the country. With all this success on its hands, the board of the Guild strangely opposed the logical idea of the next step—a professional acting school, proposed by Lawrence Langner and Theresa Helburn. Then finally the board agreed that, contingent on finding a good teacher, the Guild would sponsor a nonprofit school, with the surplus from wealthier students' tuitions providing scholarships for poorer ones. Winifred Lenihan agreed to head the school. Hamilton MacFadden succeeded her, in turn replaced by Rouben Mamoulian, the last one. Among the professionals who volunteered to direct the tryout scenes were Alfred Lunt and Lynn Fontanne. Fontanne commented afterward, "Fortunately there wasn't one with talent. If there had been any talent, we wouldn't have known what to do with them, anyway."

Lawrence Langner, in his autobiography,[2] says that the directors found themselves always stumbling over the youngsters who cluttered up the stairway of the 52nd Street Guild building. When someone suggested, "Why not dissolve the school?" the only negative notes were Langner's and Helburn's. The school came to an inglorious end, with a few talents making names for themselves because of, or perhaps in spite of, the school. In Langner's opinion, Sylvia Sydney was the most successful acting student. But Lucia Chase, Cheryl Crawford, Arlene Francis, Linda Watkins, and Florida Freibus all made important contributions to theatre. Today, fifty years later, the professional theatre school concept, now in effect in Lincoln Center, has better planned, more extensive training than the Guild's, and lasts four years as compared to the Guild's two-year program.

The drama-school experience had been more painful than pleasant. I was not comfortable with the schizophrenic problems of acting Mrs. Fair in Clyde Fitch's *The Famous Mrs. Fair,* or Amalia in Pirandello's *Right You Are If You Think You Are*—the arbitrary parts handed me for tryout. We read comedy scripts in the class called Mental Approach; Philip Loeb's Emotional Approach focused on Browning's *Dramatic Lyrics,* which was more appealing to me. Louise Gifford's movement class—the Noyes School of Rhythm—stressed the Great I Am and was hardly dancing, but had relaxing value. Florida Freibus and I concocted a duet for her, balancing music discs on our hands, spinning them and ourselves about, a "mechanique" idea typical of the twenties. Later, Florida made the *Alice in Wonderland* adaptation which Eva Le Gallienne produced delightfully at the 14th Street Repertory Theatre. "Around-the-rocks-the-ragged-rascal-ran" and other tongue-trippers in Dagmar Perkins's diction class improved my speech.

Pleasurable moments were those sitting in the balcony, as we were encouraged to do, watching the professionals rehearse. That season I saw Lynn Fontanne as Eliza Doolittle have a temper tantrum, throw herself down on the stage floor, beating it with both fists, crying, "I can't get the mood. I can't, I can't!" Dudley Digges, lovable character actor and best of directors, walked down to the footlights to murmur softly in her ear for a moment. Lynn straightened up, tried again; the return-from-the-ball scene went perfectly.

Displays of bad manners, bad temper, and egos in every state of dishabille were also part of artistic activity. Once Philip Moeller was directing from the darkened house when Miss Helburn entered from the side steps of the stage (which she couldn't see), tripped and fell. Moeller's scream of rage was deafening. "God damn it, woman, can't you be quiet?" She might have broken her leg or her neck, but no matter. The play must go on.

Hamilton MacFadden's expertise in the theatre consisted in his having managed the Harvard Glee Club's tour of Europe. His tutelage consisted in the cult of personality. We should innovate individual ways of saying "Good Morning" or "Goodby," of entering a room, of wearing clothes. Everything one did should have something unique and special about it. Unsophisticated as I was, this manufacturing of an image from the outside repelled me.

In the tomb-like lounge downstairs where we recited Browning, I looked at my classmates and thought: What am I doing here? I haven't a velvety voice, or red hair, or a distinctive nose. I haven't a fur coat; high heels torture me. I can never be a success on Broadway. One afternoon of going the rounds of the Broadway producers' offices convinced me I could not stomach the merchandising of self. Repelled by the mechanics of Broadway, I still had a great love for theatre. Fortunately for me, the theatre takes many forms. In America, the coming theatre was to be dance theatre. And by marvelous happenstance, I was to be a part of that.

Now the Humphrey group, under William C. Gassner's management (among his other artists the Hall Johnson Choir), looked forward to Sunday evening concerts at the Guild Theatre on March 31 and April 7. For me, who had been dropped from the Guild School two years before, coming back, if only for two nights, was gratifying to the ego.

The morning of the Guild concert, we were in practice clothes on stage by ten o'clock, with Pauline out in front of the house starting the trial and error rehearsal of light effects for each dance, a tedious, highly complicated affair. Pauline was uncanny in her sense of the fitness of things—the cut, texture, hue, shape and wearability of her costumes; the nuances of lighting; the suitability of the music. At all the external aids she was invaluable. "Among the three of us, Pauline is the true artist," Doris once remarked. Her sixth sense about trends in taste and style, combined with her devastating humor, made her the oracle we all listened to with respect.

"That amber light won't do," she said to Doris, who was standing downstage in front. "Doris, it makes your teeth look yellow." "That's the kind of teeth they are," Doris replied.

Often effects so painstakingly devised in light rehearsal were quite different in performance. The union could send replacements of the daytime rehearsal crew for the evening performance, and the results were sometimes disastrous. In *Color Harmony* one replacement turned out to be color blind; another, supposed to change gelatines on a music cue, turned out to be deaf. The unions were already so well organized that they could prohibit performances unless all their demands were met. A dance soloist might hire a theatre for a Sunday concert with only one or two musicians assisting. No matter. Musicians Local 802 required that salaries be paid to twenty additional orchestra players, including rehearsal fees.

The original set of folding screens, the simple step-platform which Doris had designed for the *Concerto* and used as background for other works as well, could not be moved from storage to the theatre by the Scene-shifters Union unless each piece was stamped with the union code label. Doris had to scrap the perfectly good originals to have duplicates made by a union scene construction company. Failure to comply would mean blackballing the company, not only from New York stages but from theatres across the country. Eventually of course, the theatre unions almost organized themselves out of business. When off-Broadway developed, the unions immediately began to make rules about what they could and could not do. Before the era of subsidies, this was a grim handicap to independent artists.

When giving birth to a concert, twelve to fourteen hours in the theatre were not unusual. Everything practiced in the studio had to be expanded to the size of the stage. We had to learn which parts of

Doris Humphrey and Charles Weidman in Scriabin Etude. *Photo by Soichi Sunami.*

the floor were uneven or rough and become habituated to the acoustics and the new reality of the lights, which utterly transformed the movement. We had now moved into the strange magical world smelling of cold drafts and hot dressing rooms, makeup, lighted candles and wax (we beaded our eyelids with melted mascara), becoming more and more conscious of the waiting empty space of the auditorium, where the dance would finally be realized with the presence of that negative pole, the audience. An electric excitement permeated backstage. At the Guild, auspiciously our dressing room happened to be next to Alfred Lunt's.

The March 31 concert opened with the *Air for the G String*, followed by the *Air on a Ground Bass*. Dorothy, Gertrude Gerrish and Sylvia danced a trio Bach *Gigue;* Charles premiered his new *Passion and Compassion*, contrasting character studies of violent Savonarola and gentle St. Francis. Then we danced two movements of the Grieg *Concerto*, the first plus the third allegro marcato, with the adagio played in between. *Water Study* followed intermission; then Doris presented *Speed;* and Charles, *Scriabin Study;* his solo Gershwin *Preludes; Ringside;* and *Cowboys* for Eugene, Charles and John. *Life of the Bee* ended the program.

The opening was the same for the April 7 concert, with Charles's setting of Bach's *Jesu, Joy of Man's Desiring,* a Flemish-style medieval nativity with Rose Yasgour as the Virgin and the three boys as the three kings, replacing the *Gigue*. José Limón made his debut in the *Rhythmic Patterns of Java,* choreographed by Charles for the boys, which followed the *Concerto*. Charles danced a stunning Singhalese solo drum dance; Doris repeated *Speed,* followed by the *Scriabin Poem, Scriabin Study,* and *Minstrels* (by request); the closing once again was *Life of the Bee*.

John Martin's two columns in the Sunday *Times* saluted the new achievement. His perception and elucidation of what was involved in the new influence was of tremendous value in giving the new dance recognition.

Few dancers have a gift for composition which ranks with hers [Humphrey's]; . . . more than any other dancer who employs the modern idiom, she is able to see movement in its harmonic and contrapuntal aspects. Perhaps her most outstanding talent, however, lies in her ability to externalize her vision by means of the most difficult of dance mediums, the ensemble, with a minimum of loss in the process. . . .
Miss Humphrey has built up an ensemble which is unquestionably the peer of any similar organization which has been seen in America. The Diaghilev Ballet itself presented no more exquisitely plastic an instrument for

a choreographer to play upon. It responds to her direction with equal completeness whether the demand upon muscular coordination seems almost inordinate, as in certain moments of "Life of the Bee," or whether the necessity is for such subtle mental feats as memorizing the space and its rhythmic counterpart for the "Water Study."

It is a tribute of the highest sort to Miss Humphrey that these fourteen dancers have worked together with her now for approximately a year and a half. There is no hope of emolument to hold them, for their appearances are never more than four or five in a season, and then there is not enough profit accruing to warrant paying anything like a living wage to such a large number of people. They must provide themselves with livelihoods outside . . . sad commentary on the economic situation which faces the dancer—a situation which seems to have no remedy. [The twenties, thirties, and forties were BF—Before Foundations.]

On the other hand, no member of an ensemble such as this can have much expectation of fame or personal recognition; . . . by the very nature of the work they have thrown themselves into so wholeheartedly they must merge themselves as individuals into the group. Yet by the sheer vitality of her accomplishment Miss Humphrey manages to hold them together and to increase their range from composition to composition as her own increases.

. . . At the present moment, modernism generally has reference to the method of using the body as an abstract instrument to express visual forms apart from emotional or actual experience. From this point of view, Miss Humphrey is to be classified as a romanticist. She employs the body not in an abstract manner, but rather in an impersonal manner; she is not concerned with form for the sake of form, nor on the other hand is she ever guilty in the least degree of "self expression." She strikes a mean between the two schools.

Miss Humphrey's dances are peopled with human beings, never with elements of design. They have emotional warmth, whether they are presenting waves of the sea, or bees, or nameless figures moving in response to musical phrases. They do not however express a personal emotion; they give you nothing of their private lives and beliefs. The emotional content is generic; it is of any man or any woman; . . . [it does not] evoke a response out of sympathetic experience. It is, in other words, realism separated from actuality. Because of this very quality which can scale tremendous heights of heroic and noble feeling, the greatest danger which besets Miss Humphrey is that of indefinite beauty, or to put it more crudely, prettiness. That she escapes by a wider margin in every composition indicates how surely she is building. When she has entirely downed the suspicion of softness in her strong and grotesque movements, she will have downed her last enemy.

It is extraordinary to consider the variation in approach which has characterized her four major ballets to date. "Color Harmony" was more or less symphonic in form, though it grew out of visual form and not out of music; the first movement of the Grieg "Concerto" was an inspired instance of music visualization, in which the music hovered over the dancers as the gods hovered over the actors in the tragedies of the ancient Greeks; the "Water Study" threw aside musical rhythm and phrasing and arranged natural movements into art form; now comes "Life of the Bee" which is built along theatrical lines, with its two central figures almost characters.

In this newest work Miss Humphrey may have been moved by philosophical or entomological impulses, but she has actually created a piece of dramaturgy. The mode of expression is dancing rather than words or pantomime, and it sums up into one of the most tense and beautiful dramatic ballets of our day. Never was music missed less. The humming of an offstage chorus in varying rhythmic phrases, punctuated at rare intervals by a point of open vocal tone, provides a sinister aural background for a sinister picture. A fight to the death between the two principal figures, with the chorus massed on the floor at the side and back in frenetic expectation, contains as much excitement as almost any three melodramas one can mention.

Because she adapts her method to her subject and lets the performance actually grow out of the idea, Miss Humphrey's repertoire is never likely to become stale.

In May the company had its first out-of-town date, in the Philadelphia Academy of Music for the Philadelphia Forum. The group performed the *Air for the G String*, the *Concerto, Life of the Bee;* Doris revived her famous *Hoop Dance;* Charles repeated his *Japanese Actor.* The new solo for Doris was a Rameau-Godowsky *Sarabande.* But the heavy dark-green velvet costume obscured the delicacy of her movements. Perhaps it was all not stylized enough. This was one of her minor efforts.

Again I spent a summer in Southampton, assisting Emily at the children's camp, teaching dance, swimming, diving, canoeing, life saving, but more than ever eager to resume the round of classes and rehearsals for more concerts. Charles's postcard from the Lake Placid Club to Camp Winiday: "And how goes your vacation? Mine like yours I work for. I have danced here and there and every time I do they knock it off my bill. So if I keep on I'll have one lovely cheap time. It has been gorgeous up here. Cold but stimulating. See you soon. C.W." The welcome news came on September 10: "Back from vacations and anxious to see you. Please come to our tea-party on Thursday at 4:30 and we'll compare notes and view the coming year. Lovingly, Miss Doris."

With October came the great stock market crash, which was to alter our lives in unforeseeable ways. The day the market fell I remember the excitement in the studio as we discussed what was happening. Not long after this, my oldest brother was walking past the Empire State Building and narrowly missed being killed by the falling body of a suicide. The father of a group member would be a later casualty of the crisis. Both Doris and Charles took the attitude that the best answer to stress and tragedy was work, work, and more work.

For a November 15 Women's Club program, Doris prepared new solos which definitely moved away from her innate lyricism, at the same time offering another backward excursion into preclassical music, with *Courante* (Greene): "A lady did on a merry morn / call for her horse and falcon." Charles had a new solo suite titled *Five Studies: Diffidence, Devotion, Annoyance, Rage, Resignation* (Honegger) and a successful *Marionette Show* to music of Prokofiev. The group appeared in *Air for the G String* and *Life of the Bee*. Dorothy, Cleo, Ruth, Katherine and I danced a flight-and-pursuit abstraction to Bach's *Prelude No. 2 in C Minor*. This was an etude worked out in class, partly improvised, in oppositions. Dorothy moved on the first two measures, as if fleeing in slow motion, then held, as in twos we moved after her, alternating with sustained and frozen gesture. On the resolution, the hunted one stood firm, facing her pursuers, who relaxed their tension and came to rest. Doris's program notes read:

All the first part of the program . . . including the "Air on a Ground Bass" forms an antique suite, dating from Purcell . . . to Satie, who is quasi-modern writing in the ancient manner. Most of these compositions were written in the dance forms of the day but the modern dancer avoids the exact period-style, and prefers to find a free expression for the same musical ideas. Thus in the quaint "Air on a Ground Bass" Mr. Weidman sustains the reiterated bass theme and Miss Humphrey dances the air, by this means making visible to the eye the same form that strikes the ear. In "Passion and Compassion," Savonarola and Saint Francis live again in essence through Mr. Weidman's interpretation of the contrasting methods used by Medieval Men of God in interpreting His message. All of the Bach themes have the same freedom from traditional expression.

Beginning with "The Call" and "Gargoyle (Descent into a Dangerous Place)," the old comes to an end and the new begins with two most dissonant compositions, both in movement and music; and following this lead the rest of the program is devoted to untraditional dances in varying degrees of radicalism. . . . Each of the five Honegger bits is a clearly defined abstraction of the mood indicated, so that in a few minutes a most complex array of feeling is given form. The "Valse Caprice" is a lyric study in which both veil and body move in flowing designs to supplement each other. Then Marionettes move across their tinsel stage, imitating dolls who imitate life . . . another presentation of an eternal theme.

The "Scriabin Suite" which closes the program is in a dramatic key throughout—romantic in the sense that each of the dances is a personally felt emotion, but abstract in the sense that the drama is suggested in movement and not in pantomime.

In this program the approach to the dance is from many different angles. Miss Humphrey and Mr. Weidman believe that any approach is legitimate if it is sincere and the only criterion to judge by is the value of the dance itself. In other words, the dance is the thing, by whatever path. Sometimes they find inspiration in music, sometimes in drama, but in any case they believe that the form and technique for each dance should be unique in that it grows and flowers from the original conception regardless of any previous combination of movements, and lastly they believe that motion is the language of the dance and that all ideas, from whatever source, should be translated into this

Doris Humphrey in Descent into a Dangerous Place, *at Fire Island.*
Photo by Soichi Sunami.

Processional ending from Motion Drama. *Photo by Soichi Sunami.*

medium. Hence costume, decor, music and pantomime should fall properly
into second place, so that the dance may be foremost.

Charles's sense of the ridiculous and his elegant stylization of
peculiarly wooden puppets made a delightful theatre piece: the
young princess (Sylvia's role, which she did with great delicacy)
leaning out of the window combing her long Melisande blonde wig,
the entrance of the hero, the cruel father who interrupts the flirtation,
calling his henchmen to battle the prince, the marvelous weightless
duel, and the triumphant exit of prince with lady.

At this point, the only decor used in Humphrey-Weidman concerts
was the stunningly simple set of Gordon Craig-ish flat folding
screens. Now, for the *Descent into a Dangerous Place*, Doris crouched
on a cylindrical box. She maneuvered with expertise around the
obstacle, making a strangely imaginative progression, abstract, angular, gargoylish, with unexpected spare motions, sharp accents, and
dislocations. She was philosophically years ahead of the *Chaminade
Veil* dance, inconsistently tucked into the second half of the same
program, the last time for that Denishawn piece.

That fall we strenuously rehearsed two new works, the *Drama of
Motion* and Ravel's *La Valse*. Doris's belief that "motion will flow into
new and vigorous channels if severed from music" was epitomized in
the *Drama of Motion*. Here we were launched into unrelieved silence.
True, Mary Wigman had created musicless dances in Germany, but
Doris had not seen them. This development was simply in the air of
the times.

The opening Processional was a slow-motion frieze designed for
trios, entering, crossing the stage, then exiting in unison, the arms of
the dancers on the outside rising in a curve to come to rest on the
shoulders of the one in between, like a resolving chord in music.
Letitia, Katherine and I were the opening trio. In slow motion I rose
from kneeling between them, my circling arms opened their connected arms, like a gate. Each trio had a variation so there was a
continuous interest in the design, which was what this part was all
about. The concentration required to balance on the toes, body
arched backward, head back, eyes following one arm stretched upward to infinity, without any musical support, was prodigious.

Pauline made one-piece ankle-length dresses, with rounded necklines, short sleeves, wrap-around skirts, of flesh-colored cotton
crepe—sheer, classical, sculpturesque. In that costume I modeled for
Gaetano Cecere, Prix de Rome sculptor, when he created the relief for
a capital building façade in Washington.

Doris danced alone in the second section's Transition and Interlude. She wore similarly cut light figured chiffon, and her movements were at first calm, then full of "surprising accents, all quirks and jerks," in which she was joined by the three lightest, swiftest dancers—Sylvia, Dorothy, and Evelyn—for a study in contrasts. In the Conclusion, the ensemble returned, now all in black. José, the one male, appeared with us. From opposite sides, in two groups we lunged toward each other in syncopated antiphonal rhythms, eventually joining into one black mass, making a sweep of the stage, swirling to a domino fall. This final section was marked by stamping foot accents and by great rushes of power.

At this time, Raymond Duncan, the adored Isadora's younger brother, came to New York where in a shop on 57th Street he exhibited his handmade woven garments, sandals, tie-dyed scarves, and hand-printed tracts on his philosophy of "Actionalism." Raymond, a great original, was fifty years ahead of his time. In the sixties no one would have paid any attention to him, but America of the twenties could not tolerate such eccentricity, so he lived and worked in Paris.

One of the new dancers in the group, Ruth Allred, made a point of visiting and talking to Raymond, and she invited him to attend a Humphrey rehearsal at Hunter College. When Isadora's brother entered at the back we were going through the last part of the *Drama of Motion*. In our blacks, of course, and without any sound. The first musicless abstract ballet in America came to an end. Raymond approached the footlights. He looked gravely at us in a long silence. Finally he pronounced, "Well, it's a long, hard road." Then he turned and pattered up the aisle, fillet around his head, toga flying behind him. Exit Raymond.

Raymond, symbol of liberty, might live in France and dress and act in the style of the ancient Greeks, but he was a loyal American. On Liberation Day when Paris was freed of German occupation, it was Raymond Duncan, unbidden by any general, who on his own impulse rushed to the top of the American Embassy to unfurl the first American flag in liberated Paris.

Twenty-five years after he watched us rehearse, Raymond cordially welcomed me at his Rue du Seine atelier, where on the Fourth of July he traditionally held Open House for fellow Americans. First a Frenchman read the Preamble to the Constitution in French, then Raymond in his toga repeated it in English, concluding with his Whitmanesque poem, "O You Forty-Eight States!" On the walls were photographs of Isadora. Raymond's translations of Greek tragedies lined the window, translations which he had printed him-

Doris Humphrey's La Valse.

self on his handmade printing press. Hovering in the background was Ama, his Lettish friend, in woven white nun's robe and wimple. The two together were outstanding presences in Paris.

If the soundless abstraction of the new *Drama of Motion* was far too modern for romantic Raymond Duncan, some of the Humphrey dancers were uneasy when Doris started work on Ravel's *La Valse*. In their eyes *La Valse* was not modern enough. In the increasing social distress of the Depression, whose effects were more and more visible, artists, supposed to be full of social significance, protested what was happening to their fellow men. Gertrude and Sylvia were the most concerned. Gertrude danced with the Humphrey group but studied with Martha Graham at the same time, until Martha put a stop to this doubling. Like vestal virgins, modern dancers were committed to one master. If you were a disciple of one artist, you could not study with any other. Graham dancers were even restrained from attending performances of other modern artists, lest the purity of their vision become clouded.

For the approaching January season of the new Dance Repertory Theatre, Martha's themes would be *Visions of the Apocalypse* (Reutter): Toil, Famine, Ruthlessness, Pestilence, Mourning, Prayer, Judgment; *Lamentation* (Kodaly); *Futility, Monotony, Supplication;* and *Requiem* (Krenek). In this era of unprecedented misery, socially conscious dancers would line up on the stage and literally spell out the significant word B-R-E-A-D. So what was Doris thinking of to tackle a dance of a decadent bygone century when the immediate world was experiencing disaster?

When a committee of the dancers approached me to join them in asking Doris for an appointment in which to air their view, I was susceptible. To tell the truth, *La Valse* was the first choreographic experience under Doris's direction which was more trying than joyous. The struggle to match thirty-two separate feet in the step-step-close waltz pattern with all the stylized variations Doris wanted was not easy, and everyone's patience was tried, including Doris's.

The meeting took place. If she was momentarily shaken—and I had the feeling Doris would have liked to throw us all out—she was soon calm. "There have been no compromises in my life," she stated on more than one occasion. Willy-nilly, we must learn to waltz. Gertrude defected to join Martha's group; the rest of us learned to waltz.

La Valse was an historical, sociological compendium. The group began its embryonic rhythm in silhouette, swaying from side to side in hands-linked circle, on the knees, heads touching the floor. The shape of the waltz appears as first the men, then the women, rise on one knee, arching over their partners, who sink back. Alternately lifting and falling, the couples rise from their knees to their feet, into broad, peasanty, polka swings and lunges. Charles, the Master of Ceremonies, appears, clearing a path for the entrance of Doris.

The lead couple then initiates a formal walk around before the true waltz, which we observe. They sustain a romantic duo in the center while the couples, tightly linked in a circle around them, begin to progress through the classical waltz to the heavy German, then the light tripping Viennese style, dipping bodies arched back. The rhythm accelerates to a running route. Still in a circle, facing now forward, now backward in continuous ronde, at the climax the couples break away, elbows linked, whirling themselves to the floor. Through the final maelstrom, Doris and Charles, pillars of society, walk coming forward, looking from side to side, at each other and at the audience, suggesting poles of respectability as against society's disintegrative sensuality as an aftermath of war.

This intoxicating revel Pauline costumed in empire style: the girls in filmy décolleté gowns, men with high stocks, white cravats, black swallowtail coats; Doris in floating pink mousseline de soie, Charles in black velvet. Actually we were sixteen girls, half of us taking the men's roles.

In time, of course, we came to love Ravel's rapturous "whirl of decadence," especially when performed outdoors in Robin Hood Dell with the Philadelphia Orchestra or in Lewisohn Stadium with the New York Philharmonic orchestra. The handling of the group— "sensuous, languid, playful, piquant, sentimental, showy"—was masterly; and the two central figures of Doris and Charles made their social comment by standing apart from the spectacle of society coming apart at the seams. Doris would have a social point of view; it would be expressed in her own way, not the currently popular way.

When Doris invited Letitia and Ernestine to join the group in late 1929, she sent them a carefully thought out letter reproduced here in part:

I think we may justly call our group the leading ensemble in New York and possibly America. I include, of course, all group dancing in musical comedy or opera or motion picture houses, as belonging to a different class. I am talking about the concert stage only. I merely mention the standing of the group as an interesting fact of the present, but I have in mind that this is an ephemeral state, and that the only true standard an artist can have for his work is his own valuation of it. This ideal is perhaps impossible to maintain in a material and commercial world, so I mention our present place for what it is worth.

As for myself, I want to tell you frankly what my aim is as an artist in relationship to this group—very simply it is this. I want to visualize with it the visions and dreams that make up the entire impetus and desires of my life. The group is my medium just as marble is the sculptor's material only of course the simile is not complete because the group is made of human beings who are able to add their own power of mind and body to the physical material that sculpture uses. This sometimes makes composing more difficult, by the way, because the varying powers of sixteen people must be harmonized and smoothed into a cohesive whole, and this is not always so easy.

However, the individual character of each member is most important to the whole because the group depends on the strength and comprehension and experience of each one. You must know as dancers that every move you make reveals you, even though your natural tendencies may be thwarted or changed by training. What you really are remains an easily read story even to the layman. Now you might think that in an ensemble of sixteen the individual characteristics of each one would not be apparent, but on the contrary the character of the dance is such that everyone is revealed. You can easily understand why when you think of it, at some time during an ensemble dance, through the varying changes of the pattern, every one is brought to the eye of the on-looker not as a separate entity, not as you alone, but as an individual in relation to the whole, so that if there is one who has not grasped the conception of the movement the group is doing, the eye readily detects that one and even the untrained knows that a discord has been struck.

Now for this reason in the course of composing for this group, I call upon each one to use their utmost in perception, in physical skill, in imagination and emotion; and whatever they are able to command of these diverse ingredients makes or breaks the composition, providing of course that my work of composing and training has been well done. So do not believe, put it negatively, that this group shall be formed of automatons all moving exactly like me or exactly like each other, because I think there is more power in variation than in machine-like regularity, and so my aims may be summed up like this: I am first a creative artist, thirsting to see my conceptions made visible; after that I am also interested in developing individual talent in others, in performing for audiences, educating audiences, promoting the cause of the Dance, making money, and establishing a Dance Theatre in America.

Please consider very carefully whether you would like to work with us or not because this is something very serious indeed in our minds. The girls feel they are a living part of a vital art, which they are trying with all their might to make as significant and sincere as possible. They feel a spiritual release in the dance from the pressures of materialism in a machine-made age, and to me it is everything that goes to make up life. If you come in, please think of it as a serious occupation which will demand a great deal of work and energy, and a space of at least three years in time. The rewards that I am sure of are lots of training and the satisfaction of doing dances that have been conceived and composed as works of art. There may be other rewards in the future such as fame, and money, and travel but these are only the size of a man's hand at present. Rehearsals are twice a week at night usually, but that increases to three or more before concerts, and in addition there are costume fittings during the day. I expect everyone to come to rehearsals faithfully and to arrange vacations and family events so it is possible. This year (1930) there will be four performances during the first week of January, and possibly some others out of town. In these latter I am able to pay all expenses and ten dollars to each one. The only restriction I make is that no members of my group shall belong to any other group, as this has already proven to be impractical.[3]

Already as a specifically "concert" artist, Doris was thinking ahead to an American Dance Theatre. Her aims of expressing her own concepts and of developing talents in others were outstandingly well realized, as the years would prove. The struggle to perform and to educate dance audiences would be unremitting. Fame did accrue, there was some travel, but making money was never in the cards. And where in America today is the American Dance Theatre which was the noble dream of the young dancers of the late twenties?

The Dance Repertory Theatre; 'Sacre'

R I V A L R Y between the leaders of the modern movement was inevitable. Fostered by the same artistic parents—Ruth St. Denis and Ted Shawn—Martha Graham and Doris Humphrey created a new dance for our times and contested against each other in doing it. Their goals were similar, but their natures—"Martyr Martha" and "Doric Doris," as Louis Horst put it—and their works were as different as night and day.

Martha, leaving Denishawn in 1923, spent two years as soloist in the Greenwich Village Follies. After a year of teaching at the Eastman School in Rochester, she made her New York debut two years before Doris and Charles did theirs. Charles had partnered Martha in some of the Denishawn spectacles, but the two feminine leaders did not appear together in the Denishawn tours. As independent artists they now inhabited separate islands. At this stage, Martha was all dark, introspective, angular, percussive; Doris was essentially light, lyrical and flowing.

Already Martha Graham was the priestess of a cult. The impact of her sharp percussive contractions and releases of the body, like a woman in labor, affected me so much that when her concerts ended, I walked deliberately under the thundering Sixth Avenue el to scream aloud, ridding myself of the tensions she had built up in the theatre. Had Graham been born in a primitive society, she would have been the high priestess. Her psychic power was extraordinary. No matter how many other dancers might be on stage with her, even when her back was turned you watched only Martha, so great was her concentration. She was a phenomenal psychic force, which you either succumbed to or resisted. I resisted.

1930 was an important year in the evolution of dance. Helen Tamiris convinced Martha, Doris and Charles that the four of them united in a repertory season would gain wider acceptance from the public than was possible if they continued their lonely, scattered, expensive, single one-night concerts. They accepted Tamiris's vision as realistic and desirable, so the Dance Repertory Theatre began, and the Maxine Elliott Theatre was booked for eight days beginning January 5.

Mrs. John W. Alexander, Irwin Chanin, Mrs. Ralph Jonas, Otto Kahn, Mrs. W. K. Vanderbilt, and Mrs. Ernest F. Walton were sponsors. The Actor-Managers Inc., of which Helen Arthur was director, managed the marathon event. All four artists and their companies shared the first and last two performances; each had two programs alone. The excellent idea of unifying the field of modern dance got off to a flying start, with expectations that it would increase to a two-week season the following year and that as time went on it would widen its scope to include other worthy artists.

Though all parties agreed to share equal time on the program, only Humphrey-Weidman conformed to the twenty minutes of dance time allotted. A large and distinguished audience (with Leopold Stokowski sitting in a box) had already been in the theatre two full hours before we, the last ones, came on.

Backstage the atmosphere was unusually tense. A notice on the call board—evidently Martha's paranoid directive—forbad any conversation with the Graham dancers before or after they were on stage. There was to be no communication in the theatre and watching from the wings was prohibited. Martha opened the bill with several solos; her group danced *Heretic*. Tamiris, who had studied with Fokine, danced with the Metropolitan Opera Ballet and in night clubs, and was "least experienced of the four in the ways of concert dancing," stood up well in this trial of artistic strength. Her *Dance of the City*, with siren accompaniment, and her vigorously performed *Negro Spirituals* were favored over her *Impressions of the Bullring, a Twentieth Century Bacchanale* and *Portrait of a Lady*. As *The New Yorker* put it, "these were easy to follow and vivacious to the point of being rompish."

The first movement of the Grieg *Concerto* brought cheers from the audience, as did the *Life of the Bee*. Charles performed his *Japanese Actor; Minstrels* had to be encored. The romantic sculptural Scriabin duet closed the evening, with all four artists taking a bow with Louis Horst, the indispensable pianist.

Even *The New Yorker*, which up to that time had deliberately ignored the arts, now took notice: "If the form interests you, you will discover in the activities of the Dance Repertory Theatre, and those who are going in the same direction, a sincere endeavor to make of 'the dance' an entity capable of standing on its own legs—and what legs some of them are!"

The Monday night Humphrey-Weidman concert offered six new works: a starkly abstract duet for Doris and Charles, *Salutation to the Depths,* Doris's new abstract solos *The Call* and *Breath of Fire*—these three works with Dane Rudyhar, the composer, at the piano—the *Drama of Motion* and *La Valse* for the group, and Charles's *Tumbler of Our Lady,* another medieval stylization featuring the acrobatic ability of Eugene LeSieur. Ernestine and Letitia had now joined the main ensemble, and José performed in the *Drama of Motion.*

According to John Martin:

If the Dance Repertory Theatre had done nothing more than provide an opportunity for the showing of Miss Humphrey's "Drama of Motion," it would have more than justified its existence, for here is a composition which defies adequate description in that there is nothing in the entire range of the modern dance with which to compare it . . . while others have talked [about dance being an independent medium without the assistance of music or pantomimic implication] Miss Humphrey has acted, and the result is quite the most extraordinary creation that has come from the mind of this highly gifted composer . . . from the combination of lyrical beauty both of design and movement, dramatic suspense and fantastic lightness, there emerges a dance composition that has plunged into a hitherto almost untouched wilderness of plastic potentialities, and has retained at the same time its contact with humanity and genuineness.

"The Call" and "The Breath of Fire" [were] danced surpassingly by Miss Humphrey. . . . In a spirit of frenzy she poses the mad activity of flame against its comparative fixedness of base.

. . . Less effective were Mr. Weidman's "The Tumbler of Our Lady" in which his central figure was consistently out of style, and Miss Humphrey's "Choreographic Waltz" by Ravel, in which she and Mr. Weidman and the ensemble gave an extremely decadent picture of a pseudo-Empire Bacchanale.

. . . In addition to the superb dancing of the two principals, the performance of the ensemble was exemplary. Far from being merely a group of ambitious disciples, it proved itself once again to be an aggregation of talented young artists.

Mary F. Watkins in the *Tribune* found *La Valse*

brilliantly conceived and vividly executed . . . [it] preserved with astonishing and admirable fidelity the fantastic and fateful quality of the music and revealed at the end a transparent and lovely choreographic sensibility on the part of its designers. Old and familiar numbers which called forth the evening's loudest applause were the inimitable "Water Study" by the group, Mr. Weidman's clever and subtle Gershwin "Preludes," and the utterly absurd and delicious parody of a Marionette Theatre, "Once Upon a Time."

Another reviewer found the Processional from the *Drama of Motion* "surely one of the most beautiful dances ever seen here, with all the archaic flavor of a Greek frieze and all the pliancy of the modern temper."

The second Humphrey-Weidman evening later in the week also had premieres: Doris's *Descent into a Dangerous Place*, a starkly abstract composition, was later headlined in *The Times* (to Doris's fury) as ELFIN DANCE GIVEN BY DORIS HUMPHREY. Mr. Martin found it

outstanding. She creates an elfin mood, a genuine suspense, and a choreographic design of originality and beauty entailing prodigious technical demands which she meets with ease.

Mr. Weidman has apparently taken a leaf from Martha Graham's notebook for his "Three Studies (Diffidence, Annoyance, Rage)." They are couched in her terms of composition, but are miles removed from her pungent comment. This is by no means to declare them ineffective, however, for Mr. Weidman supplies them with his own brand of humorous ragging. The third new dance is also of his creation, and is performed by him with the assistance of six men. It is entitled "The Conspirator" and tells without the aid of music a plan of convicts ostensibly to break prison. Its treatment is obvious and consequently long drawn out.

Color Harmony had its last performance on that program, but the *Concerto* was destined for orchestral performances with both the New York Philharmonic and the Philadelphia Orchestra.

In a *Theatre Arts Monthly* article, "A Study in American Modernism," Margaret Gage asked the important question, what is modernism in the American art of the dance? She spent a week at the Dance Repertory Theatre trying to find out, watching for experiments and tendencies expressive of the twentieth century, "hoping to find something akin in spirit to the scientific 'modernism' associated with the names of Einstein, Eddington, Whitehead, Jeans and Millikan;

something with a free sweep and grandeur to it that the cramped and already old-fashioned materialistic outlook of the nineteenth century had never visioned." She found

bits and pieces snatched from the nervous flux of modern activity . . . plastered on the outside of the dance like bright posters . . . angled elbows and knees that stuck out with no relation to the whole, much unnecessary versatility of hip movement—possibly to prove our modern freedom from all restraint!—reminiscent snatches from the German schools, mechanical imitations, weird noises, jazz, confusion, ugliness—not in the interest of any apparent meaning, but just because. . . . If that had been all I should have questioned my own conception of the term and wondered if perhaps "modernism" in the American dance meant mere imitative expression of the trivial, the bizarre and the disconnected.

But she saw more than that:

. . . broad creative flashes in the work of all four artists that thrilled me, made me grateful for the vision of a Dance Repertory Theatre. From the successful compositions I learned that "modernism" in the American dance means unswerving and unsentimental directness of idea presented in a style dictated wholly by that idea, with everything whittled ruthlessly away that is non-essential to the main structural lines. Abstract design is the first consideration rather than technical virtuosity or the projection of dramatic emotion . . . the elements of the dance composition are riveted together to express that design with the simplicity and strength of steel construction. Be the idea great or small, beautiful or ugly, it stands "naked and unashamed." In other words the style of presentation is absorbed by the idea and becomes transparent. Graham [is] the most consistent "modernist" . . . [a] modern psychologist in dance form, tending in her newer compositions to neglect beauty for satire and psycho-pathology.

Tamiris' joy and vitality in movement seem often to override meaning. She has a vigorous freedom of rhythm, and a straight-forward sincerity but many of her dances are manufactured from the outside rather than created from within—they lack organic unity. Her "Triangle Dance," experimenting in pure geometrical form, was completely successful.

Gage found Humphrey-Weidman covering such a wide field in the dance that the result was a confused mixture of styles and periods.

Much of their work is not strictly "modernistic"; Weidman's "Marionette Theatre" and "Minstrels," delightfully clever, finished bits of comedy. Most typically "modernistic" were the Scriabin duet, the "Water Study" and the "Life of the Bee," each expressing one central idea and unfolding it with clarity and completeness, yet with economy of detail. Graham has perhaps more originality but Humphrey's breadth of invention, variety and gift for sustained excellence make her the most significant choreographer of the repertory group. Hers is a feeling for greater and more comprehensive freedom in design. Even her failures are the result of adventurous experiment—a necessary quality in the development of a new art, or the revival and restatement of an ancient one.

Gage noted that Humphrey used twelve to fifteen dancers for the ensemble works—the number of the ancient Greek chorus. She concluded,

Surely this new interest in choreography as a serious art is the most vigorous sign of life in our modern dance movement. This subordination of technical skill and personal glamour of individual performers to the communal presentation of ideas in dance design shares in the truest spirit of dancing down the ages, and is at the same time particularly fitted to express the impersonal grandeur of those new vistas being revealed to us through astro-physics and the modern scientific view of the universe. Here it is that the vital kernel of "modernism" in the American art of the dance has its greatest possibilities for significant growth.

One of Doris's program notes elucidates the potentialities of group work:

Through the new conception of significance in the ensemble which has developed during the last ten years, the dance promises to come into its full stature, just as music flowered through the symphony. A group of bodies is as varied, abstract and colorful a medium as the orchestra, and gives the composer equally rich material to fulfill the range of his vision. The new ensemble also has the architectural and impersonal attributes of the orchestra as distinguished from the personal and expressionistic, unique qualities sadly needed in the dance to place it more seriously among the arts.

Mei Lan Fang and his company came to the 49th Street Theatre in February. I admired the exquisite subtlety of Mei Lan Fang's sleeve gestures, the abstract mime of rowing a boat, the stylization of a laughing-crying general, the rhythm pattern of the body so similar except for the reversal of breathing. This elegant company overshadowed New York's old downtown Chinese theatre, to which Doris and Charles had taken the group on an excursion the year before. There we had been so overwhelmed by the gonging din of the music we could hardly perceive what was taking place on stage. Large family parties chewing nuts, having a sociable time, and the stage manager's movements held our attention.

Unemployed apple vendors now dotted the streets of the city. It was the year of Roark Bradford's and Mark Connelly's *The Green Pastures,* that heartwarming play with music of the black man's celebration of the Bible, the glorious spirituals sung by the Hall Johnson choir. One left the theatre uplifted and singing, something only Alvin

Ailey's dance company has been able to do for me since. This was also the year of lynchings—thirty of them, not all of them in the Deep South.

In March the company took the boat to Boston, a memorable trip which proved Doris, Katherine and me good sailors, while Charles and most of the others in the group went below when we left the Cape Cod Canal and briefly felt the Atlantic surge before entering Boston harbor. The Boston Opera House performance was a big benefit affair, but the huge house was far from full. A few titters came from the audience when the silent *Water Study* began, with the group in nude-color leotards. Members of the Boston Symphony Orchestra were in the pit, with Louis Horst and Pauline Lawrence at two pianos. In one Boston paper George Brinton Beal called the program one of "drama carried to an exceptional degree of perfection: like dream figures from a world apart from reality, the ever-shifting figures moved now in dusk, now in full brilliance of reflected light, weaving endless patterns of pure beauty, designs rich in artistic content."

H. T. Parker filled one and a half columns of analysis in the *Transcript*, headed NEW WAYS OF THE DANCE TO BOSTON EYES. As if looking through a telescope, Mr. Parker elaborated on each work as if it had come from outer space and never been observed before. He was meticulous in observation:

Compared with their predecessors of the season (Argentina, Kreutzberg, and Georgi), Doris Humphrey and Charles Weidman practice the austerities of the dance. They are young, earnest, ambitious, unspoiled. They believe in what they do; work at it with mind and imagination. They minister to no decaying art but one that is rising in American regard and understanding. They seldom talk of it. When they do, they are not dispensing vague parlor "bunk." Their practice squares with their theory, since they are still honest with themselves and with their audiences. Therefore, perhaps those audiences are not yet as numerous as they might be.

Another Boston critic (E.B.) concluded, "It is a brave, pure art of movement they offer, and much of their reward must, of consequence, come from a limited group. It is to be hoped that group will find them in time."

That extremely long program began with the *Air for the G String,* followed by *Air on a Ground Bass, Water Study,* Doris's *Hoop Dance* ("an early composition, performed in every city in America and most of the Orient"), a new ensemble piece to Tcherepnine's *March,* a stylization of observers waiting for, watching, and reacting to an invisible parade as it goes by (a slight work, demonstrating rhythmic counterpoint and unison in the handling of a group). After Charles's *Japanese Actor* came the *Concerto;* then *Minstrels, Drama of Motion, Marionette Theatre, Descent into a Dangerous Place,* the *Bees* and the Scriabin duet.

On the return boat, Cleo and I, rooming together, decided to have an art gallery, pinning up picture ads from programs, newspapers and magazines onto the porthole curtains. Soon the other staterooms blossomed similarly, and we played at being gallery visitors, critics and collectors. The first prize went to a dancing school advertisement which pictured a young lady with a gauzy veil, knee-deep in a pond, arms outstretched, rising from the deep, captioned, "It is art alone that marks the prime of nations," advertising a School of Harmonic Expression which taught "Dancing as a Recreation, a Science, and a Fine Art."

A month before the Boston concert, Charles Laskey one day asked me if I would like to be in *Le Sacre du Printemps* of Stravinsky, then in rehearsal under Leonide Massine and scheduled for April performances first at the Philadelphia Opera House and then at the Metropolitan Opera House in New York. Both Charles and John Glenn were in it. "How could I be in it? I know nothing of ballet." Charles assured me that they needed one more girl, there wasn't a ballet step in it, and I could do it.

Rehearsals took place in the Dalton School gymnasium every afternoon. Massine at that time was under contract with S. L. Rothafel, supplying ballets every two weeks for the Roxy Theatre. The extra task of working on *Sacre* was for Massine a refreshing change from the grinding work at the Roxy.

Among the twenty girls rehearsing in it were Rose Yasgour and Helen Strumlauf from the Humphrey company; Lily Mehlman, Lillian Ray, Kitty Reese, Mary Rivoire, Ethel Rudy, Lillian Shapero, Anna Sokolow (my partner in the Round Dance of Spring), Hortense Bunsick, Irene Emery, Louise Preston, and Sylvia Wasserstrom from the Graham company. Martha Graham was to be the soloist, with the part of the Sacrificial Virgin. The other girls were Winifred Bagger, Betty Barr, Miriam Catheron, Jocelyn Gordon, and Rose Marshall. The men dancers were Caruso Baroto, Giles Barbridge, Etienne Baronne, John Casanova, Fred Curtis, Bernard Day, John Glenn, G. G. Jerome, Harold Kolb, Charles Laskey, Warren Leonard, Joe Levy, Buddy Niles, S. Portopovich, Jack Quinn, Oscar Reale, Jack Seulitrinic, and Alex Zarembovsky. Gerald Stevens was the Sage; Anita Bay, the Witch.

To catch up with forty dancers who had already been rehearsing a full month and memorize movements unlike any I had ever done before was quite a challenge. Massine himself was a fascinating artist to watch. Speaking only a few words of English, he directed in French and Russian with his Russian assistant's help. We worked to a piano reduction of the score. The rhythms were magnificent; the movements full of extraordinary energy and peasant stylization. Even with piano, every rehearsal was musically exhilarating; and, of course, the larger the group the more psychic power present, the more possible variation of pattern. *Sacre,* fifty-five minutes long with Stokowski's timing, was the most sustained, vigorous, demanding dance in my three years' experience.

After the long introduction with sets of girls holding ropes of flowers, and with men parading slowly in, we girls seated ourselves primitive fashion, legs stretched straight forward, the men standing behind us. With the change from oboe melody to Stravinsky's sharply accented, irregular rhythms, the girls' arms described vertical hand-over-hand grasping gestures. We swung both arms wide to the side, then moved our forearms, with fists, sharply sideward to and fro in stylizations of plucking vines and beating grain, while the boys behind us stamped and jumped as if chopping down trees. United, we stood up and danced in place with vertical leaps up, then hands and bodies swept low to the floor, hearty Russian peasant bowing. Each passage had many repetitions; the phrases themselves were asymmetrical.

Not at all sure of what I was trying to master, I happened to step into the elevator two weeks later on my way to the gym and found only one other person in it: Massine. His big black eyes regarded me gravely. He did not smile. He said, *"You* must be vairry careful." My heart sank. Did he mean I wasn't careful enough in my part? Was he telling me I would have to go? "I knew a girl in England once," he went on. "She looked just like you. She dry-cleaned a costume by herself one day, and she was burned to death. So *you* must be vairry careful."

Four of the men and six of us girls were chosen to appear in costume at the Wanamaker Auditorium with Nicholas Roerich, the old master himself, lecturing on "The Eternal Garment." The costumes he designed so realistically, with laced boots, long heavy tunics, and long wooden beads for the girls, weighed heavily on us.

Stokowski came to rehearsals periodically. Each time, drastic changes were made for the better. If there were no visitors, he was all to the point, cogent, explaining verbally to the dancers the emotions behind the music. This was much heeded since on principal, Massine, like classical ballet masters in general, never gave one word of interpretation to the dancers, who are taught steps as abstractly as mathematics. You did as you were told, no questions asked. Stokowski saw at once that we were moving like automatons, with no feeling for what we were doing. Disregarding the choreographer, he pulled me from the line, made me kneel, raise a bent arm, and vibrate it to demonstrate a prayer gesture to the Earth Spirit. If members of the board of the League of Composers—wealthy lady patrons of the arts—were attending, Stokowski would put on pyrotechnic displays. However, his theatre instinct was always right. While Massine looked on, Stokowski changed the final lift of the Virgin, rearranged the spacing of the ensemble for the ending, and in other ways tightened up the mass designs.

Another display of temperament was the puzzling attitude of Martha Graham, who had a long time to wait before her entrance in the second half. During rehearsal Martha sat in a corner, shawl over her head. When she did move it was with condescension. It was hard on Massine and on the forty dancers supporting her. Her disdain for the whole proceedings was like a damp plague over the climax of rehearsals. Finally, close to performance time, Massine, desperate, told her, "I think the part is too difficult for you, Miss Gra'm. Perhaps you are not well. Anita Bay shall do it instead." Martha tossed her head, refused to allow the substitute to take over and continued to rehearse in a half-hearted sulky way.

It was not until on stage with the full Philadelphia Orchestra and an

Scene from Le Sacre du Printemps.

Martha Graham in Le Sacre du Printemps.

audience of several thousand people that she deigned to unleash a volcanic quality so astonishing to the corps that we almost stopped dancing in amazement. This seemed to me a professionally dishonest attitude. How much fairer if she had relinquished the part to someone else, someone who would respect both the choreographer and the choreography during those months of rehearsal!

Another temperamental side was revealed to me. By accident one day a pin fell inside my shoe and pricked my foot. The Band-aid on my foot caused Massine's Russian assistant to warn me quickly, "Now you must watch carefully. Because you have enemies. You must watch everything."

"Enemies!" I exclaimed. "It can't be. It's accidental." He then detailed happenings among Russian ballet companies. One's boots might be filled with water, pins and glass spread, or costumes tightly sewn up before a quick change. Someone altered a trap door on the stage in Buenos Aires where Nijinsky was to dance and he nearly broke his leg. This kind of ballet intrigue was new to me. In the Humphrey-Weidman company there might be passionate and jealous feelings, but they were always controlled. Working with Doris and Charles we experienced a single, uniform devotion to the tasks at hand; displays of temper were almost unknown. The general atmosphere was one of total, devotional concentration.

Doris and Charles also entrained with the *Sacre* company for Philadelphia, for they were featured players in the opening work, Schoenberg's *Die Glückliche Hand*. This experimental one-act opera had Ivan Ivantzoff (baritone) as the Man; Doris mimed the Woman, Charles the Stranger who takes the Woman away from the hero; Olin Howland was a Chimera; John Glenn and Charles Laskey had bit parts as Workmen. Reuben Mamoulian directed, Robert Edmond Jones was the designer.

At the first *Sacre* stage rehearsal in the opera house, Stokowski chose to conduct seated in a saddle attached to a saw-horse with his feet in stirrups. Such antics aside, there was no doubt he knew the score perfectly, and his eighty musicians knew he knew it. They responded completely to his direction.

The big task of coordinating the scenery behind us, the lighting, and the stage effects, in addition to mastering the densest symphonic score of the early twentieth century, did not keep Stokowski from detecting the unsuitability of Roerich's costumes, which completely hid the movement. Our violent motions caused the wooden beads to break their strings, ricocheting in minor thunderclaps as they rolled over the stage. On Stokowski's insistence, at the last minute, as many animal skins as could be rounded up from a Philadelphia costumer were substituted. Instead of getting black and blue marks from wooden beads striking me in the face, I had the dubious pleasure of inhaling pony hairs, which flew into my eyes and mouth when I jumped.

But all these effects were as nothing compared to the tremendously moving sonorities of the Philadelphia Orchestra making Le Sacre an astonishing musical experience. Every rehearsal and every perform- ance, chills ran up and down my spine for the Pagan Night mysti- cal opening of the second section, when one by one kneeling girls rose as if in trance, to circle, haunted and hunting, for the chosen victim among them to appear. The violence of the Round Dance of Spring closing the first part was so consuming I had to suck on a lemon in order to swallow and ease my burning throat. Most of the dancers fell flat to the floor in sheer exhaustion between parts one and two.

Twenty-six years after its sensational Paris premiere, Sacre no longer drew hisses and cane-beatings from an irate audience. The Philadelphians were impressed: "The startling spectacle of bare- legged girls and men, whirling madly and stamping upon the stage to an orgiastic fury of sound, and a futuristic fantasy of music drama frankly and officially termed 'a symbolical hallucination of forms, colors and sounds,' scenically and symphonically shattered all histor- ical precedent of Philadelphia Orchestra performances." Another reviewer found "Stokowski (conducting without baton) flew the ensign of unabashed modernism . . . and made 'Sacre' seem the quintessence of clarity, after the stylized spree of Teutonic metaphysics."

If it was "epic" in Philadelphia, after the New York opening Olin Downs in The New York Times wrote of its deeper significance. Stokowski's curtain speech thanked the audience for its support toward a new synthesis of theatre, on the basis of a "rhythmical polyphony," of all its resources of drama, music, lighting, the dance, mime, in new ways that accorded with modern thinking, and that were perhaps to eventuate in an American form of art.

Mr. Downs found the Schoenberg work

musically meager, but undeniably atmospheric and original in its combina- tion of music, color and other theatrical ingredients . . . highly decadent . . . an extreme of pessimism, looking in fact toward death.

On the other hand, the music of Stravinsky is that of life, on however primitive or brutal a plane, and last night after the murky Poesque creation of Schoenberg, it fell upon mind and senses as rejuvenation, indeed a rebirth, from a fertile soil of new force and new horizons of power. The scenery, particularly memorable for the iron twilight of the second part, and the orchestra, conducted by Mr. Stokowski with thrilling incisiveness and nervous power, made for some the real essence of the occasion.

Sacre was the high point of the year, and Downs, the *Times* music critic, gave it two and a half columns. In the same paper Martin had five long paragraphs, featuring Massine's richly inventive choreography and Martha's performance. To Martin it was a "noteworthy contribution to the movement for a synthetic theatre art which shall include all the contributory arts on equal terms. Massine covered himself with glory with his endlessly inventive movement filled with the same pagan fire and rapture as the music." Equal to Graham's Sacrificial Dance was the Round Dance of Spring in the first section.

Martin found the setting and staging for *Die Glückliche Hand* mild, romantic and flowing where the libretto is fevered, ugly, hysterical. Against these handicaps, Doris Humphrey "labored devotedly and to some purpose, her plastique was beautiful and eloquent. Charles Weidman had little or nothing to do. Theatrically speaking, the surface of the Schoenberg was scarcely scratched."

Actually Schoenberg wanted three different sets and a play of colored light. Mr. Jones designed one set, and colored lights were omitted. Noel Strauss pointed out in his review other missing elements: instead of a dark stage with a dozen singers' heads protruding from violet hangings in a green light (shades of Alwin Nikolais), the singers were banished to the orchestra pit and six painted masks on the backdrop were flooded with white light; instead of the woman overturning a crag which assumes the form of a mythological monster, the final image was of Doris's long sleeve disappearing behind vertical panels which closed like a garage door. He found the futility of the score, with a short chorus at beginning and end and thirty-odd bars for the baritone soloist, in line with the emptiness of the fifty-seven lines of text. "Miss Humphrey's mime was exceedingly graceful. But absolutely no mood of any kind was established."

Edward Cushing decided that Nicholas Roerich's setting and costumes for *Sacre* were not altogether successful. (Roerich created the original ones for the 1913 Paris premiere.) "Mr. Roerich, when he paints, is potentially an interesting scenic artist; when he designs sceneries, he seems potentially an interesting painter." He found Graham's Sacrificial Dance failed to effect Massine's powerfully built climax.

Mr. Martin continued to dwell on *Sacre* in two Sunday *Times* columns:

The movements of the individual dancers were colored with hieratic suggestions and imbued with a tremendous muscular power which at the same time seemed to be inhibited by the mental limitations of a crude people. Through this combination of opposing ideas, the choreographer conveyed without an instant's relief the overpowering influence of something not understood—the mystery, if you will, of nature in its vernal surging. In the mass designs were creations of surpassing beauty, ingenious to the last degree, but none less stable for that.

In the first part of the ballet there was the most impressive evidence of Massine's artistry. The dance of the adolescents, in which the men perform tremendous movements before a background of girls seated and moving their arms; the games of the rival tribes and the intricate and extraordinary mass movement that closes the act—all these are choreography that ranks at the very top of modern dancing. Through its complicated visual counterpoint and its terrific energy there shines the barbaric passion of elemental human beings.

Massine had six groups of dancers moving, alternating the phrasing in figure-eight circles. My set, stamping along, began with eight beats of elbow thrusts, then nine to fifteen progressive gallops with arms curvetting in the air; sixteen to twenty-one counts on the knees, clapping the hands, swinging the arms from side to side. Each group started on a different beat. We continued this dizzy round until the curtain fell.

Another thrillingly satisfying part was the linked ensemble on both sides of the Chosen One, standing shoulder to shoulder, men facing one way, women another, vibrating in place, then alternately shuffling to make a sun-circle of the stage in a mystical, frenzied adoration of the life-force, with the most unified intensity.

When the New York performances came to an end, Massine treated the company to an Italian dinner. After the dinner, impromptu dancing. Not being tall, Massine danced a few times with the petite girls. The Russian and Italian boys ecstatically danced alone or with each other if they couldn't find girl partners. The devotion Massine inspired was very real. Our heterogeneous group from many backgrounds and schools of training looked on him as a genius, a man of such prodigious skill as to seem godlike. His black eyes, serious face, and innate courtesy endeared him to everyone.

This was the season that brought modern dancers from Germany to America for the first time. José and I saw Mary Wigman together. For Wigman, the New York audience put on an ovation before she danced a step. Much as we were impressed by her intensity and fervor, we were depressed by her taste in costuming and the general heaviness of her style. But how admirable that she could arrange her own percussion effects (she had started out as a Dalcroze teacher) and even write the flute melody for her *Pastoral!* Doris wrote her parents: "Mary Wigman was a thrill, about the only dancer outside of Kreutzberg who can do that to me. She will be hard on audiences who are still in the graceful stage though. But a magnificent artist, you absolutely must see her. She backs every other female dancer off the map."[4]

Harald Kreutzberg and Yvonne Georgi, who came next, filled us with more enthusiasm since they were younger, lighter artists. After seeing Kreutzberg's elevation, it seemed as if we too, by wishing, could leap over the Sherry-Netherlands spire. But Kreutzberg also revealed a dark strain of hallucinatory terror and pain, the aftermath of World War I, disturbingly psychotic, as it was no doubt meant to be—all those frenzied runnings and hand tremblings. An overwhelming experience, unknown in America, tortured the German psyche and was reflected in their creative dance.

It was a very simple thing, illuminating to me, to hear Kreutzberg and Georgi, at the end of their Polish mazurka, finish with an exclamatory "Ha!" The effect of the dancers' shout made everything perfect in that brief second. It made them human and complete. So often the silently moving image of a dancer transports us to an altogether idealized sphere, quite removed from reality. With the breath sound we know they are still human. This sank into my subconscious and was the basis of many subsequent dances where I combined dance and voice, from simple exclamatory vowel sounds, syllables such as "Niké!" for *Icaro,* to full-length poems by e. e. cummings and James Joyce.

The spring of 1930 was full of exitement at the studio. For a start, an invitation from Germany for the Humphrey group to appear at the first invitational Modern Dance Congress in Munich. Before anything else, the problem of funding our trip abroad had to be solved. Then Leonidoff, dance director at the Roxy, showed interest in presenting the group in *Water Study* for several weeks at the Roxy Theatre. This would help pay the way across the Atlantic. Doris was hopeful, as were we all. She wrote: "If you want to do the Roxy engagement (possibly two weeks) come Wednesday night for rehearsal, and Thursday night to show the dances to Mr. Leonidoff at our studio. Both at eight o'clock—and please telephone about the *Lysistrata* on Monday sometime—I think we can fit this all in as to time—with a little luck."[5] Leonidoff made repeated visits to the studio; we ran through *Water Study* time after time as he took notes, ostensibly for the staging and lighting. No contract appeared, but later that year the

Roxy featured a *Water Ballet* without any credit to Humphrey. A decade later the word choreography attained legal status with Hanya Holm, the first one to copyright her dances. But Doris never bothered with the procedure. Anyone could imitate a dance, change a passage here and there, and deny it was plagiarism.

Norman Bel Geddes, the designer, about to produce *Lysistrata,* engaged Doris and Charles to choreograph the bacchanale. This brilliant little fellow with a Napoleon complex, given to shouting profanity and bellowing in a large voice to make up for his size, came to the studio and chose dancers he wanted for parts in the play. He chose me first, and some of the other tall girls. The next day we attended "line rehearsal," meeting others of the cast in an old opera house on the upper east side. Later he invited us to a conference about making a film of motion, for which he wanted to use dancers. He talked about filming with a limited focus, showing only the legs. Though I never heard of his completing the project, someone else did make a successful short on just that subject. He asked for ideas. I suggested all the dreamlike reversals of gravity, where one flies effortlessly to the ceiling or soars in the air, or other upside down images. He seemed to like the concept, but again, I never heard of his completing a film on motion.

After two rehearsals, Doris—having chosen us for more important things—pulled the precious group members from *Lysistrata.* The group must be ready to go abroad; the understudies would replace us in *Lysistrata* for three weeks in Philadelphia. As it developed, Munich—where our performance time was a fifteen minute slice of a program—gave no guarantee, and there were no other European engagements to make it worth while. Before we could pack our suitcases the whole plan faded away, while *Lysistrata,* opening to sensational success in Philadelphia, moved to Broadway and stayed almost a year. For José Limón, Letitia Ide, Ernestine Henoch, Gloria Braggiotti, Helen Strumlauf, Ilse Grenau, and other "understudies," this was financial salvation and excellent professional experience. Jerome Andrews was one of the men dancers; so was Charles Laskey. The bacchanale which ended the play was vigorous, splendidly earthy, stylized, rhythmically delightful—exactly right. Charles said, "José wasn't very good in it, but he looked divine."

We did not know it, but this was to be the last summer at 9 East 59th Street. Deprived of being Greek dancers in *Lysistrata,* the rest of the group experienced a Newport garden party fête, dancing in eighteenth century Greek style. Mrs. Moses Taylor (in mourning that year) was to entertain at a small affair limited to three hundred guests, including the Greek ambassador. This was perhaps one of the last of the big parties so typical of the twenties; from then on things became ever poorer, grimmer, more depressing.

In the middle of July we traveled to Newport by boat, again delightful for those of us who liked the sea. Our stage was a green lawn in a formal garden with a pool backed by Italian-style hedges. We could hear the murmur of the Atlantic and smell the salt air. Mrs. Taylor provided canvas tents for dressing rooms. After a space rehearsal in daylight, we had light and orchestra rehearsals at night. At every hedge and tree footmen stood with trays of refreshments, including champagne.

We were not the only entertainers, for Eugenie Leontovich and the Newport Stock Company were to give Rostand's *Les Romanesques*. This delightful three-act piece featured Leontovich, Ernest Cossart, Eugene Powers, and George Blackwood with a handful of Humphrey dancers added to the spectacle as commedia dell' arte characters. It was fun being supers with elaborate capes, exaggerated face masks and eccentric hats, though our off-balance extensions of hat brims nearly knocked us down if we turned too suddenly. As night came on, the interior lights in our canvas tents produced silhouette effects. Someone reported to Mrs. Moses that now the musicians could observe the dancers dressing and undressing. The hostess laughingly replied she thought it would be very charming if they did.

The night of the fête, the guests arrived at eleven o'clock (after a *Road to Rome* performance at the Casino Theatre). Performing outdoors against nature's capricious rhythms is always unpredictable: the grass was wet and cold and slippery, not at all pleasant under our bare feet. As overture to the Rostand play, we were to dance Griffe's *White Peacock*, which Doris arranged for nine girls. Pauline designed long crinkled chiffon sheaths with trains for us. (Because of its voluptuous quality, Charles had been banished from the preliminary rehearsal sketches for this study in romantic femininity.) I had the first solo entrance, but alas! an off-shore breeze came up in time to blow away the orchestral sounds coming from one part of the glen, and the light crew on the roof of the main house never heard the music start. One by one the dancers entered, milling around in the dark before the lights caught up with the music, by which time our impressionistic postural seduction dance was three-quarters over.

Between the first and second acts of *Les Romanesques* we did Charles's *Marionettes*. There were no boys on this tour so John Glenn's role as the cruel puppet Father fell to me.

Between acts two and three came the elaborately costumed

tongue-in-cheek "satire in the manner of the ballets of the French court in the 18th century," *Les Fêtes de Terpsichore et Hymen.* Rameau's music was delightful; Doris was particularly fetching in her tambourine dance as Terpsichore, Charles was Hymen; Dorothy Lathrop, whose long-nosed face and slender body made her look like a pocket edition of Doris, was Diana. Diana's Amazons—Cleo Atheneos, Rose Chrystal and I—carried tiny bows without arrows, and wore little leopard skins slung across our low-cut bosoms; we had panniers and soft ballet slippers, and we wore our natural hair pinned up. Sylvia was Hebe, Katherine a Nymph. Helene Pons executed these costumes as if for a Broadway production.

After this gentle burlesque of ballet we were invited to the main house to mingle with the guests. As at the previous evening rehearsal, the champagne never stopped flowing. By the time we arrived, the butlers were now offering tumblers and glasses of the tallest size. When we retired to our inn for the rest of the morning, Doris declined to join our ongoing bubbly party. She went to bed. Before long the hotel management requested us to make less noise. Charles, who liked to drink, encouraged us. "Eleanor is marvelous when she has had one or two. She should always be a little drunk." Thus we had a slight taste of high life, a dying fluke from the Gilded Age.

Writing to Julia and Horace Buckingham Humphrey (her parents) as she regularly tried to do, Doris described the Newport trip as "dance in a very formal garden. We had to be careful to keep out of the flowers. We saw the dawn come up three mornings in a row and

Dorothy Lathrop as Diana with Eleanor King, Cleo Atheneos, Rose Crystal, as Amazons in Doris Humphrey's Les Fêtes de Terpsichore et Hymen, *at Newport, R.I.*

when we got back we were dead. It was no vacation."[6] She also revealed what was to become an increasing conflict between her extraordinary gifts as a solo dancer—blessed with "a body sculptured like a greyhound" as Tom Borek described it—and the impulse to create for ensemble. In the same letter she tells: "I want to do something alone that is really worth while, but as long as I have this group I either can't or won't resist composing for them and ideas for solos remain unborn."

Next we rehearsed for the August 17 performance with the Philadelphia Orchestra, in Robin Hood Dell, a natural amphitheatre that seats eight thousand. The stage shell is graced by overarching tall elms which make a fine frame for the stage. Sitting in a front row, watching Alexander Smallens conduct the musicians in rehearsal for that week's program, I lost another illusion about artists.

I had naively assumed that all artists shared the quest for perfection of form and were also perfect people. But here were these great, these famous musicians, laughing and joking among themselves during the repetitions in Ravel's *Bolero*. Worse than that, on the stroke of noon they put down their instruments, never bothering to finish the measure, let alone the phrase. Union musicians, they seemed to care more about minutes than music itself.

Still, among our dance group we agreed the ideal husband would be one of these Philadelphia Orchestra men, who naturally would be able to accompany rehearsals and classes, besides inspiring us with music. If this paragon were also a masseur, it would be perfection. Later one of the dancers did marry such a one; it ended in divorce.

The idea of a full dance evening had not yet taken hold in Philadelphia, so our program was preceded by Mozart's overture to *The Marriage of Figaro* and Beethoven's *Symphony No. 2 in D*. The *Air for the G String* opened, followed by the Tcherepnine *March;* then came Charles's new *Commedia (Burlesca)* to music by Coppola. In this farcical absurdity, as Captain Mala Gamba he wore puffed slashed sleeves and a hat with long, long pheasant feathers. Cleo played a Zany, and Sylvia and Evelyn had extravagant hats and false noses, which were pulled in the contest over the Inamorata, a part for me. Charles designed and made the costumes, mine a tan Renaissance dress with painted gold figuring and a tiny hat with single feather. I carried a glove, and dropped it to entice the Captain, who of course was afraid of his own shadow. Pauline checked from the last row and said the mime carried that far. Charles's nickname for me during this work was "Pie-face." He threatened to make us perform the whole piece as a real improvisation when we had an audience. But fortunately this

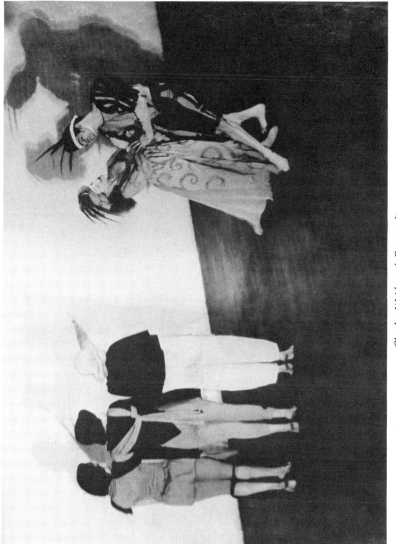

Charles Weidman's Commedia.

Doris Humphrey as the Eldress in the original production of The Shakers.

didn't happen; at that stage of my career I would have been frozen with horror. With the check for the Philadelphia Orchestra performances, Doris wrote: "Dear Eleanor the Inamorata—And here is something to buy you a new hat (but be sure it has a feather in it)."[7]

Water Study followed the *Commedia*. Then Charles premiered his new *Danse Profane* to Debussy. When he first proposed doing it, Doris dismissed the idea with a scornful, "Why, you haven't a profane bone in your whole body." This stung Charles; he determined to show her. He went ahead to produce a strong excellent dance. The group finale was *La Valse*.

In the studio, after choreographing *La Valse*, Doris had played Scriabin's *Poème de l'Extase* for us. In a letter to her parents she described it as "a tremendous work which I will labor over long and lovingly,"[8] and we expected it would be the next large group work. Instead, she began rehearsing an ecstatic theme that was quite opposite in style—*The Shakers*, which was primitive American. Pauline found some old Shaker melodies, then improvised a theme on a harmonica, singing a wordless melody while Doris beat the drum.

When we started working on it we thought the movements hilariously funny. The crisp marching steps, the hopping with hands shaking lightly from the wrists, the bouncy rhythm, seemed singularly primitive, yet light and happy. But we soon ceased being amused and in no time were caught up in the compelling mood so masterfully built to an ecstatic climax, with Doris, as the Eldress, whirling in the center and the "brothers" and "sisters" leaping joyously forward until they ended on their knees, hands clasped, all faces turned up to heaven. As she commented to her parents in the same letter: "The subject never is the point. Starting a new work based on religious cults—the general theme being Shakerism. The subject is fascinating to read about—but is chiefly important as a starting point."[9]

She organized *The Shakers* in an open square with women on one side, men on the other, the Eldress seated on a bench up center. The dance builds on the idea of an invisible line down the center of the room, which keeps the celibate Shakers separated. At first swaying from side to side on our knees, with palms clasped, the arms gradually extending, the body lifts grew deeper and higher till we stood.

Posed to face the center, each man in turn meets a woman opposite. The two nearly touch but draw back in the body as they progress up the center, to break off into walking circles, inner arms extended like spokes of a wheel. From the circles, broken lines with individual gestures, some pointing upward, some crossing then opening the arms, and stepping and hopping with the legs. With a light tapping step, shaking the wrists downward (to shake themselves free of sin), the two sides facing front move toward the center and back.

Against an 8/8 rhythm, first one then another breaks into a galvanic 9/8 phrase, a strong reaction to the forbidden line: first dropping forward over it, pulling up, falling back, reaching up with one arm—the body suspended—then falling away with running steps into a jump and rebound. From the 9/8 we burst into a 10/8 pattern, which added a flying forward leap.

Doris used three voice effects: Pauline's singing, Katherine's interpolation when she stopped in her tracks (while we held still) to say: "My God, my God, my carnal life I will lay down, I will lay it down because it is deprav-ed!"; then Doris herself in a "speaking with tongues" phrase—actually some mixed-up Japanese words—before she started whirling in the center.

At this point, we dropped forward on our knees surrounding her and began an ecstatic lift, falling first forward then backward with breath suspensions which finally brought us to our feet for the concluding rush forward: jump, jump, jump, leap, repeated until we were continuously leaping. With Pauline's "Amen" on the harmonium, we ended on our knees, Doris standing with arms out and head up.

Shakers was the most infectious of all Doris's compositions, because the simple rhythms to drum beats were so well built. These decorous Shakers controlled within fine boundaries the tension inherent in their lives, clearly stated in the pull and attraction to the straight line down the center of the room, the movements always drawing toward or away from it as an irresistible magnet. It was good Americana, good religious ritual, excellent theatre, and just long enough to establish the mood, make its point and build to an exciting climax. It would have been easy to prolong it and spoil it, but Doris often said "all dances are too long," and she knew when to stop.

In September, for financial reasons Doris and Charles gave up the fine 59th Street studio. "The Unholy Three," as Doris, Charles, and Pauline had been called in Denishawn, took an apartment down on 12th Street to live in and found for their studio a third floor loft at 151 West 18th Street, above a machine shop on the first floor and a shoe factory on the second floor. They put a special wooden dance floor in the whitewashed brickwalled 32 by 38 foot space with four skylights and seven windows—a kind of upstairs barn with three old brown rafters. Pauline hung brown burlap curtains at the windows; wooden chests containing costumes were spaced around the walls for seating;

there was room for the grand piano, two small dressing spaces, a shower, a storage space for costumes, and an entry hall that doubled as the office. Rental for this out-of-the-way haven was seventy dollars a month.

At the housewarming party we danced the Virginia Reel and Pop Goes the Weasel. Doris taught us the English country dance Gathering Peascods. She had received a splendid education in folk dance from Mary Wood Hinman, and she believed all choreographers and dancers should know these forms, created by generations of unknown dancers.

After general dancing, Charles entertained with his satirical sketch of Miss Ruth reciting Tagore's poetry; his satires of famous dancers, from Isadora to Martha Graham to Tamiris, were hilarious. Pauline did a perfect burlesque of a stark "modern" dance to Sibelius's *Finlandia*. Then the two of them, their faces dipped in white flour, performed a Kabuki scene: Pauline making incredible sounds as a geisha with a baby, Charles samurai-ing about, pulling Pauline by the hair.

Walking alone at night on West 18th Street between Sixth and Seventh Avenues was enough to make strong men look twice, as Charles Woodford would declare later, when he came to know it. But then, he added, "Dancers are fearless. They aren't afraid of anything." Someone broke into the studio one night and made off with the few dollars in the cash box. After that we were cautioned not to work alone at night in the studio. But occasional evenings were the only free time for composition.

I locked myself in one evening to work on a new dance. Hearing footsteps in the hall, I thought to outwit the intruder by producing the sound and motion of a group rehearsal, so I ran about, jumped all over the place, clapped my hands, pretending to be half a dozen people. After an hour of this exhausting make-believe, I dared to open the door and fled past the empty landings down the narrow steps to the street, where the dark silent warehouses and lofts seemed less threatening than the hallway at 151 West.

In the new barnlike studio, with machinery clanking away below, Charles started work on his first big group project, Max Beerbohm's *The Happy Hypocrite,* to Herbert Elwell's music. Nura designed the masks for Lord George Heaven and Lord George Hell, Charles's dual roles, challenging and delightful parts for his pantomimic gifts. Cleo was a flashing wicked Senora Gambogi, Letitia a perfect Jenny Mere, Sylvia the Merry Dwarf, "sometimes a Cupid, too."

All of us participated in the opening banquet scene. The low

comedy mime of eating celery I remember as being particularly unre-
fined and absurd. The setting was half a dozen of the rectangular
boxes, which became now tables, now walls, now benches. Charles
cast me in the additional role of Mr. Aeneas, the Mask Maker, a role I
did not at the time appreciate. It would be decades before I visited
Asia, learn to value the discipline of the mask, and understood the
virtue of learning to perform all types, sexes, and ages, instead of
being merely oneself. As pantomime *The Happy Hypocrite* may have
lost Beerbohm's fantastic verbal wit, but Charles's response to it was
exactly right in movement and prankish gestural comedy.

The Institute of Arts and Sciences at Columbia University sponsored a concert on December 20 at the McMillin Theatre. Six of "the
concert dancers" performed the *Air for the G String*, the *Marionette
Theatre*, the *Commedia*, and the premiere, with Doris, of *The Shakers*,
billed as *The Dance of the Chosen*. Charles danced his *Profane* and the
Japanese Actor; Doris the Bach *Gigue,* the *Scherzo Waltz, Hoop Dance* (by
request), and *The Call;* together they offered the *Air on a Ground Bass*
and a quick-paced *Burlesca* (Bossi).

This last concert of the year was portentous, being the first time the
doors of academe opened to sponsor this company of modern dancers. Increasingly in the years ahead, as dance struggled to survive,
colleges and universities across the country would welcome the arts,
and the dance would ultimately reach American students and the lay
public.

For Doris, 1930 was a peak year of artistic innovation never to be
surpassed. She would compose larger works of first magnitude later
on, but she was the first American choreographer to assay the complete independence of dance, without music or other aids except
minimal costuming and lighting. She progressed further than anyone else with the idea of unaccompanied motion.

At the same time, with her musical gifts she was able to handle
symphonic scores admirably, so that appearing with the Philadelphia
Orchestra gave *La Valse* the scope of accompaniment it deserved. She
could turn from large scale to miniature with the Rameau garden-
party trifle, spoofing the Greco-Roman Frenchified court ballets, and
at the same time create the totally respectful serious Shaker ritual, a
modern dance classic of nineteenth century American folk art that is
today revived as often as *Water Study*.

Many dancers followed her lead in composing, abandoning musi-

Doris Humphrey and Charles Weidman in Air on a Ground Bass.

cal support. But hers is the honor of being first in America. Like all
true innovators, she leaves us with a kind of breathless wonder at the
daring and the accomplishment.

CHAPTER FOUR: 1931

The Little Group

IN THE CIRCULAR BASEMENT ROOM with a round dance floor at
the newly opened New School for Social Research on West 12th
Street, John Martin inaugurated a new course on the art of the dance,
originally suggested by Henry Cowell to Doris Humphrey and
Martha Graham. Mr. Martin lectured informally on principal tendencies, which were illustrated by leading exponents of the new American dance. The series of twelve sessions served the public so well that
it continued for eight years, a force in building understanding for the
pioneer movement as well as making usually nonverbal dancers
clarify basic concepts and methods of work. The New School was to
be a bastion of modern dance for years to come.

In the same place Paul Boepple offered Dalcroze Eurythmics, and
Henry Cowell conducted an exposition of what the twentieth century
had added to music, offering six lectures on the science and six on the
materials of the new music. Upstairs Ralph Pearson's pictorial analysis planned to answer the burning questions: What is modern and
what is academic art? What is the value of creation as against imitation? and even What use is modern art? Freda Kirchwey lectured on
the independent woman, Sidney Hook on Karl Marx, Robert Frost on
poetry. Julian Huxley came to speak on heredity and environment;
Dr. Koffka lectured on Gestalt psychology.

The first musical concert featured Leon Theremin's laboratory
demonstration of his new electrical instrument which produced
sounds from "beat-tones." Henry Cowell's recital of new piano

works included his famous tone-clusters produced by pressure of the forearm (elbow to flat hand) on the keys, and use of the back strings of the piano, muffled, percussively beaten or plucked with the sound board removed.

Doris had the honor of being first on the dance series. We were called upon to demonstrate her analysis of movement as having three divisions (opposition, succession, unison) and three qualities (sharp accent, sustained flow, rest); no dance being well balanced without two elements from each division, the best dances having them all. We have been assigned design problems in class; my little exercise on the theme of parallels was one selected by Doris for demonstration.

Graham and her group were second on the series, an evening made memorable by the attendance of Michel Fokine. Fokine, who had seen Isadora Duncan in Moscow and revered her because "she gave her dances the whole scope of human emotions," could not appreciate the Graham mystique or the movements of her dancers. In *Novoye Russkoya Slovo*, March 31, 1931, he described what they did:

The girls lay down, sat down, walked on flat feet, and . . . that was all. The arms either hung limply or tensely pushed upwards with their elbows. The chest was always pushed out exaggeratedly or else sharply sunk in. In these two movements was the essence of the dance. The tempo was only slow. The expression was sad, and almost always evil. Clenched fists. A somewhat barking movement of the torso and the head. The barking girls!

To him it was monstrous in form and evil in content, especially since legs were placed arbitrarily with the feet pointing inward.

When someone asked Graham's opinion of the ballet she replied that she recognized the ballet as one form of dance; she liked Pavlova, especially when she bowed—she bowed very well. "But when the ballet begins to approach the Greek dance, it is horrible." Fokine, struggling to keep quiet, must have expressed more than he wanted to show, for Miss Graham not knowing who he was, turned directly to him. "It seems you have a question?"

"Yes," he said. "In working with your girls, do you have in mind the development of natural movement or do you disregard naturalness in your art?" Long, long silence. He repeated the question, then asked permission to illustrate his point.

It seems to me that your girls, in order to raise the hand, first of all raise their shoulders, then their elbows, and only then the whole arm. . . . If I want to take a hat from the hanger, I do not raise first my shoulder, then my elbow . . . no. I simply raise my whole arm and take that which I need. But according to your system one must do exactly the opposite.

Fokine went on to say:

I showed how the simple movement would be performed according to the system of Miss Graham. It was funny. The public laughed, and so did Miss Graham and I.

"But I still insist that you do raise your shoulder in order to raise the arm," said she.

"I? Never. . . . Is it from here that your movements originate?" and I also pointed to my stomach, [noting] that nothing extraordinary happened there when I took a book from the shelf.

"But you breathe?" she said.

"I always breathe," I said with conviction. . . . Movement becomes more beautiful the less we feel the tenseness in its execution. Such is the aesthetic of the ballet, such is the aesthetic of any dance. The teaching of the dance is based mainly on constant elimination of unnecessary tension.

The theory of Wigman and Graham is exactly the opposite. They seem to say: Be tense as much as you can. Without clarifying the question about natural movement, Miss Graham unexpectedly said: "You know nothing about the movement of the body!"

Answering that I had been concerned with this question for more than forty years, I asked: . . .

"Did I understand correctly that all the movements are divided by you into two categories, those with the chest pushed out and those with the sunken chest?"

"Yes."

"Is it true that the chest expresses, in your opinion, anger and hatred?"

"Yes." . . .

"Can I ask another question?"

"No," said Miss Graham, "we will never understand each other. Besides, it is not very nice of you to stop the lecture by your questions."

"Why is the ballet horrible?" I asked.

Miss Graham assumed the fifth position and . . . said, "How can anyone dance the Greek dances in this fashion?"

"You know very little about the ballet. Many ballets . . . are not built around the five positions, but every movement is built on natural expression, on purely Greek lines and style. I myself have choreographed *Daphnis and Chloe* and *Narcisse and Echo,* Nijinsky has done *Afternoon of a Faun,* Pavlova was famous in *Bacchanale.* Is it possible that all of this does not entitle me to a question—why the ballet is becoming horrible when it treats the Greek subject, why the monopoly of Greek dances must belong to the dilettanti?"

. . . Ballet is an art like music and painting, and modernism is a temporary condition, a period of evolution in art. The Diaghilev Ballet . . . or Ralph de Mare's Swedish Ballet were so modern in some of their works that the German dancers or modernists like Graham are left far behind.

When someone in the audience revealed Fokine's identity, Miss Graham said, "I did not know I was speaking with Mr. Fokine." Ending the discussion she said, "We will never understand each other."[10]

Fokine's attitude illustrates perfectly what ballet people think of the insurgents: we are "dilettanti" because we eschewed the classical five positions, the barre, the turnout, the conventional pas de deux with its display of the saccharine ballerina, her partner a prop to hold her up and push her around, the ballerina herself a projection of mindless femininity idealized to the point where believability vanished. The rescue of this vapid puppet was one of the missions of modern dancers. Doris and Charles were the first to establish truly democratic treatment of men and women as equal partners in their duets. The Scriabin, later the *Rudapoema* and the Roy Harris *Quartet*, choreographically affirmed the healthy balance between and co-equality of the sexes.

Artistically, at this point ballet was in a sickly state. Could anything so decadent have a future? We moderns could not conceive of it. Ballet would succumb in five years' time, we thought. Yet it was to be revitalized by the innovations going on outside of ballet. Eventually Balanchine, the great classicist, would incorporate the revolutionary vocabulary of the moderns into his elaborately laced movements.

Contrariwise after the first flush of puritanical independence from all elements of tainted theatricality, the crusaders a decade later relaxed their aversion to ballet barres, and basic classical discipline slowly crept into the once revolutionary studios. Thus the modern revolt added new life to ballet, gave it new horizons, released it from its nineteenth century bonds, and assured its survival, a revolution Fokine lived to see.

The second Humphrey demonstration at the New School was on composition. Though this was Doris's metier, she had remarkably few rules to go on. The time-honored and, so far as it went in vaudeville, quite successful Denishawn formula was simply this: to make a good entrance, be sure of a stunning exit, and, when in doubt, *turn.* As she wrote her family:

I was brought up in the theatrical school which used the audience's pulse to tell whether a composition was good or not, consequently my ideas of composition were something like this:
Never let down in the middle.
Surprise them at the end.
Never turn your back.
Save the star for a good entrance.
Use the ensemble for a background to the solo.
Express every musical beat and phrase some way—the high notes up, the low notes down. They can follow it better.

Follow a slow step with a fast one.
Never stand still or lie down.
A slow process and one that really should be done by someone else.[11]

At the end of the exposition of elements taken from her choreography Doris admitted frankly that when it came to composition she never thought of any of these formal theoretical things. The way she composed a dance was to sit in a chair and think the subject through as if nothing had ever been composed before: The idea alone determined the form.

Our second Dance Repertory Theatre season—which was to be the last—ran from February first to the eighth and included Agnes de Mille as an additional artist. The first night's mixed bill included works of Humphrey, Tamiris, De Mille and Weidman. Humphrey dancers opened with the *March*—that "charming trifle in which a number of peasant girls watch a troop of soldiers pass," Mr. Martin described it. Doris's intention was an abstraction of people watching people on parade. Later she confessed it was "on the cute side."

Following Tamiris's group in *Woodblock Dance* and Agnes de Mille's character study *Ballet Class* after Degas, we appeared in Doris's striking new work *Dances for Women,* to music composed and played by Dane Rudyhar. The first half ended with *The Shakers* (first time in the theatre).

Charles Laskey and José danced *Ringside;* Tamiris's group appeared in *Revolutionary March* to percussion accompaniment. De Mille with Warren Leonard for partner mimed *May Day,* a picnic scene to Beethoven. Charles performed his inimitable juggler's *Scherzo,* substituting that for the *Marionette Theatre* because Sylvia was ill. De Mille and Leonard concluded with Offenbach's *Cancan.*

The *Times* listed the audience as of substantial size and warm responsiveness to Humphrey's three new works; De Mille's *May Day* was most popular with the audience; Tamiris's works were not particularly distinguished. Martin acknowledged the striking originality of the subject and treatment of *The Shakers* but called it "more a purely theatrical form than a dance, for it involved spoken phrases in unintelligible jargon and a hint of a linear plot," and went no further. Modern dance was at this moment supposed to eschew everything theatrical. It was *concert* art; from that narrow view *Shakers* was overstepping the bounds. *Dances of Women* Martin found "of more substantial stuff than the March, with cloudy moments in the composition, especially the opening"; the whole a "highly stylized treatment of the elemental experiences of birth and death, with a passage of formalized triviality in between."

Doris considered *Dances of Women* her most serious new work, in which she tried, as she wrote her mother, to "include us all both before and after the industrial revolution."[12] It impressed other reviewers as the finest work on the program, but it did not long remain in the repertory. In retrospect I think the content was not connected enough—the biological and sociological parts needed some link to make the point.

Part One, the abstraction of birth, was the most realized and graphic. Costumed in long red wool tubes of jersey, with black chignons, we were spaced in contracted positions in a line ending upstage at one of the Humphrey boxes. Like the stem and branches of a tree form, we moved in spasmodic rhythms, with individuals breaking out to the sides, like leaves. At the climax Letitia and Katherine bore Doris folded like a bud to the top of the box where she rose to flower, gesturing in successions through the finger tips. The group below rose, each in turn touched the ground reverently, then with thumbs and first fingers touching to make a symbolic triangle, hands placed on the pelvis, we moved forward into a massive highly stylized mother-rocking. To Rudyhar's expressive accompaniment beaten on exposed piano strings and gongs with an Eastern effect, the dance had powerful poetic imagery.

Opposed to this menstrual-flower symbolism, the second movement made a sociological comment about women as objects, as dolls—"pink ladies" Doris called them. This was a tiny mincing dance for a quartet dressed in pink, up on their toes, little fingers arched, moving in a boxlike space to tinkling music, a sketch which could have been developed more, perhaps with a strong oppositional group for contrast.

The third section, too, was rather a sparse statement of rebellion requiring a frantic costume change, enveloping ourselves in huge black tarpaulins, shooting one arm up in the air as if striking, while against our repetitious cogmill procession, Doris made a valiant solo attempt at freedom, representing woman as militant, only to be stepped over by the tide of resisters and, forty years before women's lib, being brushed aside; a negative ending.

The generous Wednesday evening program began with Doris's and Charles's dramatically stark *Salutation to the Depths*; her solo *Gigue*, his *Profane*; the group in the three-part *Drama of Motion*; then the delicate Purcell *Air on a Ground Bass*, with an added robust companion *Burlesca* duet; then *Steel and Stone* for the first time. Mod-

Doris Humphrey and Group in Dance for Women, Part One.

Charles Weidman's The Happy Hypocrite. *Photo by Soichi Sunami.*

ern architecture and modern dance were recognized as the new arts in America, and their conjunction was inevitable in dance. This abstraction of the thrust of modern architecture, to Henry Cowell's music, was performed by Weidman, Limón and Laskey. In the absence of male students, Charles had sometimes used me in working it out, a cause for strengthening my arm muscles, for most of the dance was designed from floor level, balancing on one hand and one or both feet, striving upward. In this "vehemently composed and executed expression of the machine age" along with the excellent design of his *Danse Profane*, Martin found convincing proof that Mr. Weidman was "growing apace as a composer." We repeated *Dances of Women*.

Saturday matinee Charles premiered his newest, most ambitious work, that charming "Fairy Tale for Tired Men" by Max Beerbohm, *The Happy Hypocrite*, to music of Herbert Elwell. Mr. Martin hailed it as the first "ballet d'action" to be devised by any of the modern dancers of this country, "a well-constructed little work of exceptional clarity of form, the pantomime happily translatable, and the choreography suitable, though of lesser importance. The choreographic substitute [for Beerbohm's words] is witty, however, if it is not subtle." Again the screens and boxes were used to imaginative effect. This was the most elaborate of all the Dance Repertory Theatre's offerings.

But Graham's new group work, *Primitive Mysteries*, overshadowed the rest of the Repertory. Thanks to a small Guggenheim grant which permitted her to visit the Southwest, Martha had been inspired to create an evocative ritual of Spanish and American forms such as can be seen in remnant form today. She dramatized the celebration of the Virgin in rugged simplicity and purity, and the group danced around her like so many wooden santos—monumental, stark, robust. Some dancers consider that Graham never surpassed that lovely composition with its breathtaking intensity.

Decades later when it was revived at Connecticut College, collated from the memories of the original group and passed on to the young dancers of the 1960s, Martha saw that the current training of modern dancers had so altered their physiques that they no longer had the earthy quality of the pioneer moderns. To make today's long-lined, elegant figures look somewhat heavier she added flounced petticoats to the original skirts, thereby making baroque what had been a classic of primitive simplicity.

Audiences were slowly growing, dance was receiving more attention. The Shuberts even approached the artists of the Dance Repertory Theatre with an offer to send them on the road across the country. Since the Shuberts owned most of the commercial theatres in the land this was a good opportunity for the consolidation of the new American dance to add momentum to the whole cause. But it was not to happen; Martha refused to go. She feared they were all in danger of losing their individuality by appearing together.

Martha herself was later to gain a great deal of publicity as the mysterious "Miss Hush"; the identity of her voice kept many people guessing for weeks on a radio contest. Thus that curse of the modern dancer, individuality, reigned supreme; the idea of repertory, which could have saved them all, lay dormant then as it does today.

February 9 we were presented at the Philadelphia Academy of Music by the Philadelphia Forum. One critic summed up the evening as a paradoxical triple demonstration—"that dance is triumphantly emancipated from need for accompanying music [*Drama of Motion*]; that accordion and drum are just what the dance needs for accompaniment [*Shakers*]; and that the dance ought always have the aid of a complete symphony orchestra, last night's closest approach to that being a piano and a violin [*Air for the G String*]. The dance in which that violin helped out won about the warmest applause of the evening." Charles's work was noted by another critic: "More than any other dancer, perhaps, he maintains a sense of humor and a gift for satiric comedy; in the dancing preludes of Gershwin he elegantly caricatured the foibles of our time, from the cocktail shaker to Mr. Jolson and his 'Mammy.'"

Doris appeared before the curtain ". . . in a clinging robe, with outfloating hair, as little lame as the Winged Victory of the Acropolis," to explain that a strained tendon barred her from dancing on the program of February 12, when we were in Washington for a Community Institute program at McKinley Auditorium. This had happened at the last Repertory performance. Sylvia was still absent because she was ill, so I had her center part in the *Air for the G String,* which opened the concert. To the Washington reviewer, we might have been "as many saints from a Raphael fresco." Dorothy Lathrop substituted for Doris in the *Air on a Ground Bass.*

After *Water Study,* Charles performed his *Danse Profane,* then came *The Shakers,* Dorothy again in Doris's role. Only the third section of the *Drama of Motion* was given. The program note for *Steel and Stone* and *Ringside* read: "These two compositions are based upon the movements and rhythms of those who unconsciously dance. The first, men at work, the second, professional fighters." For one reviewer, this was the climax of the program, "watching the two lads, Laskey and Limón, joined with the male star, for the hewing of granite and the smelting of metal. The second dance, mimicking all

Doris Humphrey in The Lake at Evening. *Photo by Soichi Sunami.*

the actions of a prizefight, stealthy, stertorous, or ferocious . . . exactly like a prize sparring contest, only far more beautiful."

Doris was able to dance again on March 9 in the Humphrey-Weidman and Concert Group program at Smith College, matinee and evening. We danced the newly titled *Passing March*, the Ritual of Growth from the *Dances of Women*, the *Dance of the Chosen* and *Water Study*. Doris's and Charles's duets were the abstract *Salutation to the Depths*, the delightful *Air on a Ground Bass* and the romantic Scriabin *Suite*. Charles did his marvelous juggler to Borodin's *Scherzo*, then the Debussy *Profane*; Doris her lyric *Lake at Evening* and *Night Winds*.

We were back at the Washington Irving High School on March 13 for the Students' Dance Recitals, which had been initiated at low prices. *Passing Parade, Steel and Stone, Rituals for Women*—now with helpful subtitles of Growth, Restraint, Struggle for Freedom; the *Scherzo*, and *Dance of the Chosen* for the first half. Then Doris's lyrical dances to Griffes, Charles's *Profane*, the *Air on a Ground Bass, Water Study* and the Scriabin *Etude No. 12* duet.

For Doris, spring held a personal triumph in her solo performance as the protagonist in Irene Lewisohn's Neighborhood Playhouse production of Ernest Bloch's *Quator A Cordes*. A Coolidge Festival of Chamber Music commission, this opened in Washington and later came to New York at the YMHA Kaufmann Auditorium. I noted Ruth St. Denis in that audience, wearing a large picture hat, carrying a book which she diligently read until the lights went down. Miss Ruth drew her august tallness together and left when the lights came up in the interval, not waiting to see the whole work. A little modern dance went a long way with the "Mary Baker Eddy of the Dance."

Doris's impatience with Miss Lewisohn's scenario—"She goes in for the most minute psychological changes every four bars," she wrote her family[13]—must have communicated itself to John Martin, for he disdained its neurotic concept, evidently a theme much loved by Miss Lewisohn. In the last two seasons she had presented similar works, one with Blanche Talmud leading a "group force" against a similar pair of protagonists (Charles being the male defender), and the year before similarly Martha Graham and Charles in Strauss's *Ein Heldenleben* (memorably and passionately danced by both artists). Miss Lewisohn spared no expense in her annual springtime events, bringing the Cleveland Orchestra to the Manhattan Opera House for productions of Debussy's *Nocturnes* and Borodin's *Polovetsian Dances*, with dancers from the Grand Street Theatre Neighborhood Playhouse.

Martin, vehemently against the use of a string quartet for dance—

Doris Humphrey and Group in the Bloch Quartet. Photo by Vandamm.

"music with no suggestion of physical movement in it"—
nevertheless saw Doris's apparent struggle to reconcile her native
style of movement with the larger subjects which interested her as a
choreographer. He acknowledged that she had recently given more
to the group than to herself—and now,

In the Bloch quartet she has definitely found herself. Nothing of her lyricism
is lost, but under it there is a tenderness that has nothing whatever of
sentimentality about it, a fine and gracious femininity. At no time previously
in her career has she touched such a deep simplicity.

The first two movements of the composition he found thoroughly
admirable:

In fact, the season has furnished no performances more lucent in beauty of
conception, freer and more devoid of artifice. In the second half the plot and
the music conspire against the composer, and invention takes the place of
creation. The choreographic line had rounded to completion while there
were yet pages and pages of music to be played, so that the protagonist and
her male defender were faced with many repetitious battles with the powers
of evil, or "the consciousness of the group force," as the program calls it.

Charles danced "with taste and a becoming subordination of himself
to the central figure." We were all deeply moved by Doris's shining
spirit in this work. She wrote her family: "I think that I did the best
work on my own part that I have ever done. It was so good to have
nothing to think about but myself for a change."[14]
    For the officers and delegates of an American Federation of Arts
meeting in the Brooklyn Museum's sculpture court, John Martin,
who gave the preliminary address on the art of the dance, invited
Charles to present his works: two Pierrot pieces (Pauline Lawrence at
the piano playing the first of the Cyril Scott pieces); the Scherzo;
Minstrels with Cleo and George Steares (José having no gift for
comedy or pantomime); Danse Profane; the Sengalese Drum Dance;
Gershwin's Preludes; Ringside (Laskey and Limón); Steel and Stone
(Pauline Lawrence at the piano assisted by me beating a drum); the
Scriabin Study; and the Marionette Theatre with George Steares in the
part of the Father.
    Two nights later at the St. Bartholomew Community House on East
50th Street, Cleo, Ernestine, José and I made our own debut. The girls
opened with the Sarabande from Bach's Fifth French Suite. The program said, "A group arrangement of solo composition by Doris
Humphrey." It was one of the minor pieces taught us in class; we
simply expanded it for three. Cleo danced the Quasi-Waltz (Scriabin),

Eleanor King and José Limón in B Minor Suite. *Photo by Marcus Blechman.*

Eleanor King and José Limón in Mazurka. *Photo by Helen Hewett.*

another Humphrey solo choreography taught in class. Ernestine danced her Mozart *Fantasia;* I performed *Two Little Sonatas* of Scarlatti (Charles's choreography), which I loved. Our first trio—Ernestine, José and I—was Debussy's *Cortege.* I suppose the music, as usual, led us around by the nose—I can't remember one movement from it.

José and I opened the second half with a duet to the Polonaise, Rondeau and Minuet from Bach's *B Minor Suite.* Cleo danced another Weidman piece, a Scriabin etude; Ernestine her Schumann *Novelette.* José had found a Scriabin mazurka which he liked to play on the piano, and he and I danced it as a duet. Ernestine, José and I finished with a musicless *Danse* in which we hurled ourselves to the floor and up again in breathless fashion.

For the Bach duet Charles helped with costuming, fitting some fine tan cotton crepe (ten cents a yard at the 14th Street fire-sale fabric store) to make a simple long-waisted bodice for me with round neck and long sleeves and a circular skirt hanging from the hips, beautifully flowing in movement. José wore a reddish tunic with a shoulder drape of tan. Both of us barefoot, and he barelegged, made no visual concessions to the baroque period of the music.

Dancing with José was strenuous and demanding. He was very forceful, with a geometrical angularity about his designs which contrasted with my femininity. When he extended his arm in a straight line from the shoulder to the side, I opposed my arm in a parallel curve. The sprightly melodies made us move in space—the Polonaise dignified and courtly; the Rondeau mostly using arm gestures in a small area; the Minuet gayer. Later we substituted the Badinerie for the Minuet—to the joyous flute we scampered about the stage.

The Scriabin *Mazurka* which Mr. Martin insisted should be retitled since there wasn't one mazurka step in it—"all moonlight and honeysuckle"—was an extremely bound composition. José wore long black trousers and a shirt for the *Mazurka.* Similar to the sheaths which Pauline had designed for *White Peacocks,* I made a gray crinkled crepe-de-chine sheath, slashed at the leg, round neck, no sleeves. I stood in front of José—he was about five inches taller—and we proceeded to move almost from a fixed base, like a long-stemmed goblet, our torsos, heads and arms doing most of the pattern, in deplorably symmetrical fashion, conditioned no doubt from standing in front of the mirror when composing, a habit fatal to the development of movement.

In both the duets our upper bodies were superior to our lagging legs and feet. Nonetheless, Pauline Chellis, a Boston dancer friend of Pauline Lawrence's, liked these duets better than those of Kreutzberg and Georgi. We worked at night on these pieces until we were ready to drop. José would gasp, "I am dying, Egypt, dying," then add cheerfully, philosophically, "of course we are all dying from the minute we are born."

In the *Danse*, Ernestine and I wore off-one-shoulder tunics of pongee with short flared brown skirts; José wore a long-sleeved short red tunic. This musicless trio exposed our limited sustaining powers. Short in itself, all the rhythms were choppy, repetitious, not much development and one single dynamic—if we didn't have complexity we had youthful vitality, and everything was simple and *strong*. Ernestine remembers my bossing them all around, but like all the duos, trios, quartets, ideas were contributed at any time by anyone involved.

Danse began with Ernestine and José supine on the floor. I stood between them summoning them to life with a commanding arm gesture. Soon we were alternately and together hurling ourselves to the floor and rebounding like rubber balls with the indestructibility of youth.

Later that season a job came along for some of the girls in the group to model fur coats at the opening of the Capitol Theatre in Pottstown, Pennsylvania. Rose Yasgour persuaded the management that, while the models were changing from one series of coats to another, The Little Group could dance in between. To save musicians' union fees, we chose the unaccompanied *Danse* and *Tango*.

The truck was crammed with racks of fur coats and had no springs. We were packed into the back, huddled in jackknife positions on the floor. In that way we rode for hours without seeing a sign of the country outside. The theatre opening was scheduled at the close of Yom Kippur, and the holiday Pottstown audience was restless and curious. When the curtain rose on a bare soundless stage with two seemingly dead bodies lying on it, me standing stiffly upright, there were immediate catcalls, whistles and taunting remarks. Waiting until this uncouth audience would simmer down to respectful attention as proper concert audiences did, I stood adamant until the stage manager appeared on the stage himself. "What are you waiting for?" he roared. "Get on with it."

After the performance, young people stood at the stage door to follow us about in the small streets, José the main attraction. We were fascinating freaks to them. "What kind of dance is it? Is it still dance without any music at all?"

We were invited to dance at the Brooklyn Ethical Culture School. Cleo had dropped out, too busy now as an assistant studio teacher and secretary to be with us. So Ernestine and I contracted the Bach *Sarabande* to a duet. She danced her *Fantasia* and *Novelette;* I repeated the Scarlattis; José and I did the Bach and Scriabin duets. The three of us united in the *Cortege* and *Danse.*

Financial problems were acute at the end of the spring season for Doris. "It has been a very bad year for me," she confessed to her parents.[15] It was a bad year for everyone, economically, psychologically and morally.

While some twenty-three hundred banks were failing, the George Washington Bridge, the Empire State Building, and the new Waldorf Astoria were rising in the air. There were a few glowing highspots in the theatre. Katherine Cornell's success in *The Barretts of Wimpole Street* was matched by the appearance of the Lunts in *Reunion in Vienna* and the monumental *Mourning Becomes Elektra* with Nazimova and Alice Brady. Chaplin's *City Lights* was an isolated work of cinema art.

Eight million unemployed men in America meant bread lines in the cities; on the outskirts, towns made of cardboard and tar paper sprouted where homeless vagrants slept. Men who had the price of a subway ride wrapped themselves in discarded newspapers and huddled in the trains all night to keep warm, considering themselves lucky if they were jailed for a day or two, which meant they would have shelter and care.

Stewart's Cafeteria on 14th Street in New York—"the artists' Paris cafe"—was the eating place we all knew. William Matons, "Wild Bill," who slept at the studio in exchange for janitor's chores, dined exclusively at Stewart's. He could be seen there with a text of Schopenhauer spread out on the table, faithfully copying the philosopher's words or else recording his dance lessons into a notebook, while he consumed his twenty-five-cents-a-day meal—a bowl of vegetable soup mixed with crackers plus the entire contents of the nearest sugar bowl and ketchup bottle.

The painful image of John Glenn coming to rehearsals wearing a red-dyed tunic which barely covered his hunger-swollen stomach burns in my mind today.

Helen Savery wonders how she survived that period. She didn't have a coat and nearly froze to death with her nursery school baby-sitting job, taking children of neglectful parents to Central Park. It was sheer agony until her roommate lent her a torn, frazzled raccoon coat. "Through it all, how terribly devoted, inspired and believing we were in this new venture of Modern Dance."[16]

To give Doris a much-needed rest, some of the Orientalia collected by the Unholy Three on the Denishawn tour was sold to provide a ticket for a Caribbean cruise. When she returned she looked transformed: relaxed, radiant, happy. We soon discovered why when Charles Woodford, a broad-shouldered British seaman, walked into the rehearsal room, sat down in a corner, and quietly went to sleep, while Doris, conducting her group of dancers, waxed more eloquent and luminous than before. We stared at her in amazement.

"Leo," as Doris called him to avoid confusion with the other Charles, was everything the men of the theatre usually were not. Solid as Gibraltar, he was—strong, silent, masculine, utterly dependable. If there had to be a man in Doris's life, as evidently she had decided there should be, she had picked out the ideal arrangement. Leo was an officer with the Furness-Withy Line who would only be in port every now and then, so that her schedule of constant classes, rehearsals and performances could remain the same. Leo would be on call, so to speak.

Doris picked up the habit of smoking on that trip, a habit which grew on her with the years. No doubt she smoked to assuage some of the tension and some of the physical suffering she came to bear when she was afflicted with crippling arthritis in her hip.

The summer courses for teachers, undertaken in desperation for living expenses, went so successfully that they became an annual institution. Some twenty teachers from all over the country would show up for three weeks of intensive three-hour daily training sessions, with weekly performances by the group thrown in, thus keeping us up to concert pitch and giving us a chance to show our own works too.

Doris wrote her family: "The first recital [for the Summer Course] consisted of original dances given by about half a dozen members of the group. To say that I was proud of them is putting it in the mildest terms. I've always taught dance as a creative art and tried in every way to stimulate my girls to do things for themselves. About a year ago I gave up teaching them for a while because we weren't getting anywhere, and refused to tell them what to do except in rehearsals."[17] I remember Helen Strumlauf's strangely beautiful dance with halting rhythms to Schumann's *The Prophet Bird*; even Letitia composed a silent *Nocturne* with a swooping fall.

But it was true we had not been getting anywhere in her classes, except, as always, preparing for the new compositions. Doris was finding it more and more difficult to teach technique per se because she had little patience with it and little interest in it; composition and creation were more important to her. To solve the problem she made it a creative challenge to us that we should begin to construct etudes to develop each part of the body and to take turns directing each other. No one enjoyed this discover-your-own-way very much.

When Charles offered to give technique classes to the girls, not every one could or would come, some because of the hours. But Cleo, Katherine and I were happy to work with him. "Dear 4 o'clock class" he left a note on the hall desk one day: "Before I left I spoke to as many members as I could get in touch with concerning the continuance of your class and those I did talk to were in favor. If only from a technical standpoint a lot can be accomplished with José's aid, and although it may be asking too much, I had hoped that each one would have an antique dance to show me upon my return. I really do not think it is asking too much—what you all probably need is most likely a good spanking and a little class *spirit! Please, please* continue with your work. My best regards to all of you."[18]

Pauline was giving us a class in music which helped in many ways. To fulfill both Pauline's and Charles's assignment I began work on

Eleanor King in Gagliarda.
Photos by Marcus Blechman.

Eleanor King in her first solo, Study*(Brahms, Edward Ballade). Photos by Helen Hewett.*

Galilei's *Gagliarda,* intrigued that this was Queen Elizabeth's favorite morning exercise—to dance five galliardes on arising, and that in Tudor days, prostitutes preferred to dress in men's attire so that they could more easily spring and kick their heels for that dance. Following Pauline's design, I made a red tarlaton neck ruff, tight black bodice and scarlet-lined black duvetyn circular skirt split down the front, with a flat black square of a hat tied on under the chin. To Respighi's *Siciliana* I danced a formal series of lyrical bowings and turnings, skirt lowered; one skirt end lifted and fastened to the shoulder, I bounced and capered to the gay galliarde.

My parents, who had not followed our every concert in New York, were acutely unhappy about my choice of a career. Once, I entered the apartment in time to hear my mother saying on the phone, "Oh,

Eleanor King, Ernestine Henoch, José Limón in Danse. *Photo by Helen Hewett.*

she's fine, except she's completely bewitched by Doris Humphrey."
That shocked me. I was indeed devoted to Doris and Charles, but it
was as much their ideal of dance that held me in thrall. They were the
catalysts bringing it about. Dance was simply the most vital, satisfying expression in the whole world.

I summoned up courage to invite my parents to see a studio
rehearsal of my first real solo, to the *Edward Ballade* of Brahms. I called
it *Study*. Mother declined; Father came. At the end he said, "Well,
kiddo, you seem to have the right conformation of figure for dancing.
And if that's what you want to do, go to it."

I could now begin to feel I was making progress after four years of
struggle. When Doris saw the Brahms for the first time she said,
"That's a grand dance." I could hardly believe it. Charles's criticisms
were always pointed. He told us our movements were too choppy.
He told Ernestine to work on her long arms and hands, always a
problem for a dancer. I was afflicted with relatively short arms and
was astonished to hear Charles say they were superb in the Bach with
José. Compliments from our teachers were so few and far between
that these were momentous words when they came.

On August 7 the Contemporary Arts Studio in Westport sponsored
the members of the Doris Humphrey-Charles Weidman Concert
Company. The program offered the Bach *Sarabande* (Letitia,
Ernestine, and I), the *Tango*, José's two DeKoven *Preludes*, the Bach *B
Minor Suite* duet, the four of us in Medtner's *March Funebre*, my
Brahms solo, Ernestine's *Novelette*, the duet *Mazurka*, and the trio
Danse. Whoever wrote the review which appeared the next day in the
Westport paper was obviously carried away with José's masculinity:

ENCHANTING DANCE PROGRAM AT CONTEMPORARY ARTS
The Little Group was met with amazing reception. Encore after encore rang
through the studio from the audience of intelligentsia and aristocrats,
including a number of socially prominent and professionally important New
Yorkers.
The dancers were superb in their ultramodern interpretations. A symmetrical sway of the body with a movement of the arm stirred the innermost
elemental of the most cold-blooded humans. In "Funebre" the dancers, who
were dressed in a death-like gray, went through the most unusual
contortions of dejection—the audience was spellbound—several moments
passed—silently—what emotions these dancers with their exciting
movements stir.
We are unquestionably going to hear more of José Limón. Limón is of
splendid build, powerful but fine, and is capable of awakening the utter
fundamental, effortless. In the finale, the "Danse," the group danced to the
accompaniment of a tom-tom. One could hear the savage beat of the jungle,
the slap of a bare foot on the floor—the most unreal dance—Limón with

Ernestine Henoch, Letitia Ide, Eleanor King in Marche Funebre.

movements would draw the bodies to him, they slept—they would awaken through his apparent hypnotism—it was glorious.

The high spot of our performing so far, Westport, was an exciting event. Florence de Cromer was our accompanist, and Doris, Charles, and Pauline accompanied us there. We were all the house guests of Mrs. Walton, Doris's friend.

A congratulatory gray-haired gentleman came up to me afterward, introduced himself as G. Mortimer Lichtenauer, and asked if he might film my solo, identifiable to him as "that dance with the three folds in the skirt." He also wished to film the Bach and Scriabin duets and José's solo, the next afternoon.

Because of the warm reception we had received and the general afterglow, I proceeded to relive the dances all night long, my heart still racing with excitement. I was too tired the next morning to get out of bed and join the others downstairs for the breakfast I could hear them enjoying. I dozed for a while, then, through the open cottage windows, could not help overhearing a private conversation between Doris and Mrs. Walton on the porch in the otherwise deserted house. "I do not consider myself a genius in the sense that Mozart was," Doris was saying. "I'm not that prolific."

"José has a narrow range," came next.

"Narrow rivers cut deep," Mrs. Walton murmured.

There were indistinct sentences, then Doris: "Of course, if I already had a child, I wouldn't have felt the need to compose *Dances of Women*. After all, what are these organs for, if they are not used; how can we be complete? I haven't many years left if I am going to have a child." (She was thirty-six years old.) I tucked that away in the back of my mind and forgot about it until later.

Charles accompanied us to the Lichtenauers' large house with a beautiful meadow and much rolling ground. We were received by Mrs. Lichtenauer, an impressive lady, a Dalmation Countess who owned a villa at Ripoli, near Florence. Lichtenauer was a successful mural painter. Among his works were the Puvis de Chavannes-esque murals at the Washington Irving High School, where we had recently danced. He had been all over the world and had filmed Balinese dancers, among others. He had started a reel of close-ups of the Spanish dancer Teresita's hands; our dances would follow.

We returned to the Westport Barn Theatre of the night before, where he filmed the Scriabin duet, the Brahms, and the DeKoven, partly indoors and partly on the porch. Then we went on the grass in the afternoon light to do the Bach suite and the last section of the

José Limón in his first solo, Two Preludes. *Photos by Marcus Blechman.*

Brahms, wearing the Bach costumes. At the end, Charles stood between José and me, we linked arms, and José puffed on an unaccustomed cigarette. I hated to look at the camera and was glad when the close-ups were over.

When we returned to Mrs. Walton's, Charles, with a finger on his lips, beckoned to Ernestine and me upstairs, "Come see how Doris sleeps—she dances in her sleep, too." Doris, having a nap, flung out on top of the bed, lay on her side, auburn hair floating on the pillow, her body and legs relaxed in leaping position.

Martin's Sunday article in the *Times* approved of these artistic sproutings, saying we had complete justification for having elected to be dancers; that the compositions, while strongly influenced by our leaders, showed considerable individuality; that we moved excellently and were equal to the demands of the compositions; and that many more formal concerts of the season lacked the verve and finish of this debut. He quoted one of our principals' endorsements of this activity: "For years I have been trying to make them create for themselves so that I can be freed from the necessity of telling them every move to make and how to do it."

Martin saw clearly the problems of the secondary dancer in a modern dance group, comparable not with the corps de ballet but with secondary principals in the classical school, the corps de ballet of the old school being merely background and filler-in, while the modern group is more a foil for the principal dancer.

The group dancer who is an individual in the best sense is the one who is able to grasp quickly the style and content of the composition and to fit himself into it as an animated participant instead of allowing himself to be moved about like a robot . . . active instead of passive . . . he gives indications of mind as well as of body. The problem of the young dancer is that he has been a self-sentenced amateur, lacking all individuality.

The secondary dancer in the modern group must adapt his talents to the requirements of the dance, and then be merely one of many, except in those rare instances where he is allotted a brief solo passage. He has not the privilege of putting his best foot forward or projecting himself into special favor. He must be able to respond to all demands and take as his sufficient reward the satisfaction of work well done. These increased responsibilities, to which he is not always able to measure up, have militated against the progress of the modern dance; and the limited opportunities have made considerably harder the young dancer's career. There is no intermediate step for him; he is either a member of a group or an independent soloist. Frequently he takes upon himself solo status before he has proved himself capable of fulfilling group requirements. It is about time, therefore, that he awoke to his predicament and took just such well-ordered steps toward independence as those which are now being made.

We had the joyous experience of a return engagement to Robin Hood Dell on August 18 and 19, moving to the superb sonorities of the Philadelphia Orchestra, Smallens conducting again. After Cherubini's *Anacreon* and Mozart's *D Major Symphony*, the Humphrey screens and platforms were set up on the stage, the orchestra withdrew to the pit and we danced the Grieg *Concerto*. During the second adagio movement we could clearly hear the crickets making their own cadenzas. Pricks of stars shown through the night sky and a light summer breeze lifted our silk tunics. In this enchanting atmosphere everybody danced with extra élan for the 6,500 capacity audience.

Charles premiered two little dances to Pick-Mangiagalli's sprightly *Piccoli Soldati* and *Notturno*. These were revue-ish dances for himself and Sylvia, with Cleo and José the second couple. Doris repeated her Rameau *Tambourine* solo from the Newport garden party of a year earlier. José and Charles danced together in Satie's *Gymnopedia*—"that modern interpretation of an ancient Greek ritual," the physical training for Greek youth to flute accompaniment. *La Valse* was the spectacular group closing dance.

Ten days later, Letitia, Ernestine, José and I, now calling ourselves The Little Group, danced a two o'clock matinee at the Bedford Hills Montefiore Sanitarium. New works were Ernestine's and José's unaccompanied *Tango*; my solo, which I called *Study*, to Brahms's *Edward Ballade*; for the four of us *Marche Lente* to Medtner. Florence de Cromer was again our pianist. Old numbers were the Bach *Sarabande* and the *B Minor Suite*; the Scriabin *Mazurka*; José's first solo to the two preludes of DeKoven; and Ernestine's *Novelette*.

Rose Yasgour, José and I had at different times modeled for sculptress Emily Winthrop Miles, daughter of Grenville L. Winthrop, donor of a million dollar Chinese art collection to the Harvard Fogg Museum. Mrs. Miles, descendant of the early governor of the Massachusetts Bay Colony, had the beautiful head of a French marquise and a delicious laugh, and she was so thoroughly democratic that she eloped with Papa's chauffeur. Papa thereupon refused to speak to her husband and cut her off.

"On the one hand Pa gave Lennox, Massachusetts, a library, but he can't be gracious about the consequences when informally educated people take advantage of books to improve themselves," she complained. The enterprising ex-chauffeur soon became pilot and owner of his own small commercial airline. Mrs. Miles's studio apartment in town was on 55th Street, but her great love was the country place at Sharon, Connecticut, near Amenia, where she raised swans,

Pekingese, goats, flowers and herds of cows. A new barn had just been built for the cows, and Ernestine, José and I were invited to dance for her friends at a private soirée in the upstairs hayloft on October 18. Guests sat around in mink coats on bales of hay while we danced on an imported ground cloth to the mooing of the cows in their immaculate white tile bins below us.

We opened with the *B Minor Suite*, José danced his DeKoven and a new *Danza* (Prokofiev) solo. My Brahms solo followed the duet *Tango*, and after the *Mazurka* we ended with the trio *Danse*. A string quartet played before and in between. If Mr. Miles was among the guests he remained in the background.

My friendship with Emily Miles continued for three decades until her death. She was not only my friend but my only patron, presenting me with fine books on art every Christmas. After lunch at the Gorham, on two occasions she quietly wrote out a hundred dollar check, once to assist in costuming my group works, the second *Brandenburg Concerto* and *Beasts and Saints*; and once as a bon voyage for my first trip to Europe.

She adored Franklin D. Roosevelt and his policies, much as her father disliked "that man." She was a classical artist (having had drawing lessons from Meissionier in Paris years before) who readily welcomed an old bearded Communist model from the Brooklyn Museum's WPA life model class. The old man used his long hair in a variety of ways: shortened, with a hat, for a Kentucky colonel; nude to the waist, John the Baptist; unrolled, as Tolstoi. And always the *Daily Worker* was brought out of his coat pocket to read while he munched his single luncheon sandwich.

Remarkably, Emily Miles's generosity was without strings. She arranged singing lessons for her maid's daughter, Kathleen, a beautiful young person with a gifted voice, funding a small opera company so that Kathleen could have more experience. The company played two years in a downtown theatre. Never once did the patroness interfere in any way with the director's choice of operas or of the casting of them. She enjoyed hearing Kathleen sing; the politics involved did not interest her in the least.

She was an artist's artist. When sculpting became too much for her battered physique after several operations, she continued to pour out and publish poetry, illustrated with fine line drawings or with her sensitive photographs of nature. Her zest for life and taste in beauty were equal; she was one of nature's aristocrats.

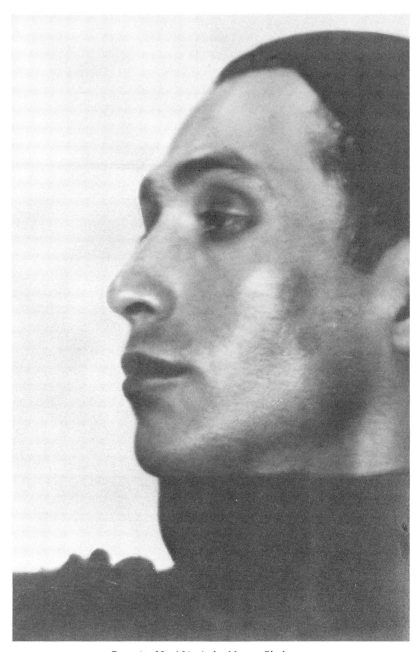

Portrait of José Limón by Marcus Blechman.

The first fall concert for the big company came in November. One critic wrote:

Mature, intelligent, finished dancing filled the stage of the New School's auditorium last night when Doris Humphrey and Charles Weidman and their concert group came together for their first recital of the season. Miss Humphrey and Mr. Weidman have concluded that clarity and simplicity are worth considering; that movement for its own sake is as satisfying in restraint as in orgiastic ecstasy. The grace of their bodies has been illumined by the stability of these conclusions. They now seem to dance for the spectators as well as for other dancers.

    Mr. Weidman has that rarity among male dancers, the combination of grace and power. Last night he seemed to have met with new self-assurance. His "Passion" and "Compassion" were little short of masterpieces of bodily portraiture, made of the sheerest artistry. . . . some present found the "Burlesca" which followed "Air on a Ground Bass" crossed the border from the humorous to the coy, and is, therefore, unworthy of such dancers.

    . . . Regardless of their group experiments and their rough edges, [they] themselves seemed riper, mellower, more agreeable masters of body and mind last night. They now promise to humanize the modernism with which the dance has lately been saturated, and to mold and project their results with exquisite excellence.

    One of the most felicitous programs they have offered since their partnership began . . . if they fail to bring the dances which they gave last night . . . to an uptown theatre it will be a distinct loss to Broadway.

In the *Times,* Mr. Martin found that the New School's open apron stage without a curtain detracted from *The Shakers* and the *Bees,* as well as from Charles's dramatic contrasts of St. Francis and Savonarola, but he thought the striking architectural background enhanced the processional from the *Drama of Motion.* He was the one critic to discern in Doris's new abstract solo, performed in simple white costume to music of Medtner and Malipiero, some of the finest composition she had yet achieved.

In her *Two Ecstatic Themes (Circular Descent, Pointed Ascent)* he found the dancer at the top of her form. Also her new solo Brahms's *Variations on a Theme of Handel* he found excellently built and full of charm. Charles's *Puerto del Vino* (Debussy) ". . . was his best work. The *Two Gymnopedias* with the very promising José Limón was somewhat ambling and overlong for the material it contained."

The *Circular Descent* was a tour de force of voluptuous successional movement, performed in one spot, with lifts and sinkings in the body to the lowest level. *Pointed Ascent* was angular, brilliant, striving and triumphant. Repeating this dance two years later at Bennington,

Doris wrote to Leo, "Anyway, *our* love dance, the Two Ecstatic Themes made a big impression. Some of the ecstasy that was and is ours must be in it."[19]

The Brahms *Variations* was another of her excursions into the romantic music of the nineteenth century. In a yellow underdress with a blue brocade overskirt, the slanted and elegant movement had subtle stylizations of the arms and hands. Charles's *Puerto* was stunning: masculine force and grace which only his long arms and longer legs could fashion. It had Spanish dignity and flavor but it was more than an evocation of the music and could have stood apart from the accompaniment as a modulated rhythmic masterpiece.

It was a prestigious year for all of us. Doris's triumph in the Bloch quartet was only surpassed by the more concentrated *Two Ecstatic Themes*, of which Martin later said: ". . . there is no other dancer in the field who could have conceived it in just this form or who could dance it with such a complete sense of fulfillment. Miss Humphrey's style is seen perhaps here at its best. It is like steel and velvet; strong, resilient and accurate, with an exterior of the utmost delicacy." For Charles, his success with the Beerbohm *Happy Hypocrite* marked a big step forward in commanding a concerto-length ballet-pantomine for group.

The Little Group had managed to appear four times, with a return engagement by request to Westport. Ernestine's Schumann piece included a passage with her whole body vibrating from the feet, perhaps the strongest dynamic point the four of us achieved. José had made great strides in assurance—even his first solo, right-angled elbows and all, revealed his essential strength and fire. Letitia was so beautiful she didn't have to move at all, everyone gasped just to look at her. As for me, I felt I was losing my pin feathers, so to speak, and was beginning to feel like a dancer who could sometimes fly.

CHAPTER FIVE: 1932

Climbing

''WE'VE DROPPED the D[ance] R[epertory] name so as to be able to drop Tamiris, who is a grand girl but a bad dancer. Too bad,'' Doris wrote her parents.[20] The united front of four modern dance leaders jointly performing opening and closing bills was abandoned. Now a series of separate concerts by the artists with their groups was scheduled at the Guild Theatre. Perhaps the reason for the emphasis on concert dance was that New York State law permitted only "sacred concerts" on Sundays; Sundays were the one time Broadway theatres were available to dancers. Billed as benefits for the New School for Social Research, the Humphrey-Weidman group appeared January 17, repeating the November 2 program except that *Water Study* replaced the *Drama of Motion* processional, and Charles, omitting his beautiful contrasts of *Savonarola* and *St. Francis*, substituted a new *Danzon* (Debussy) for the *Puerto del Vino*.

Mary F. Watkins of the *New York Herald Tribune* thought:

"Water Study," perhaps the most remarkable of earlier group works, proved itself still the peer of much that has come later. The "Air on a Ground Bass" and "Burlesca" still remain as engaging a bit of theatre divertissement as may be found on the recital stage.

Using the strategy of billing students only for classes they missed, Charles had succeeded in achieving a men's group. He said later that none of them ever missed a lesson. Led by José, the group also included Gene Hirsch, Marcus Blechman, George Esterowitz,

William Matons, Irving Lansky, Hugh Saunders, Lewis Stilzbach and Gabriel Zuckerman. Some were husbands or beaux of girls in the company. Marcus was a Yale-trained artist, Gene had a physical education degree, Bill Matons had blown into the studio off the sea. With this set of nine men, Charles held the stage at the February 14 concert. New works were large group abstractions: *Prologue to Saga* and *Studies in Conflict*. José led the group in a satirical Stravinsky *March*. Charles's solos were the *Scherzo, Danzon* and *Profane*; together he and José danced Satie's *Gymnopedia*. The Beerbohm fantasy, *The Happy Hypocrite*, concluded with additional "Lords and captains invited to Lord George Hell's party"; the principals were the same as before; José did the maskmaker, Mr. Aeneas.

Mary F. Watkins noted:

Mr. Weidman is one of our most distinguished leaders of the left wing; he and Miss Humphrey have long been looked to for the pace setting of progressive seasons. Of late, however, this gifted and intelligent young man would seem to have overreached himself in his assault upon the abstract. Of the various ensemble compositions submitted this season, few stand out above the general level of confusion and obscurity. But Mr. Weidman has another view in which he is easily past master, the vein of antique, faintly satirical and grotesque humor. This has served him well, but never better than in the revival of "The Happy Hypocrite" . . . here is a real modern ballet, one which fulfills all the requirements in a difficult and recondite idiom. Here is pictorial quality, clarity of pattern, dramatic integrity, overlaid with a delicious fantasy which carefully avoids almost all the pitfalls which beset the experimentalist today.

In a long Sunday column discussing Weidman's successful ballet of humor, Martin wrote,

. . . humor is his natural endowment. He is none of your "devastators" though he can cut with a telling blade in his satin; nor is he a clown in the broadest sense of the word, though he is by no means above good, healthy slapstick methods when he sees fit to use them. It is whispered that he has built up a large repertoire of burlesques of his colleagues in the dance world, both male and female, with which he is wont to regale his intimates upon occasion. Indeed, his comedy obtains its vitality from the penetration with which it focuses upon human foibles and the adroitness with which it points at them the finger of genial scorn.

"The Happy Hypocrite" finds him at exactly the right spot. Here are characters worthy of his ridicule and a plot that calls for just such fantastic originality as he can supply.

If the ballet d'action is to be developed as the next stage in the modern dance—and there seems to be a strong likelihood that it will—Weidman will find himself a unique contributor to its well-being in that he can achieve lightness and laughter without sacrificing any of the principles upon which the modern dancers have reared their structure.

Doris Humphrey and Group in Dionysiaques.

Directed by Gluck Sandor and Felicia Sorel, *The Happy Hypocrite* moved to the Dance Center at 105 West 56th Street for three Sunday evenings. In that tiny crowded studio theatre, aficionados of modern dance could see performances given without theatrical union restrictions.

For Doris, probably the most taxing concert she ever gave was the March 13 Guild Theatre performance; exclusively her afternoon. The new major opus was *Dionysiaques* to the orchestral score of Florent Schmidt. The idea had been incubating a long time, at least since the 59th Street Christmas present from Charles of Evans's beautiful book on explorations at the Palace of Knossos in Crete. Then she had talked about a Cretan bull dance ballet to be projected through an opening between two screens so that the beginnings and endings of the movement would be hidden (a device she never used, but one I gladly picked up years later in staging the third section of *Miracles* to electronic music and the poem of Walt Whitman).

Now further inspired by Nietzsche's *Birth of Tragedy*, finding a consonance between his cult of the ecstatic and her own movement-the-arc-between-two-deaths theory of dance, for the first time incorporating two men in the ensemble of girls, she achieved another theatrical work of large dimension. Pauline's felicitous costumes of bias-cut long skirts banded in purples, greens, and blues translated the elegance of the Cretan ladies in style. Between José and Gene, also costumed after the frescoes of Knossos, she stood as the chosen one, the virgin about to be sacrificed for the good of the whole, in a gold mesh tunic with a copper-banded kirtle, leading a long line of women out of dimness into bright light onto a cleared stage.

At first all Apollonian, the chorus move to seated orderly rows. Doris states a theme of balanced harmony. A gradual fervor takes hold; she moves through the archaic attitudes of the group with more and more impulsive gestures, beginning with odd curls of the fingers, ending with the whole body ecstatic. The group swirls around her, becoming eccentric in action and space. Finally, Doris, leaping against the linked arms of the group on one side, runs and jumps upon the thighs of the opposite group, and from there runs to leap upon José's arched-back chest, where she balances for a moment before throwing herself off to destruction. When the victim falls, the group goes mad, with individual fall-and-recovery variations for twenty-seven accented beats. The boys lift up the sacrificial burden as the dancers return to Apollonian order.

Gene always caught Doris safely in her dive to the ground—though at the first performance she scraped her lip—and José always stood firm as the Rock of Gibraltar. It seems that at the moment of his birth, José had frightened his mother by the vehemence with which he arched his chest. He was tremendously strong. Katey said she never could look at that moment of take-off, it was too unsettling, a real risk.

In a note for an article in *Trend* (1932) Doris defended her theme by stating:

My ballet *Dionysiaques,* although stemming from ancient days is a modern psychological drama about ourselves. Being an American I am party to our morbid liking of spectacular danger, that is the Dionysian passion for unbalance, and this characteristic expressed in original movement makes the dance veracious. This is an example of race experience in material. . . . Given that dancing is limited to known experience, personalized and racial, there must be correlation and evaluation of these experiences and then a meticulous selection of just those experiences which will give meaning to the evaluation with the most succinctness, and simplicity. Here there can be no rules, especially for the American, not only because of his conglomerate racial heritage without a common folklore or mythology, but also because his environment has divested him of his religious faith. To other people in other times and countries a common religion has been so well established, at least during the span of any one artist that he was provided with a ready made attitude about experience. He knew what the past meant, what he could expect the future to hold, and therefore with what it was important to concern himself in the present. But the modern artist is adrift in a maelstrom of conflicting interpretations of life and must determine what is true for him by a conscious struggle. Some sort of philosophy is implied in all human activity, and no matter how the artist symbolizes or represents it in form there must be implicit some attitude toward the meaning of existence. If his conclusion is that human existence has no meaning, that too is an attitude toward the meaning of existence.

Whether or not the audience related the theme to the American passion for speed-racing and for violence of all sorts, the critics were impressed aesthetically. Henry Beckett judged *Dionysiaques* "fascinating, gripping and marvelously worked out." He noted that

in their own person and in their refinement of motion these girls exhibited a physical aristocracy which delighted us. At some recitals of late we gained the impression that the leaders of the dance movement were deliberately selecting the most plebian and bovine females to be found and training them thoroughly in the ways of awkwardness. Surely that is not right. Surely a pretty face, a straight leg, a light step and a graceful way of getting from place to place have not become liabilities in the dance. Miss Humphrey herself is superb in pictorial value. In the "Two Ecstatic Themes" she was ever interesting and significant.

For Mr. Martin, *Dionysiaques* was the outstanding event of the afternoon in which Miss Humphrey touched new heights as a composer.

It is strong, simple, pagan in feeling and its mood is matched in design of sheer magnificence . . . a contemporary restatement of the "Sacre du Printemps" with all the force and passion which must underlie such a subject, yet with no tinge of emotionalism in its projection and no taint of self-consciousness in its hieratic suggestion. Though Miss Humphrey ranks as one of the great choreographers of the day, she has here outdone herself.

Where *Dionysiaques* courted danger, risking everything, *Pleasures of Counterpoint* was essentially rhythmic order: a playful shifting of accents shared between three girls in white and the rest of the group in red. Pauline costumed it in long transparent tarlatan dresses with Elizabethan ruffs. After the dance was worked out, Joseph Achron wrote the score, itself a counterpoint to our movement.

Ernestine had the solo part for the first presentation, Doris took it for the repetition given at the end to close the concert. Light, quick, pointed, "with her unfailing sense of balance in design and her faculty for delicacy of style" (Martin); "an exquisite study in rhythm and accents" (Henry Beckett); "its weaving and revelling of rhythms, its brightly threaded designs" (M. F. W.)—*Pleasures of Counterpoint*, a mathematical exercise to do, was not my favorite to perform.

"Me-You, You-Me, Me-You!" Doris called as we shifted toward and away from her. My verbalization to the opening was:

> Moi, je suis ici, viola!
> Il n'ya pas de quoi,
> Mais tout la même,
> Moi, je suis, ici!

The initial measure was a spring in the air with arms and one leg circling, then arms pressed against the meridian center line of balance, one high, one low, the opened leg arrested on half toe, the body rebounding to the side, an open frontal curtsy.

In addition to *Dionysiaques*, the *Counterpoint* and *Water Study* the group performed *Dances for Women*, now subtitled: The Fruitful, the Decadent, the Militant. The opening was still the best abstraction; the Decadent was fragmentary, not developed enough; the Militant still needed more introductory material.

After the matinee a reception to honor Doris and her group, given by Lucy Rosen, sent us hurrying with great expectations to the off-Fifth Avenue chateau of this lady-musician, first performer on Theremin's theremin at Carnegie Hall and a League of Composers board member. When we arrived, the distinguished guests, Stokowski included, had just left. Mrs. Rosen in a flowing gown descended a spiral staircase to usher us into an empty dining room. As many servants as dancers stood about to offer cups of hot chocolate and sweet cakes from a table littered with crumpled linen napkins and used plates. The greatest need for dancers after a performance is something to cool dehydrated throats and bodies. We ate in isolation, then fled to the nearest Nedicks on a street corner for lemonade and hamburgers.

That season Uday Shankar, his wife, and his dancers, with his brother Ravi leading the musicians, came to grace the dance world. Shankar's radiance, his sublimity of face, body, and gesture, could not be matched by us of the West. Dancing the gods, they were godlike, divine beings.

Now came the Kurt Jooss company from Germany by way of England, with their international artists and their eclecticism. They blended modern dance with a classical base, *then* a daring and risky idea, today the commonplace aim of most companies. For ballet people it wasn't balletic enough to use soft ballet shoes and eliminate the pointe; for the moderns, any concession to ballet at all was still unforgivable.

But no one could have reservations about *The Green Table*, Jooss's bitter masterpiece whose propaganda was perfectly balanced by the humanity of the concept. To an insinuating tango rhythm, a group of international diplomats meet over a long table, with masks, white gloves and spats, to mince and bow in their places, becoming more and more aggressive. Finally, leaping onto the table, each pulls from his pocket a pistol and fires into the air the shots which start the progression of danced and mimed scenes—war's train of losses, hunger, rape, and blackmarket scavenging—with Death always triumphant. O, that *The Green Table* were performed every year at the convocation of the United Nations!

John Colman was with the Jooss company now, playing one of the two pianos in the pit. His *Ballade*, a Renaissance court intrigue plot, was in their repertory. Through John I met some of the dancers, Atty Van den Berg and Bethene Baldridge, who became real friends. Several times with the Jooss company we tripped up to Harlem, fascinated by the dancing at the Savoy, which we would vainly try to duplicate.

On March 21 The Little Group performed at Briarcliff College, with

Les Choéphores from the Oresteia.

Karl Young as accompanist. Karl was a friend of Howard Selsam, whom I met through Harrisburg cousins. Howard, who was himself from Harrisburg, had taught in Beirut for several years and was pursuing an advanced degree in philosophy at Columbia. He lived in the Village and seemed an exotic figure to me, with his Arabian dress, his pipe, his love of music, and his dreams of a better society decidedly Marxist and Leninist in tone. He was much taken with our dance concerts; we were grateful to him for the abilities of Karl Young.

Group rehearsals that spring centered on Darius Milhaud's *Les Choéphores* (The Libation Bearers) from Aeschylus's *Oresteia* trilogy. Doris relished this most profound of all Greek tragedies and hoped to complete the preliminary *Agamemnon* and concluding *Eumenides* when they too would be recorded on disk. Milhaud had written this astonishing score when he was in his twenties, working at the French Embassy in Brazil; *Les Choéphores* was sung in French by the Antwerp Chorus with Mlle. Croiza as soloist, the orchestra conducted by Louis de Vocht. Equal to *Sacre* in its intensity, with magnificent speech rhythms and primitive power, this was hair-raisingly dramatic. Doris chose Ernestine for Chorus Leader, José for Orestes, and me for Elektra, saying she might do the role herself later.

Ernestine's entrance with outstretched arms, thumbs extended, followed by the chorus racing after her until they dropped to their knees, lifting their arms to heaven, with fingers clawing at their cheeks, was enough to strike terror in the beholder in the Vociferation Funebre. To solo voice, almost in a trance of emotion, Elektra enters to pour libation over the tomb of her dishonored father, then leads the chorus in a frenzied round which ends with all sinking to exhaustion. While the singers invoke the savior Orestes, the group dances an expectant rocking rhythm, a lullaby for the honor of the house.

Orestes and Pylades enter. The brother and sister are wary at first, then with recognition they rush to meet over the tomb, where Elektra mimes how Clytemnestra struck their father down. Overwhelmed, Orestes falls to the earth. Elektra takes him by the hand to lead him to the far end of the group, where he becomes the focus of the magnificent Exhortation: the group stands in two long diagonal lines at first facing the pillars of the palace up left; they mark with heel beats the spondees and dactyls of the impulsive chanting until the phrase culminates in explosions of gesture, head and arm oppositions signifying yes, no, dissent, frustration, rebellion, urgency.

The Chorus Leader works on the group, Elektra on Orestes, who finally, after a reluctant false start or two, picks up a spear to rush into the house. Leaping upward to incite him, Elektra is carried in running position through the air and set down on top of the tomb where she awaits the sound of the ax blows.

When they come, shuddering, in the orchestra, the double murder has been done. The group freezes in horror as a cloth representing Clytemnestra's blood-stained robe is lifted upon spear point above the parapet. Orestes creeps out, dazed, bewildered by the Furies already appearing to his tortured vision. As he runs off, the chorus and Elektra slowly shift their eyes and bodies to follow the direction of his flight toward eventual cleansing of the blood guilt.

In April Doris wrote her mother: "Orestes is coming along nicely. I am plotting to get the three or four likely producers of this sort of thing down—Stokowski of course, and Sokoloff, who has just come from Cleveland to take on a N.Y. orchestra, Koussevitsky, who has the Boston orchestra, and Hugh Ross, who heads the Schola Cantorum."[21] Optimistically, she later wrote, "Stokowski is coming to take a look at Orestes on May 1, so I'll still be here for that. I am also hoping to get some others down who might be interested in producing it, but want Stokowski to have the first chance."

We all felt that the *Choéphores* from the *Oresteia* was the best work that Doris had yet done. The movements were terse, staccato, full of dramatic tension; the sylized hands with thumbs extended, the straight alignment of the feet and legs and body, rooted to the ground, had primitive strength, and throughout the dance one felt an inexorable sweep of the power of human emotion.

When we heard that Stokowski was coming to the May 1 rehearsal, we were prepared to dance as we had never danced before; maybe at last Doris would have the right musical support and staging worthy of one of the supreme tragedies of the Western world. Consequently, we were dashed to find a telegram at the studio announcing that Stokowski was departing on a ship for Europe that evening. Rumor had it that Greta Garbo was also aboard.

Sol Hurok made an offer in May to manage the Humphrey-Weidman company. Unfortunately the firm was tied to the Gassner contract, which the latter did not wish to release. People invited to see rehearsals of *Orestes*, as it was called, were impressed. My oldest sister and brother attended a rehearsal. While we were talking afterward Doris came by to comment, "She is one of the lucky ones. She can stand perfectly still and project without moving at all."

Greenwich House on Barrow Street asked Doris for some dancers to contribute to Greenwich Village Week. Doris turned the festival

Eleanor King, Letitia Ide, Ernestine Henoch in Dances for Saturday, Sunday, Monday. *Photo by Marcus Blechman.*

date, May 25, over to The Little Group, so we made our official New York City debut in the Provincetown Playhouse, the famous barn theatre where Eugene O'Neill, Edna St. Vincent Millay, and others had their plays produced. The stage was minuscule, the dressing room downstairs was primitive, and we climbed to the stage itself by means of a ladder. A low-ceilinged door led directly on to the stage, so that in turn we struck our heads against it and made our entrances wide-eyed, looking stunned.

José had three solos: the DeKoven *Preludes*, a new *Cancion* (Mompou) and *Danza* (Prokofieff). Ernestine had her Schumann *Danse*; together she and José performed *Tango Rhythms*, with percussion added. José and I danced the Polonaise, Rondeau, and Badinerie from Bach's *B Minor Suite*, and the Scriabin *Mazurka*. Letitia appeared with us in the opening group *Scherzo* (Prokofieff), in the Medtner *Marche Funebre*, and with Ernestine and me in our new trio *Dances for Saturday, Sunday, Monday*, to Peter Warlock's arrangement of dance tunes from the sixteenth century found in Arbeau's *Orchesography*— that delightul treatise on dancing written in the form of a dialogue between a monk and his pupil, a source book on the preclassical dances: Basse, Pavane, Tordion, Gailliarde and Mattachines. We wore tan leotards, full-gathered skirts of a transparent brown material, long brown sleeves, matching collars around the rounded necklines. Saturday was sprightly and gay; Sunday mannered and quirky with bowings and prayings; Monday a washerwoman's frolic which Charles said was "like red meat." Perkins Harnley made a wash drawing of me in the costume, as seen from the rear.

My solos were the Brahms *Study* and a new *Notturno*. *Notturno* came about in Charles's class. As we were listening to him urging us to compose I happened to be seated on the floor, knees drawn up, arms stretched forward between the knees. "That's a good position to start from," he said. "Go on from there." Like a strange creature in the night, full of slow-motion and fast-motion falls, turns, and suspensions on one or both knees, I hovered over the ground trying to evoke atmospheric emanations of night. Pauline arranged a percussion score including the sliding whine of a flexatone with other small instruments. A 14th Street dry goods store supplied costume material for a hooded tunic, a blue-gray metallic knit fabric and a dollar's worth was all that was needed.

The Provincetown Playhouse audience was friendly, the house so intimate I could recognize a brother's cough and family voices shouting at the end of the Brahms. This embarrassed me, making me wish they had been unknown voices. Receipts from the box office totaled

$125. After expenses and the contribution due Greenwich House, the five of us, including Karl, received eighteen dollars and nineteen cents each.

I was sleeping soundly next morning when my sister Lucile opened the bedroom door, shouting out the *Times* review heading: " 'The Little Group in Dance Debut / Four Members of the Humphrey-Weidman Company Appear at the Provincetown / Fine Technique Is Shown / Eleanor King's Solo Work Proves a Revelation / José Limón an Artist of Ability.' Wake up and read the rest!" My parents were pleased; after all, it was *The New York Times*. Mr. Martin commended the recital:

Many a performance given far less modestly has had far less to recommend it. These young dancers have the excellent judgment not to attempt anything beyond their capabilities, and if as a result the evening is slight in substance it is on the other hand full of skillful composition and admirable technique.

Mr. Limón has presented all of his solos on the programs of other dancers whom he has assisted, and it is no new discovery that he is gifted beyond the average. Eleanor King, however, who has had no opportunity heretofore of showing her solo work, proved to be something of a revelation. She moves beautifully and exhibits considerable imagination in her compositions. Her "Notturno," in spite of the fact that it is in effect a combination of Wigman's "Gesicht der Nacht" and Miss Humphrey's "Descent into a Dangerous Place," has character and strength.

The group compositions are less satisfactory than the solos. The Medtner "Marche Funebre" manages to mistake the entire form of the music, and the "Bacchanale" seems cold and choppy. "Polonaise, Rondeau, and Badinerie," danced by Miss King and Mr. Limón, and "Dances for Saturday, Sunday, Monday," danced by the three girls, are charming bits of formal design.

On happy feet I flew to the studio later in the day where "Ah, Revelation King!" and "Ah, No-News Limón!" greetings were exchanged. When the big group rehearsal ended, Doris called the four of us aside to tell us of her pride and joy in our success the night before. "I want to speak seriously to you, because you have proven you are of the elect—you are the creative ones. You will not always want to be with me, and when the time comes I want you to remember this, and it is the most important thing—never forget that *loyalty stinks*." The four-year-past Denishawn crisis of loyalty had so completely disappeared from my mind that I stared at her in amazement. The word "stinks" did not sound like our Miss Humphrey; the idea of leaving her at that stage never entered my mind. That she was very serious and meant to impress us was clear.

Occasionally Doris invited group members to dinner at the 171 West 12th Street apartment where she and Pauline lived. Doris was a firm believer in Dr. Hay's theory that the human stomach cannot simultaneously digest proteins and carbohydrates, and she posted menus in the studio, hoping her dancers would avoid colds by not eating meat and potatoes at the same time. Once we found her lying on the dressing room floor, Pauline massaging her stomach until she recovered and stood up. She had gone off the diet and it had tied her in knots. I remember dining with her when the menu was corn on the cob, potatoes, succotash and pudding. For a joke, Ruth Allred and I sent her a basket of Park and Tilford's biggest lemons with a Guess Who? card. I don't think any of us followed Dr. Hay's prescription, and Charles and José, who had appetites like horses, supplemented their diets with malted milks several times a day.

A few days after the concert, Doris invited me to lunch with her at Alice Foote MacDougall's on Eighth Street. I could hardly taste the delicious food for excitement as she talked about our program: "You're the one Mr. Martin is interested in."

"Aren't you going to write and thank John Martin for his review?" the family wanted to know. I knew Mr. Martin by sight, his distinguished strawberry-blonde head always looming above any crowd. Partly shy, partly fearful of meeting him, partly arrogant, I never did. Keeping an impersonal distance from the press seemed more appropriate to me.

Mr. Martin's follow-up Sunday *Times* article cited our quartet as a

healthy and encouraging enterprise, for it makes clear that the American dance field is not an army consisting of generals. . . . The four dancers have been working under conditions of ideal artistic discipline. . . . They have had the advantage of dancing in compositions which grew out of the mature emotional experience of older artists, and their function was only to interpret the creations of their leaders. Thus, without the strain of having to create prematurely, they have been able to devote themselves to the development of both their physical and their choreographic techniques.

As a group they still have things to learn in both departments. Their musicianship is by no means as thorough as it should be. In the Medtner funeral march this was most obvious. Their grasp of form in the large sense is also shaky. Ingenious as many of their sequences of movement are in themselves, they more frequently than not follow each other like beads on a string instead of growing from a beginning through a middle to an end. This is more apparent when the substantial support of music is taken away from them and they are left with only percussion accompaniment. It is not always true, to be sure, but it is true often enough to be remarked. The Scriabin mazurka should certainly be retitled at once. The fact that the composer wrote that title above

his music and put his accents in the right place does not justify the retention
of the title for a dance composition that is all moonlight and honeysuckle and
that completely disregards the mazurka spirit.

As an individual, Eleanor King is the outstanding member of the group, if it
is permissible to single out anyone from so small a number. She has unusual
authority in her movement and a rather wider range than is evident in her
colleagues, even without excepting the admirable José Limón. If she is
sentimental in the above mentioned mazurka, she reveals strength and
character in her "Notturno." When she has broken the habit of apparently
singing or talking as she dances, she will be much more effective and her
work very pleasing to the eye.

Mr. Limón has been seen previously in solos on other dancers' programs
[he assisted Grace Cornell for one] so that his excellence is no longer a
novelty. He has still to acquire variety in the quality of his movement,
however, in order to do his capabilities full justice. He has at present a
tendency to confine himself to the use of swift, sharp impulses and of a more
sustained movement characterized by an almost leonine dynamic intensity.
The lower ranges are as yet unexplored, and consequently when employed,
are a little false, a little assumed. The same criticism applies to the general
type of design to which he is partial; it is bold rather than subtle, and inclined
to be sweet when it approaches the regions were delicacy is indicated.

Miss Henock acquitted herself with less interesting material. Vitalization of
the hands will greatly improve her movement. Miss Ide was seen only in two
ensembles and therefore is more vividly remembered as the Arcadian Jenny
Mere in "The Happy Hypocrite" than for anything she did with the Little
Group. Presumably in other programs she has her own solos to offer.

. . . Their program is from all angles sound, fresh and healthy. Though
their work with the larger groups of which they are members must of
necessity require the bulk of their time and energy during the season, it is to
be hoped that these four young people will find it possible to give recitals of
their own from time to time. Not only is their work interesting for itself but it
gives them a possible creative outlet which so many group members are
denied and for lack of which they frequently break away from their moorings
before they are ready. They have much to contribute to the Humphrey-
Weidman organizations, but they have still much to gain from association
with them.

Doris was teaching classes for children at the Dalton School once a
week, and had taken on a twelve-week session at the New School for
Social Research. I went along as her assistant to these places, demonstrating the movements and the dance studies she taught. After one
of these sessions when we were early at the studio getting ready for
the next rehearsal, and alone, Doris began, "I have something to tell
you which will surprise you." I waited. "I am going to be married."

"Doris, how wonderful!" I embraced her immediately.

"It's the expedient thing to do," she said coolly, as if the whole idea
were distasteful to her. She said nothing further about when, where
or with whom this event would take place. We were getting used to

seeing stalwart, broad-shouldered Leo sitting in the corner dozing off while we rehearsed. I knew it must be Leo. She never mentioned the subject again. On July 11 *The New York Times* carried a two-inch box on the front page:

Doris Humphrey, Dancer, To Marry. A marriage license was issued today in Doylestown, Pa. to Miss Doris Humphrey, dancer of 151 West 18th Street and Charles F. Woodford of Hull, England. Miss Humphrey's age was given as thirty-seven and that of Mr. Woodford as twenty-nine. Miss Humphrey has appeared in New York for several seasons and performances have been favorably received by critics. Her latest performance was at the Provincetown Playhouse on May 25th when her Little Group made its debut.

It was a hurried secret affair from which the groom immediately returned to his ship for the next ten-day run. By the time the Monarch of Bermuda steamed into port again, Charles and Pauline had some-what recovered from their first furious reaction. "Why did she have to go and *marry* the man?" Charles complained.

The group took part in a wedding party at the studio, transformed for the occasion into a royal setting. Two chairs were placed on the platform used in the *Concerto,* a length of red cloth down the center of the floor, the golden hoop from the *Hoop Dance,* with a white satin ribbon tied around it, hanging from the middle rafter.

Rummaging in the costume trunks, Sylvia, with a Bea Lillie touch, found some large dress shields. Pinning these to the outside of our long evening dresses, with feathers in our hair and long gloves, we made a pretense at elegance, while the boys dressed up as admirals, generals or ambassadors. When the bride and groom appeared, looking carefully blank, Pauline at the piano struck up the Wedding March, and Charles, the Master of Ceremonies, conducted bride and groom through the hoop to their thrones, before which we paraded in a grand march ending in formal bows. In a travesty of a sailor costume, Charles performed a prodigious sailor's hornpipe.

Leo never changed face. Whether he thought he had descended among a bunch of fools or was too embarrassed we could not tell. Doris, looking tired, maintained a calm exterior, while we ourselves were hysterical with laughter over our burlesque of British royalty. A white cake and punch added to the charivari festivities. After his brief weekend, Leo returned to the ship and Doris continued with her life.

In mid-June, Doris and Charles went to Cleveland to choreograph the summer operas there; they took José with them to dance in *Carmen.* Doris offered me the 12th Street apartment to live in for the weeks they were gone—an oasis of peace and independence away from the home pressures: Mother continually urging, "If you want to dance, why can't you dance at Radio City, wear pretty costumes and get paid for it every week?" and five brothers and sisters still convinced I was "crazy to go on dancing."

When José returned from Cleveland, Charles took him, Sylvia and me up to Westport to try out for the dances in Lawrence Langner's production of Molière's *School for Husbands*. The tryout version, titled *School for Lovers*, had verse written and adapted by Arthur Guiterman and Mr. Langner, together with delightful music arranged from old French airs by Charles Rickett. The play was to run for a week in August. There was no question that José would be selected; it was a tossup between Sylvia and me. For the audition Sylvia danced one of her light quick solos; I think I performed the slow dramatic Brahms, because it was my best work. A mistake—Sylvia was selected. José invited me to see the last night of the show, so I watched the play and thought it charming.

The next year most of us were to be in the New York run of *The School for Husbands*, our happiest theatre experience. But by that time Sylvia had left the group, and José, dancing in one show, was busy choreographing another.

Unexpected economic salvation was just around the corner. In May, J. P. MacAvoy and J. J. Shubert visited the studio. After we performed *The Shakers* and *Water Study* and the boys did *Ringside*, "Poker-Face" Shubert gave in. We were signed into show business for the J. P. MacAvoy *Americana Revue*, rehearsals to start in August. Don Barclay, Lloyd Nolan, George Givot, Peggy Cartwright, Georgie Tapps and Albert Carroll were the other headliners. Although it had no connection whatever with the theme of Americana, a Royal Tzigane Orchestra led by Alfred Rode was also to be in it, thanks to an about-to-expire contract with the Shuberts, who faced a law suit unless they quickly employed the Hungarians.

Americana 1932 had the honor of bringing modern dance to Broadway. It was one of the last of the old-fashioned revues concocted of topical humor, show girls and blackouts. Instead of receiving ten dollars for our few-and-far-between concerts, we would be professionally employed six nights and two matinees a week at Equity salaries. We soon learned that we would earn our wages, for not only were we booked to dance the concert works, but we helped fill the stage and joined the singing in both opening and closing choruses for the two acts.

"Uncle Sam Needs a Man Who Can Take It," the theme song for

the opening, was set in Central Park at the unveiling of a statue to the Common Man, borrowing from Chaplin's *Modern Times.* At the conclusion of the unveiling, with burlesque speeches, "Wild Bill" Matons threw a revolutionary bomb for the blackout. Parodying a Greek ambassador, putting the em*pha*sis on the wrong sy*lla*ble, George Givot orated from a side box nearest the stage and concluded by falling out of it. Georgie Tapps, a thin, energetic young man, performed his specialty tap dance down in "One," the front strip of the stage closest to the footlights.

Then came *The Shakers.* When Lee Shubert accepted the group it was with reservations about the gloomy Shaker costumes. He proposed that purple and white would be more cheerful, a suggestion Doris scornfully refused, telling him, "Keep your predatory hands off my dances. And I don't suppose you even know what predatory means!" While Charles got along well with Broadway managers and producers, Doris's contempt for them was only too apparent. Her uncompromising nature could not accept their standards, an attitude which did not go down well with the tycoons of Shubert Alley.

At the last minute in Philadelphia, when the producers wanted more humor in the show, *Shakers* was to be taken out and a comedian put in its place. Doris threatened to remove the group from the show unless *Shakers* was restored, at least until the critics had seen it. Mr. Lee, called the Cigar Store Indian because sun-lamp treatments had turned his face a mahogany brown, thought this over. *Shakers* went in and stayed to become the talk of the town.

"Brother, Can You Spare a Dime?" the featured song by Harold Arlen, was the climax of a grim bread line sketch. *Amour à la Militaire* began a change of pace; then came *Piccoli Soldati* to a new (union) score by Bernard Herrmann, then a burlesque of *Reunion in Vienna,* with Albert Carroll as Lynn Fontanne. Carroll, gifted mime and parodist, had gone to school with Doris in Oak Park, Illinois; they had in fact danced together in high school shows. His witty impersonation of Moissi in Reinhardt's *Jedermann* had been one of the high spots of the delightful *Garrick Gaieties* a few seasons earlier. On the heels of this sketch, the gypsy orchestra appeared at one side, and the group came on to dance the *Blue Danube,* a ballroom waltz scene directed by Doris. (Doris had not, like Charles, been signed to dance in the show. The volatile Hungarian conductor refused to play any music but his own arrangements, so there was no opportunity for her.)

At the opening in Philadelphia, neither costumes nor masks had arrived until just before we went on for the first act finale. Since all the girls were masked Lynn Fontannes and all the men masked Alfred Lunts, it was a guessing game to find the right partner, especially as in my case, when the mask moved sideways just enough to block my good eye, and I found myself stumbling about near-sightedly, unable to see anything except the other side of the stage.

Thousands of Shubert dollars had been spent on an overhead revolving wheel of colored spotlights, in which we were supposed to maneuver in three-four time, couple by couple. The girls, in long white evening dress with hazardous trains, long white gloves, and high heels, waited for the right Alfred Lunt to come along. Even after Charles found me I was completely lost, unable to focus with one eye. Squeals of surprise poured out from Fontannes mistakenly lifted aloft, while Fontannes expecting to rise in the air stood helplessly stranded.

At the conclusion of the two-week run, the gypsies departed from the show. We missed seeing the mad conductor shredding his violin bow strings every night.

The second act opened with a topical newsreel, closer to home than old Vienna, followed by the *Water Study*. For this Albert Johnson conceived a blue cellophane backdrop which, in one unbroken piece, became the ground cloth as well. In our nude-colored leotards under blue lights behind a front scrim, we danced with delight on that smooth, slightly crackling surface. Not trusting a Broadway audience to sit still through something so new as a musicless dance, Doris compromised to the extent that she had Pauline stand in the wings to beat softly on an orchestra-size gong, adding a muffled roar.

Naturally one of the hits of the show was *Ringside*, with Charles in the added role of the Umpire between the boxing-dancing of José and Gene Martel. Charles also staged a group dance for Harold Arlen's *Satan's Little Lamb*, a speakeasy scene. I didn't mind the other show numbers but felt uncomfortable in this jazzy, supposedly decadent dance. *Doom Over Kansas*, with characters named Alfalfa, Anemia and Mope confronting the banker foreclosing on the mortgage, made its acid points on the condition of Midwest farmers. The show ended with an appeal to "Get That Sun Into You."

I enjoyed our tryout in quiet, sedate Philadelphia. In back of the theatre, in the eighteenth century alley with its iron hitching-posts, we could enjoy 65-cent tea house dinners; on another street we lunched at a Russian restaurant for 35 cents. On the platform circuit that season the Philadelphia Lecture Assembly was offering Thornton Wilder, Princess Cantacuzene (General Grant's granddaughter), Clara Clemens (Mark Twain's daughter), John Drinkwater, Daniel Frohman and even Lewis Carroll's nephew, Prof. B. J. Collingswood. Nazimova and Claude Rains were touring in *The Good Earth* and Grace George and Alice Brady were in Jacques Deval's *Mademoiselle.*

That was a strange world of six nights and two matinees per week spent largely in the basement dressing room of the Shubert Theatre among the steam pipes, attended by elderly ex-chorus girls with dyed hair and rouged faces, who peeled us out of and into costumes for quick changes; the stage crew who played a never-ending pinochle game; the stage manager who kept one eye on the clock and hurried us on and off so the production would not drag one half-second over the allotted time decreed by the union, lest the salary of the stage-hands double. All this was show business discipline, very different from the concert stage. Doris or Pauline watched every performance; regular rehearsals were called to keep things tightened up. Doris was also busy with the understudies, who had become essential.

Creative work at the studio suffered a lapse while we were on Broadway, but was not allowed to cease. Mrs. Miles invited The Little Group to come again to Sharon to entertain her friends in her elegant cow barn, so in September we had that chance to perform our compositions.

October 19, after two brush-up rehearsals, Doris took the group to the New Jersey College for Women in Montclair for an afternoon lecture-demonstration. Demonstrating technique is far more strenuous than performing dances, with more strain involved and without any of the emotional release of dance. I had been rehearsing my *Notturno,* that low-level dance performed largely on one or both knees; nightly we were falling to our knees in *Shakers,* sliding on them in *Water Study.*

We returned to the theatre for the evening show very tired. At the end of the last Shaker jump, my knee buckled under me. I fell on it and the knee swelled. The next day it was too stiff to dance on. The official Shubert theatre doctor told me to apply heat to the "bursitis." Heat treatments in his office and hot water bottles at home aggravated the condition, which, undiscovered by the doctor, was also one of infection. I could no longer walk because the whole leg swelled. Finally the family doctor came, took one look, lanced the swelling, painted it with Mercurochrome and inserted a drainage tube.

During the days of enforced lying about at home, Marcus

Blechman came out to cheer up the invalid, whose knee looked like a Cezanne red apple with a stem on it. He brought letters from the studio. Doris wrote:

Enclosed is fifteen dollars for last week which is half of two-thirds, if you know what I mean.

So glad to hear that you are progressing toward health—you'll be a better dancer than ever, you'll see. I am the veteran with four sprained ankles and a knee! C'est la guerre. Anyway you must have had lots of time to think, or didn't you like what there was to think about? If I remember rightly, Charles Laskey came back with ten ballets and four dances completely laid out. Which reminds me of the remark he is said to have made, "I hear they are doing one of my dances in Americana"—the "Ringside," which further reminds me of Pauline's inspired test for dancers. "Throw them off the Empire State Bldg., and if they bounce, take them in the group. If they splash, refuse them."

Needless to say we miss you, and want you back as soon as possible.[22]

Doris was used to cheering up invalids. Her father had had a stroke, her mother's health was not robust. She was invalided with arthritis too, as Doris would be later. For years the daughter, who supported both parents, wrote them as regularly as possible, trying over and over again in her brief notes to cheer them up with some whimsical or funny saying.

I cannot recall who replaced me but the understudy received part of my salary. A letter from Pauline, written four dashing words to a line, was a boost:

How are you getting along? The "Shakers" will never be the same without you and I miss you very much. I wanted to come to see you one of the past Sundays but what with the understudies and Charles try-out (He did the "Cowboys" and "Marionettes" for "Walk a Little Faster," which came to nothing, after he and José had worked out two chorus dances for them.) I couldn't make it. I want to make the trip to Brooklyn though, and I will. Have you had any news of us. Helen Savery sprained a toe ye Gods! and amid much tears by all left the "Shakers" in the middle last night. I told them that the next time we chose an understudy we would take them up to the tower of the Empire State and throw them out, if they bounce we'll take them, if they splash they're out. This certainly is like the war what with all the wounded lying about. And I did the most horrible thing. I *missed* the "Shakers" the other night. Imagine me, of all people.

My knees could hardly carry me down the stairs when I heard everybody yelling "My God, where are you they are on." Well, try it once it makes you feel rather insane. I staggered to my accordion and was able to get in and finish up with them. Then Pete Davis punched Allen in the eye for missing the finale or something so you see its quite wild here. Get good and strong before you come back.

D. began a new rhythm dance for the group, just barely started so you won't have missed much. And we began work on a "primitive tree ritual" for the 100% Kosher Xmas at the Dalton School. I am reading the letters of D. H. Lawrence. You would love them, they are delightful and richly human. I am going to dig around my family tree and see if I can't claim him for a relation.

P.S. Will miss you on Sunday at Henry Street. (A benefit performance.)[23]

Doris' next letter was about my return to the group:

Here's the situation as I see it about your coming back into the group. I need you, as one of the best dancers to do the "Water Study," because it is a difficult dance and because it is the one number that represents the group. Almost anybody can do the speakeasy scene, and anyway I think you should be dancing for me and with the group primarily—also in the rest of the show when possible. So I feel that you should work on the knee gradually until you can do the "Water Study." Meta can do the speakeasy and Letitia will be back too and can do that. Please keep on coming to see me—just anytime—there will be no rehearsals this week.

Hope you have a nice Thanksgiving—mostly with the refrain (I guess) "I'm glad I have a leg again."[24]

Going about with a cane had subway advantages—someone would usually offer a seat. I visited *Americana* several times as an observer out front and discovered all over again how immensely different the dance appears from the way it feels, and in the case of *Water Study* and *Shakers* how much greater was the whole than the sum of its parts. But the knee mended slowly. When I joined rehearsals at the studio it was disappointing to be cast with the doleful slow-moving ground-bass group while Tish and Katey leaped and darted about us. There was no excitement for me in the new dance.

The Broadway engagement helped solve financial problems only temporarily; after four months *Americana* would close in December. Doris, still on the Hay diet, wrote her family in November, "We have two gas radiators in the studio to use at night for people who don't live on the Sun-diet and get colds."[25] Earlier she had told them, "Did you know that cabbage once a day makes up for many other dietetic sins? Yours for science."[26] Another November letter to them revealed the real stress they had been through: "Am wondering if the gas will be turned on at the studio—it was off all summer for the lack of funds to pay the bill. We use gas radiators on Sundays. You may have thought you were poor, but I'll bet you never had the gas or electricity turned off."[27] For two or three weeks that summer Pauline in the 12th Street apartment had used Sterno cans for cooking and candles for light. The telephone was also cut off. As if the utilities were not enough, they also had a law suit over the apartment rent.

Americana, with its mostly gloomy topical content, did not offer

enough of the ingredient of escape or romance to lure many customers. The show closed in December. Lowered admissions helped to
keep some theatres open. Buying the cheapest seats I saw Walter
Connelly and Pauline Lord in *The Late Christopher Bean,* Osgood
Perkins and a young James Stewart in *Goodbye Again,* Katharine
Hepburn captivating in *The Warrior's Husband,* and Katharine Cornell's stylized production of Thornton Wilder's adaptation of *Lu-
crece*—the kind of poetic theatre that most attracted me. Wearing
half-masks of silver and gold respectively, Blanche Yurka and Robert
Lorraine, alternating as narrators, spoke their lines from each side of
the proscenium. Basil Rathbone was a sinuous Tarquin, sneaking
around Roman pillars. Martha Graham directed the mime of Lucretia's serving women, as they rhythmically sewed.

Down at the Civic Repertory on 14th Street, Eva Le Gallienne
gallantly continued to offer the classics at low prices. It was a joy to
see the delightful *Alice in Wonderland* (Florida Freibus's adaptation),
Liliom and *Camille.* Uptown Cornelia Otis Skinner offered her witty
monologues. She did not match the inimitable Ruth Draper, but she
had a sense of period, humor and style. That a single woman artist
could hold the stage alone fascinated me.

The year before, movies had added double features. More than one
movie house kept the reels turning twenty-four hours a day. For
twenty-five cents people could see film or sleep the hours away in a
bad-smelling semidark but warm place. The cheap houses were
always packed. Garbo with the Barrymore brothers, Jack and Lionel,
made a good thing of *Grand Hotel,* and the Lunts appeared in their
much loved *The Guardsman.* Radio City opened its doors to the largest
auditorium in the world, seating 6,200. I went only once in my life,
and got a headache. Too much of everything.

The last year of Herbert Hoover's presidency was marked by the
Bonus Army, made up of unemployed veterans of World War I who
had been promised, then denied, a bonus. With their families and
children they had taken up residence on the mud flats of
Washington. General Douglas MacArthur led an attack against them
with tear-gas, bayonets, and tanks. This was also the dark and tragic
time of the kidnapping of the Lindbergh baby.

Supplementing their incomes, Doris and Charles taught outside
classes at the Allied Arts Studio uptown, from whence would come
later company members such as Kenneth Bostock and Sybil Shearer.
For her children's class at the Dalton School, while she directed
sitting down, I demonstrated succession patterns (wave motion) to
MacDowell, or led the children in running, swinging and falling sequences.

Teaching at the most permissive of progressive schools had its problems, since the program each day was determined by what the students felt like doing. One day we arrived, dressed and waited until someone came to the door to inform us that the class had chosen that day to visit the museum instead. Ten-year-old Sonya Stokowski, pert and gifted, announced one day, "Mother is arranging my schedule so I can come to class again."

Doris urged, "Splendid, but you'd better hurry. We're getting ahead of you."

Sonya, disappearing down the hall, replied, "O.K., Colonel." During these sessions or traveling to and from, Doris said little. Her thoughts seemed far away from the children. I felt that what she really wished to be doing was composing.

In December the Dalton School put on a prodigious pageant which might have competed with Broadway. Olga Samaroff (the former Mrs. Stokowski) conducted the chorales; Gloria Vanderbilt (the then current Mrs. Stokowski) planned the costumes; Mr. Vandamm, top theatrical photographer, directed the lighting; Doris handled the movement. An infant Stokowski was to be the bambino in the crèche. He howled unmercifully in the wings until he was brought on stage center and held aloft in Mary's arms, when the family theatrical instinct took over; he cooed and beamed at the audience on the musical beat.

Doris, who by this time was pregnant, was less in evidence at the studio. Charles met Martha on the street one day and told her the news that Doris was having a baby. Martha was glad to hear it. Then she said, "Doris can have her baby; I have my technique!" As Mrs. Charles Woodford, Doris more or less turned us over to Charles, now launching his largest, most ambitious project of making a full-length dance-pantomime of Voltaire's Candide. Ian Wolfe was set to adapt the text into rhymed couplets to be spoken by a narrator. In the Bees we had the experience of humming while we danced; in Shakers three individuals had lines to speak, the Eldress's being a simulation of speaking with tongues. Orestes was dance-mime to sung-text in French. Now in Candide, in the Eldorado scene, the dancers chanted nonsense syllables: "Za zee zum za zee." In the rape scene by the Bulgarian soldiers the men shouted, "War, that is our business; rape, that is our job!" and we girls, tossed into the air, used our own voices in screaming protest.

Rehearsals for Candide were underway while Americana was still on the boards. Helen Savery remembers going to the 18th Street studio for late rehearsals after the show at the Shubert Theatre. For José and me, on whom Charles developed the group themes, it was every day,

Sundays included, throughout the winter until the run in May. *Candide* was a test of endurance and devotion to Charles's gifts as America's leading male dancer. Full of innovation, he added sets of gray boxes, which, laid end to end, became a garden wall; upended, fortress walls; separated, tables or chairs or beds. These bits of abstract furniture and scenery were pushed into place by the dancers.

Doris, looking better and happier than we had ever seen her, was achieving her goals of being a wife and mother. Charles was in a fever of creativity. For The Little Group it had been a kind of graduation year, from apprenticeship to professional engagements, with our successful New York debut. And having been given the plum part of Elektra, I was now to have another choice role, that of Cunegonde in *Candide*.

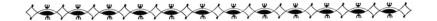

Plateau; 'The School for Husbands'

E X C E P T T H A T she was more radiant than before, Doris's approaching maternity was not apparent. Her last performance in public before the baby's birth was on February 4 at Columbia University's McMillin Theatre, where indefatigable John Martin was launching another series of Modern Dance in America programs. The group danced *Pleasures of Counterpoint, Water Study, Parade* and *Shakers.* Doris appeared in her elegant Brahms solo *Variations on a Theme of Handel,* then risked the central *Counterpoint* role with its jumps, bounces and spins. Nothing happened. Ernestine, Tish and I contributed *Dances for Saturday, Sunday, Monday*—the only time a Little Group composition appeared on a Humphrey program—to fill out the evening, which ordinarily would have had more Humphrey solos.

In March, Stanley MacCandless, of the Yale University Drama Department, invited Doris to choreograph movement for the stage lighting demonstration: "A Mobile Composition blending light, music and motion (dance)." Preceding the Humphrey experiment, an academic exploration of theatre lighting would demonstrate procedures and functions, the evolution of lighting from the manuscript to the lighted scene in romantic, classic, and expressionistic styles. Lighting for the Mobile Composition was in the hands of young graduate student Jean Rosenthal, later the indispensable lighting artist for major New York productions. For music Doris chose Debussy's *Nuages* and *Fêtes.* The dance was a solo; she chose me for it.

We rehearsed in the studio, then took the train for New Haven, making a three-day visit with the MacCandlesses. Mrs. MacCandless, companionably enough, was also large with child. We rehearsed the first day and had two performances. I could hardly visualize how the lighting was to be mobile, too, except in a vague Scriabin-esque curtain-of-light sense. It was disappointing at rehearsal to find that a static cyclorama was hand-waved while a cut-out silhouette of sun-

Debussy's Fêtes, *experimental light-sound-motion program at Yale University, directed by Doris Humphrey with Eleanor King as soloist.*

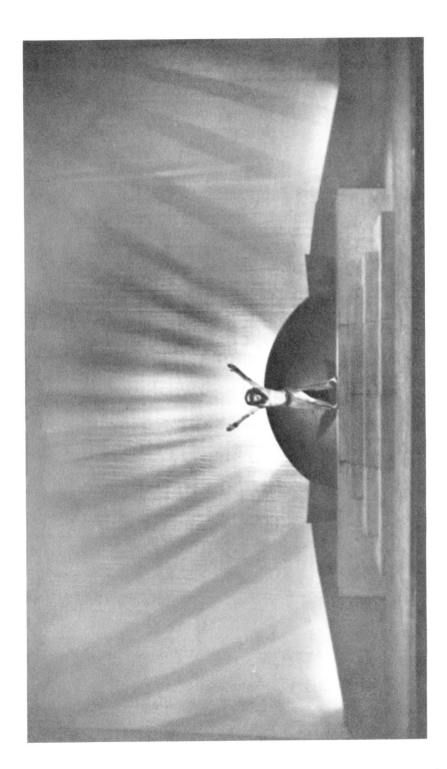

rays was projected upon it. Mr. MacCandless explained that only Severance Hall in Cleveland, with a newly installed Izenour board, could fully cope with their ideas.

I could not see the first part of the program because I was warming up, then being costumed. Yale supplied a long silver-edged transparent costume, also a series of step levels on which to dance. The Debussy was thrillingly satisfying to me. There had been some despairing moments in my life when my existence seemed futile and hopeless. At those times the thought of Debussy's orchestration consoled me; a world containing such magnificent sounds was a world worth living in and for.

The theme of the dance was the evolution of light from dawn to dusk. From a horizontal position on the steps I woke, gradually stood, then crossed the stage with high lifts of legs and arms; at the climax I mounted the highest platform and became part of a projected light form on the cyclorama. I loved the dance, though I knew my legs never went as high as Doris wanted. With some alterations and a title change to *Renascence,* I kept the dance in my solo repertory for several years.

Doris wrote her family, "[at Yale] everything went increasingly well up to the performance and at that point the electrical mechanism that controls the victrola record went wrong, so that the tone wavered horribly ruining the whole thing."[28] Sitting out front she "died by inches." Poor Doris was not in a good mood; she had gone off the Hay diet. On the train returning to New York she volunteered the comment that Charles did not live for ideas, but for sensation.

MacCandless wrote Doris later:

I can hardly express appreciation to you and Miss Eleanor King for the time and enthusiasm which you devoted to our recent Light Show. While I feel that there is considerable to be desired in the point which we tried to make, I am sure that the proficiency with which the dancing was done raised the experiment to such an extent that people were more inclined to accept it as a distinguished effort than something which otherwise might have fallen flat. As soon as I can recover my point of view I want to analyze the results more thoroughly and would love to talk them over with you.

He mentioned the possibility of attending the *Run, Little Chillun* show on Broadway (featuring the much-loved Hall Johnson Choir), which had opened on March 1; Doris had staged its Voodoo number.

As increasingly happened, this was another theatre event I had to miss, with *Candide* rehearsals required every night. If you were a Humphrey-Weidman dancer, you spent your life within studio walls preparing for rare performances, missing many contemporary theatre high points such as the Bel Geddes *Hamlet,* for which Charles had directed the players scene.

At this time Pauline went to Boston to help Pauline Chellis with a concert. She wrote Doris from Boston:

> I've decided that what really ails me is my perfection complex—the only satisfaction it ever realizes is in my imagination—both art and people including P.L. herself . . . I behave very successfully, I am quite an improvement over last year, and my costumes are stunning, ready on time and make a big hit. My ideas are priceless too, even I know that. If this were to be all though, I couldn't bear it.[29]

"Cassandra Legree" at the studio, Pauline had been living through the end of a complicated love affair. Her life of devotion to Doris was total, and to Charles too, if not so consistently. She shared their art, their lives, their poverty. No matter what the difficulties, thanks to Pauline's help in the background, the two leaders were able to receive fame and recognition, while reviewers seldom mentioned her costumes, which were usually ideal for movement, or her lighting, which could make or mar a performance. She was prescient, intuitive; she could nag, she insisted, and always aesthetically she was right.

"How can one ever repay devotion like that?" Doris commented once. "Pauline has been my friend for years. I always enjoy her company." This was long after she had forgotten the bad moments. Once at rehearsal at the New School, Pauline's fingers at the piano slipped on one note. "It's G sharp, not G flat," Doris turned on her in fury. "Why can't you practice enough to get it right?" Pauline answered sharply; the air was electric with tension. But such an outbreak was exceptional.

What the pregnancy brought out in Doris was a strong domestic instinct, aborted for so many years by the demands of teaching, rehearsing, performing. She wrote her parents,

> If people only knew how domestic and stationary most artists are, all the nonsense about Bohemianism would die out. I assure you there was more rejoicing over a new couch at our house than there usually is over a new dance . . . I am almost perverse, annoyed with people who think it lovely for me to bring up at least two children and so give up working so hard! Also when the opinion is I am a perfect fool to go in for an infant. The thing is, I want it all, and I hope I won't bust trying to get it . . . my health is ok, thanks for inquiring, in fact I am more ambitious and stronger than usual, who says babies aren't good for dancers?[30]

Eleanor King and José Limón in Candide. *Photos by Edward Moeller.*

Later that spring she addressed a remarkable letter to herself, headed "Dearest Doris," signed, "lovingly, OM."[31] A carefully thought-out epistle, she alternately castigates then encourages herself, disparaging all the time she spends directing, composing, even writing when what she rightfully should be doing is having the supreme happiness of dancing: "To be moving oneself is the greatest satisfaction because the whole self is both engaged and liberated." For Humphrey, of the perfect body "sculpted like a greyhound" as Tom Borek says,[32] having to abide sitting and watching others move must have been a disturbing experience. As the child trapped her body, the pull of her personal drive as a performer must have intensified as it was threatened.

The amusing touch is the signature. With her Congregational background, Doris had taken an appraising look at Denishawn's Messianic cult with its excursions into Oriental philosophy, and would have none of it. When Miss Ruth and Shawn instituted twice-weekly readings and talks on the literature of the East for the benefit of the Denishawn dancers, Doris flatly refused to be impressed. The mysticism of reincarnation as expressed in the *Tertium Organum* was not convincing to her. The OM letter, revealing her inner struggle of the self divided against itself, invoking the name of the Brahmanic-Buddhist deity as a protective counselor, seems a consciously humorous return to Denishawn metaphysics.

While Doris was being domestic and loving it, we devoted ourselves whole-heartedly to Charles's new *Candide*, day after day, night after night. Helen Savery remembers Charles's movement phrases running ninety-seven counts or more, all the dancers counting with him, for the music wasn't yet written.[33] Once Charles became more and more annoyed until he screamed, "You're doing this as if it was the third part." The poor dancers, who had nothing but drum beats and counts to go on and were quite lost, answered, "We thought it *was* the third part."

Along the way, musicians came and went. John Colman, whose melodies poured from his fingertips, could not write down what he felicitously improvised. Ruth Wertheim came, tried, and faded away. Finally Genevieve Pitot solved the problem, composing and completing the score.

Compared to Elektra, the role of a victimized Cunegonde, passive object, was neither so intense nor so compelling. Both characters experience love, shame, grief, despair, hatred and hope. But Cunegonde is acted upon, while Elektra's depths of feeling impel her to act on others. In the Milhaud *Les Choéphores*, the Elektra role lasts perhaps fifteen minutes. Cunegonde, on stage much of the evening with Candide, suffers most of the disasters of man and war but in a fairy-tale way. Since Charles was engrossed in whipping the company into shape for this, the first full-length modern dance work, he rarely stepped in to perform his own central part. I spent a great deal of time standing about waiting to be carried off by José in his multiple roles as Fate, Judge, and Spanish Don. He was also a priest in the church scene. An effective mime was the quartet of characters, Candide, the Lord Inquisitor (José) and a wealthy Jew (Bill Matons) fighting over Cunegonde, all at cross purposes and all beating on the walls, the doors, the tables, in rhythmic counterpoint.

After many difficulties along the way, Charles announced that instead of Sol Hurok, as we had been given to hope, Michael Meyerberg, with assistance from J. J. Shubert, would produce the piece for a week in May at the Booth Theatre. Meyerberg emphasized Don Forbes's line drawings of the Bulgarian army rape scene used for announcements. Perkins Harnley made the theatre lobby posters. A few weeks before the opening, Charles announced that Doris, who had long absented herself from the studio and to whom all of Candide was new, would come for a runthrough. We gave everything we had to this important rehearsal. Doris gave no sign until the end, when she observed, "It needs a lot of work," then bowed herself out. This was disheartening and crushing.

We moved into that charming theatre the Booth, in Shubert Alley, hoping for the best. To be in one theatre for a whole week was a giant step for modern dancers. Cleo, Katey and I shared the number one dressing room, reveling in the auspicious fact that on other occasions it had harbored such artists as Ruth Draper and Angna Enters.

Charles not only adapted and arranged Voltaire's Candide, he also designed and in some cases executed the simple, ingenious, effective abstractions of costumes. The piece itself was divided into two acts with four cantos. The first canto, "Under the Influence of Optimism," opened with a vision—a conflict between pessimism and optimism (John Glenn as Pangloss and Charles as Candide); a pantomime of a day's routine at Castle Westphalia (a duet by John as Pangloss with Cleo as Pacquette); followed by a dance of Candide's awakening, a gambol with Cunegonde, then discovery and pursuit of the lovers from the garden (where the boxes represented hedges); the entrance of the Bulgarian army with orgy, plunder and rape; and a closing Fugue.

The introductory narration and occasional couplets were spoken by an actor whose voice represented that of Voltaire—a large gilded

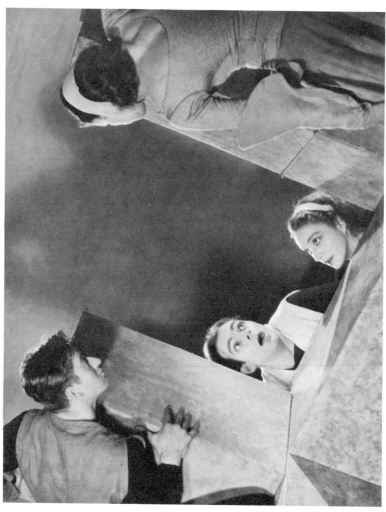

Bill Matons, Charles Weidman, Eleanor King, Katherine Manning in Candide. Photo by Edward Moeller.

Bill Matons, Katherine Manning, Cleo Atheneos, John Glenn, Eleanor King, Charles Weidman in Candide.
Photo by Edward Moeller.

mask of whom was set over the proscenium. In addition we dancers also used our voices. At one time or another the whole company sounded off.

The second canto's visionary prelude—in which Candide embraced religion—was a scene set in a church: files of people on their knees in praise and supplication, until a priest of the Inquisition (José) appears in a mixture of love and wrath, rousing the group to a complete frenzy.

The boxes upended become walls of a room wherein Cunegonde is forced to become the mistress of the Lord Inquisitor, then of the wealthy Jew. Beating on the walls, the doors, the floor in a rhythmic battery, Candide in the ensuing brawl kills a man. He and Cunegonde flee. The interlude, "Optimism Explodes," was a trio for Pangloss, Martin (Bill Matons), and Katey, cast as a Materialistic Hag.

The vision of the third canto was a travelogue in which Candide and Cunegonde meet the South Americans, who speak a strange language of "Za, zee, zum, za, zee" syllables. Enter Don Fernando, seeking new fields to conquer. He abducts Cunegonde, leading to a dance of pursuit. Then molto dolce, the utopian dream city of El Dorado—distinguished by Colman's sole surviving music in 9/8—followed by a disintegrating wrangle and a fugue.

The fourth canto's opening vision beholds Fate intervening again. "Through shipwreck and disaster, Candide finds himself back in Europe on the way to Paris and in Paris meets Parisian Mannerisms," a highly stylized seduction scene by the girls. Fate intervenes to present Cunegonde, veiled as idealized womanhood, then mockingly substitutes an alluring flesh-and-blood adultress (Cleo) to Candide's eyes. Pessimism (Martin) joins Candide. Fate acts again to bring optimism back to life, allowing Candide and his companions to settle down in the country along with Cunegonde, now a little the worse for wear. Candide, deciding the best thing to do in this best of all possible worlds is to cultivate one's own garden and keep silent, dances a soliloquy before the final group fugue.

The opening went very well; we were elated by the response of the audience. The reviews next day were mixed—many of the Broadway reviewers not knowing how to review this pantomime-comedy—but Charles was exuberant. Backstage talk was that the production would go on to Chicago, then holding its Century of Progress Fair, and that *Candide* would go to London. Several people came back for second looks, and one attended all eight performances.

Grena Bennett hailed it:

. . . that classic work, familiar in its original guise to every student of literature, was cloaked, danced, spoken, illuminated and otherwise unusually and
unsuspectedly conditioned and brought to the attention of an eager and
inquisitive audience. But if they came in a scoffing mood they undoubtedly
remained to applaud. . . . This version of the Voltaire romance . . . should
run not for one but for many weeks, and so provide a delightful and delectable entertainment in "this best of all possible worlds."

Mary Watkins thought:

Voltaire must have glanced down from his celestial seat and chuckled . . . an
orgy of energy and pace, and extravagant stylization, if brought down to the
level of low farce, achieved with a fine simplicity of line.

Burns Mantle wrote:

The opening had the importance of an event, with quite impressive dancing,
with Weidman particularly good in all the episodes in which Cunegonde, the
heart of his adventure, was opposite. And particularly amusing in his meeting with the Bulgarian army in which the soldiers have the most diverting
habit of standing stiff and straight and falling full-length upon their faces by
way of salute.

He singled me out as talented, José as vigorous, Cleo as a flashing
young person.
Bernard Sobel approved *Candide* as

in the spirit of the original manuscript—satirical, bitter, disillusioned . . .
replete with beauty, freshness and inspiration. The respectful attention of the
audience; the burst of applause and laughter; and the great enthusiasm at the
close of the curtain bore out this impression. Charles Weidman, as Candide,
dominated scene and story, while lost in the sincerity of the illusion he was
creating, sensitive and agile.

On the other side of the fence, John Mason Brown summed it up as
an evening which did little for dance, added nothing to the theatre,
and took everything away from Voltaire.
Richard Lockridge conceded:

an interesting experiment, with moments of visible wit, to be recommended
to those who like to see Mr. Weidman dance and do not mind having Voltaire
reduced to words of one syllable. On the credit side is an excellent use of light

and color, several sufficiently exciting movements and some deliciously impish pantomime on the part of Mr. Weidman.

To John Anderson, the spoken passages were appallingly trite; the Bulgarian army and church scene highly inventive and incisive; the large group scenes better than the smaller ones.

José Limón outshone the whole stageful by the energy, precision and superb style of his performance. Mr. Weidman was often amusing though he relies heavily on facial expression for his points and Eleanor King, as the luckless Cunegonde, had moments that were interesting.

Robert Garland saw it as "missing Voltaire's prime impulse," if with "merit in the interludes—in Candide's awakening, the gambol with Cunegonde and the fugue in which he solves a trying situation, but the dancing and pantomime failed to fuse into a happy whole."

Arthur Pollock objected that "too little [was] done in the way of making the words that tell the story the words of Voltaire himself . . . they are better than Mr. Wolfe's. This 'Candide' is frolicsome and it has novelty. Last night's audience remained after the final curtain to applaud and cheer with enthusiasm."

Whitney Bolton qualified his seeing it

as a step in the right direction which will lead to new forms in the theatre, new dimensions and new force. If the step were a toddle rather than a vigorous stride then that is a fault I can't trace since the guilty person is not discernible in the program. Somewhere between the impulse to say that it is a refreshing step in the right direction and the truth of having to say that most of it is curiously unbalanced and some of it feeble lies what rightfully ought to be said about Mr. Charles Weidman and his company. . . . Mr. Michael Meyerberg, with commendable ambition but faulty discernment, presents it at the Booth Theatre. It had been expected that "Candide" would be brash, unholy, impudent and suggestive. The sidewalk gossip, before the curtain rose, had it that something very sooty could be expected (in the name of art) and that unbelievable, not to say indescribable things would take place right on the stage. . . . Nothing of the sort took place . . . a few scenes of seduction in two-four time, a few bold antics by the Bulgar soldiers. Any single one of the events could have been staged by the Mosholu Parkway Civic Uplift Society without causing resignation among the members. Several of the ladies and gentlemen of the First Night audience seemed bitterly disappointed that nothing untoward took place.

And what of the *Times*, the oracular voice which automatically spelled victory or disaster for the dance? Three small paragraphs appeared under Mr. Martin's signature. They did the play in. John Martin, who had so recently urged Charles to undertake a "ballet d'action," accused the dancer of "suffering a disturbing relapse."

The mixture of ballet d'action, dance recital, Broadway revue and little theatre morality play must seriously have disturbed the shade of the Squire of Fernay. The evening's most egregious burden was the sophomoric couplets issuing from the large golden mask. Mr. Weidman and his attractive company of youthful dancers work with commendable energy and high spirits, but in a vain cause. Neither the patchwork musical accompaniment, the sketchy production nor the choreography help them to do much besides miss the point rather completely.

No place in the world is more iffy than Broadway. Would it have gone better if we had been ready sooner and opened before the hot May weather set in? If Arthur Guiterman had adapted it? After the opening full house, audiences fell off toward the end of the run. The last day, cursed with a violent spring storm, people stayed away in droves from the matinee and evening performances.

When the final curtain came down, Charles met us all on stage, confessing there was not enough money in the box office to pay us anything. To cultivate his own garden he would have to borrow money to get himself to his farm in New Jersey for a rest. The musicians and the stage hands were paid. Later we learned that Richard Abbott (narrator), in a breach of etiquette, had stepped in front of the curtain before the second act to announce to the audience that he would not continue until he received his salary. From somewhere Meyerberg found money to pay him. We, who had worked for a year and performed for a week on Broadway, had total experience as our reward. Thus this extraordinary endeavor "in the best of all possible worlds" came to a crashing end.

Two years later under the WPA Dance Theatre Project, *Candide's* ten-week run was a resounding success. Coupled with Tamiris's *How Long Brethren,* with new costuming and orchestral accompaniment, this more adequate production could have run longer, but Congress, squeamish about dance and especially irritated because Eleanor Roosevelt had a young dancer friend on the Project, suddenly curtailed all money for the theatre and dance projects. Both Doris and Charles had been named to the directing board of the Federal Dance Project. I had not gone on relief; Cunegonde was danced by Katherine Litz.

During the 1974-1975 season another *Candide,* this one with music by Leonard Bernstein, had a successful run on Broadway.

From the ashes of *Candide,* we were soon fanning the flames at the studio harder than ever, for we were booked again with the big symphony orchestras—the New York Philharmonic at Lewisohn Stadium and the Philadelphia at Robin Hood Dell. The dates were in August, time enough for Doris to have her accouchement and be ready to dance again. She wrote her parents: "I'm rehearsing so as to have everything in the best possible condition, but working over old things is quite a bore. Charles is still in Cleveland, Pauline is giving a music course to the little darlings in the studio, and Leo is running the plutocrats to Bermuda and back."[34]

Pauline's course, perhaps in emulation of Louis Horst's "Preclassic Dance Forms," consisted of studies in rhythm and in the early dance forms. We all enjoyed it; there was always something amusing and enlightening with Pauline. Stravinsky's Minuetto from the *Pulcinella Suite* haunted me with its strange dark melody, and I made a dance for that, wearing a long brown dress banded in black, with a headband and chin strap. As usual, Stravinsky's modernized eighteenth century Venetian music led me around by the nose. Doris said, "That's the strangest dance I ever saw." José's reaction was, "You amaze me."

In June Doris wrote her parents:

The sight of José and Charles driving in from New Jersey with the load [of baby furniture—crib, scale, table, drying rack] and carrying it upstairs from 12th Street was a proof of devotion I never thought to witness. Both of them heartily disapprove of the whole business you know, as being highly dangerous to me, inconvenient to others, and an act of injustice to the child.[35]

It was true—Charles was of course alarmed for Doris's career, as was Pauline; José hated all babies on principle.

As Doris wrote her parents, "Finding the right orchestral work which must set the right keynote of dignity and vigor, it must not be a royalty piece, must be a suite of dances—or at least have a program—must include a part for me, not too strenuous but telling [a problem she solved with the choice of Roussel's *Suite in F*]—antique dances in the modern manner. These must be conceived and composed next. Charles will help me—and after I get them sketched out will go ahead while I am occupied with my biological composition."[36]

Doris calculated the baby would be born in plenty of time before the first Stadium performance. According to plan, the baby would come in June. June came; June went. The doctor ordered her to take long

Eleanor King in Minuetto. Photo by Marcus Blechman.

bumpy rides in the car that José had recently invested in. She accomplished the sketch of the Roussel. "I finished up rehearsals Thursday night with quite a satisfactory feeling that the whole stadium program could be done without me—if necessary—even the two new numbers have been blocked out enough so Charles or Pauline could finish them. I take a great joy in being able to stay at home and putter—something I have never been able to do in New York."[37]

Charles composed the Prelude of the *Suite*, "a series of greetings, a leading couple salute each other and the on-lookers, and then present the group in a lively series of greetings." The role which Doris would have had was given to me. Greeting Charles was of course delightful; greeting the 12,000 onlookers stretching north and south for two city blocks was quite a projection test. The Sarabande provided a spot for Doris, holding a rose in one hand, standing almost still in the center, while the girls undulated around her. But the Gigue made considerable demands on the company, the boys vying in leaping and jumping after they brought on a tall maypole with ribbons. Pauline made unbleached cotton tunics for us; with flowers in our hair and the weaving of the colored ribbons it was a gay fertility folk-dance, scenic enough for the large outdoor space of the Stadium. Rehearsing the maypole was tedious, if there was one mistake of going under and over, the whole thing had to be unwound and started again, a mechanical process.

Water Study followed the *Suite in F*, then Charles with seven men (Marcus Blechman, Jack Cole, John Glenn, José Limón, Gene Martel, William Matons and Gabriel Zuckerman) performed the Farandole from the Cleveland Opera production of *Carmen*. The *Piccoli Soldati* had to be encored, being just what the popular audience liked. *The Shakers*, with Dorothy Lathrop in Doris's role, was enhanced by the singing voices of the Hall Johnson Choir.

Having shaken ourselves free of sin, shaking just our wrists in the gentle Shaker way, we came on next in the bacchanale "Satan's Li'l Lamb" from the *Americana Revue*—courtesy of Lee Shubert—shaking our shoulders and hips too. Charles and José danced the Satie *Gymnopedia*; Ravel's *La Valse* was the grand finale, with Cleo in place of Doris. Printed on the program in both opening and closing numbers, Doris was listed with Charles and the group, the supposition being that the contract would be null and void if her name at least did not appear more than once.

The thirteen girls in the company now were—besides Cleo Atheneos, Letitia Ide, Ernestine Henoch, Katherine Manning,

Dorothy Lathrop and me—Debby Coleman, Rose Crystal, Ada Korvin, Frances Reed, Hyla Rubin, Gail Savery and Helen Strumlauf.

Mr. Martin's Sunday column, devoted to the Stadium concert, was encouraging:

In the opinion of the present writer there is not an ensemble anywhere in Western Europe that is its peer; for it has the rare combination of two first-rate "stars," an unusually strong line of soloists, impeccable teamwork, and one of the most gifted choreographers of the day.

He spoke of Miss Humphrey's yearlong withdrawal from public appearance, during which she composed the Roussel *Suite* and three of the nine parts of the projected *Oresteia,* which

bids fair to eclipse everything that its composer has previously done, if its remaining movements continue in the vein of those already completed.

The "Dionysiaques," the Roussel, the "Orestes" mark a new period in Miss Humphrey's creative methods . . . achieving a balance between form and substance which has been the most elusive of all the goals sought by the modern dance. . . . a delicate balance in which the true classic spirit and the romantic are reconciled without compromising. . . . she has no stereotyped vocabulary of movements which are repeated in varied combinations. Each phrase seems to evolve as a whole rather than as an assemblage of parts. Yet with all the conviction of originality which runs through her compositions, there is never any straining after novelty, which disfigured many of the later Diaghilev ballets and is an outstanding characteristic of some of the sensational modernists' creations.

The "Suite in F" is a light and charming example of its composer's fluency. Its first movement is literally an introduction. . . . This involves as neat a bit of contrapuntal design as anyone could wish, perhaps a trifle too closely knit to be readily grasped in so large a place as the Stadium. The central roles were danced most ingratiatingly by Mr. Weidman and Eleanor King (vice Miss Humphrey).

Henry Beckett considered the performance "probably the most freshly entertaining and clever of all the dance programs given here."

The same program given on August 16 and 17, in Robin Hood Dell with the Philadelphia Orchestra (Alexander Smallens again conducting), pleased the Philadelphians too: "The work of the evening devolved principally upon the men and women of the group and they were worthy of the assignment. It is an extraordinarily well-trained, competent ensemble," wrote one critic.

The symphony program included an announcement of a new Philadelphia Studio of the Dance for Humphrey-Weidman, who were branching out: "[they] have an approach to training of modern dancers which is unique to them. They believe in a foundation of natural movement followed by a study of distortion and stylization

which leads to composition and professional performance. Students
. . . trained in this way . . . who merit it will be engaged to augment
the ballet directed by Doris Humphrey and Charles Weidman in the
American premiere of *Iphigenia.*"

Distortion was a frightening word to professional dance educators
meeting in New York, when Doris addressed them in November. It
caused such a ruckus that Martin came to her defense in his Sunday
column. "The so-called 'natural dance' is not and never was an art
form but merely a type of play-dance whose function is the discharge
of energy or emotional surplusages in the dancer." Distortion as a
means of emphasis, of accentuation, was an inevitable hallmark of
Humphrey-Weidman composition.

Broadway, as if to make up for *Candide,* now beckoned to Charles,
and a series of auditions went on at the studio. Charles was signed to
do the dances for *As Thousands Cheer,* the sequel hit to the great
American musical *Of Thee I Sing,* and for *Let 'Em Eat Cake,* later called
I'd Rather Be Right, which ran for only three months. *As Thousands
Cheer* played for nearly a year. The group was divided up: José and
Letitia were to be the featured dancers of the group in *As Thousands
Cheer* with Debby Coleman, Katherine Litz, Irene McBride, Margaret
Sande, Helen Savery, Helen Strumlauf; Robert Gorham, Harry Joyce
and Bill Matons.

Ernestine, Katey Manning, Ada Korvin, Hyla Rubin and I were to
dance in the dream ballet interlude of the Theatre Guild's *School for
Husbands,* [38] our partners to be Marcus Blechman, George Bockman,
Kenneth Bostock (from the Cornish School, Seattle, and Herbert
Gellendré's Theatre School in New York) and Jack Cole, ex-
Denishawn. Cleo and Frances Reed were also to be in the Guild
show. Cleo, while doing most of the assistant teaching at the studio,
was to understudy Doris; she and Frankie appeared in the mob
scenes.

Everything about the Molière was a delightful experience. We
loved the play, the music, the production; the cast, who tried every
night to improve their performances; and the director, Lawrence
Langner, who treated us always with courtesy and respect as "ladies
and gentlemen of the theatre." "The Dream of Sganarelle" ballet
interlude had songs, verses and a variety of dances centered around
Osgood Perkins as Sganarelle. Ada and I were handed plum parts of
the two Egyptians, roles originally danced at court by Louis XIV and
one of his noblemen. As soon as Doris completed the ballet
choreography—with Charles doing his part of the Dancing Master

and the dancing lesson with the old man—we went to the theatre to show it all to the board of the Guild. Langner, rubbing a hand over his extra-long side locks which covered the top of his bald head, chuckled and laughed at our "Twiggy bit," approvingly.

Doris's delicate burlesque of Egyptian style was just right. We had to mock Sganarelle, look up to the heavens, stand on one leg, touch the floor, then make mumbo-jumbo hand gestures to mystify and confuse the old Pantalon. The mime scene with Perkins was not easy on balance; our Egyptian trappings were heavy and monumental. We wore mitred and plumed priest headdresses with long curls attached, grand long gold-fringed dresses of white satin banded with copper, and heavy epaulets, also fringed.

For the first time in my life I was wearing ballet slippers. A canvas tent of a change booth was set up backstage, and both Doris, who had to change from shepherdess into bridal finery, and I, switching from Egyptian to Olympian, used it. The tent sides bulged and flapped while wigs, robes and shoes with laced ribbons were exchanged for the Olympians' white curled wigs, satin hats, and tonnelets of white satin garnished with red ribbons and gold fringes—a far cry from our usual bare feet and black leotards. As for the wedding pavane, I still had not had a ballet lesson in my life and the turnout which Doris wanted was hard to produce.

Everyone in the play appeared in the act one finale. Floating about backstage in our silver dominoes ready "to attend the Dauphin's fête," we were a happy family enjoying our masquerade. Only Marcus pined under his furry costume and mask as the dancing bear for the street dancers' scene with Doris and Charles. Kenneth Bostock had a link boy's part in the second act magistrate-and-notary scene, a perfect commedia dell' arte vignette. Years later Kenneth was voted Victoria, British Columbia's favorite character actor, and Vincent Massey, the national Canadian adjudicator, chose him as the best in all of British Columbia. Gentle Kenneth, with his long neck and the blond beauty of a Sir Galahad, was full of refreshing British-style understated humor.

George Bockman also had humor, as well as ideals about theatre dance. Richard Wagner and Noel Coward were idols of his because both of them composed words as well as music and thus had complete control of their perspective and creative ideas all the way.

Jack, who was intensely devoted to Ruth St. Denis, was the most dedicated dancer of the boys, the most sophisticated in his acute sense of style, the one who demanded most from himself and everyone else.

Backstage at "School for Husbands"

Don Freeman's drawing in The New York Times *of the two Egyptians with Solomon and Socrates, backstage at* The School for Husbands.

But it was Ada Korvin-Kroukovsky[39] who fitted most perfectly into the courtly atmosphere of the play. Ada with her star-sapphire eyes, her mystical smile, the gaze always a little above and beyond—Ada reigned like a queen wherever she was. How different her European background from ours! She was born in Tiflis, the most southern part of Russia. After her family moved to St. Petersburg, at the age of five she was accepted into the Dowager Empress's Gymnasia. Graduating seven years later, she received a gold medal from the mother of Tsar Nicholas II. Very young, she married a military aviator. When the war began she followed her husband to the front as a nurse. When all the officers were being shot, she, her husband, her mother and her brother escaped the revolution. They traveled by Siberian Express to Harbin, from Harbin to Fusan in Korea, and eventually to San Francisco. She took degrees in Russian and French at Berkeley. Boris, her husband, took a further degree from M.I.T. before joining Sikorsky, the aeronautical engineer.

Ada's first dance studies were in Germany, where she visited her mother, her teachers being Rudolf von Laban, Hanya Holm and Mary Wigman. When she returned to America she had an interview with Ruth St. Denis, who advised her to join Doris Humphrey and Charles Weidman. So Ada came to the 59th Street studio and soon was in the company. Her delicacy, refinement, mysticism and fatalism set her apart from the general run of our sturdy American extroverts. She and Boris lived in the country on Long Island, where she tenderly cared for her garden of strawberries and cucumbers and a plant unknown to her—we recognize it as poison ivy vine—that she had planted by the side of the house. Obligingly, it grew as high as the chimney in gratitude.

In the lobby of the Empire were portraits of Daniel Frohman's greatest stars: Ethel Barrymore, Modjeska, Mrs. Fiske, Maude Adams. The dignified house, with its maroon velvet, had an unmistakable air of tradition. The number one dressing room, which Doris shared with June Walker, was big enough for the two of them, along with their maids and their voluminous costumes. From the ceiling hung the special flyropes for Maude Adams's *Peter Pan* flying costume. Even the stagedoor man had style: once, during a Saturday morning rehearsal on stage, he appeared with a telephoned message, delivering it on a silver tray with so proper a bow that the whole group burst into applause.

There was a delightful history, too, in Molière's *School for Husbands*. Its premiere occurred in 1661, the year that Louis XIV instituted the first Academie de la Danse. From it, in unbroken descent, our present day ballet training derives. Three years later at the Louvre Molière himself directed a ballet titled *The Forced Marriage*, with music by Lully and with Beauchamp as choreographer and conductor.

The ballet followed Molière's one-act comedy of the same name. It had nine speaking parts, taken by members of Molière's company, as well as one song and two ensembles. Later, at the Théâtre Palais-Royal, Molière condensed the two parts into one act and suppressed the entrées.

The original entrées of the ballet danced by the court itself were: first, Jealousy (solo); Troubles and Suspicions (duets); second, Four Clowns; third, Two Egyptians, danced by the king and a noble, accompanied by four additional courtiers; fourth, a Magician, plus four demons; fifth, a Dancing Master (represented by M. Dolivet) who comes to give Sganarelle a lesson in the Courante; sixth, two Spanish Couples; seventh, a grotesque Charivari, with eight dancers led by M. Lully (who composed the music); eighth, Four Gallants, who flirt with Sganarelle's young wife. The Duc d'Orleans (brother of the king), Mme. Beauchamp, and Reynal took part in this.

Mr. Langner had every justification for inserting the ballet interlude between the two acts of the play, for Molière himself, true child of the commedia dell' arte, habitually introduced ballet interludes throughout his later works. The situation of an old man wanting to marry a young girl paralleled Molière's own experience. There is a poignancy about the dream ballet in which Sganarelle, uncertain what to do, asks guidance from the shades of Solomon and Socrates and from two Egyptians, all of whom confuse him further.

Sganarelle watches the shepherdess (Doris) and her dancing master (Charles) as they perform a gavotte and cries, "If I could dance like that! But here's my chance! I'll get this man to teach me how to dance." The shepherdess exits; the dancing master begins with a minuet which Sganarelle cannot follow. The dancing master claps his hands and two assistants come who try to help limber up the old man's legs. Finding him hopeless, they leave him sitting on the floor.

The shepherdess, now dressed as a bride, enters attended by four young girls, dancing a gavotte. The Goddess Athênée, comes center; Solomon, Socrates and Egyptians return, with Tircis, father of the bride. Sganarelle asks, "My friend, I'm well-born, rich and keep a carriage; so may I have your daughter's hand in marriage?" Tircis nods consent; four couples enter performing a wedding pavane. When Sganarelle begins to dance with his bride, the music quickens to a fast contradanse. The dancing master enters and dances away with the bride.

Doris Humphrey and Charles Weidman as Columbine and Harlequin in the Theatre Guild's The School for Husbands. Photo by Vandamm.

Sganarelle tries to pursue the couple but is continually blocked by the young men and girls circling around him. Getting angry, he stamps a foot, then duels in pantomime with the dancing master, who runs him through. The young men bear him aloft and put him down on the bench. The bride pauses to kiss his head before dancing gaily off with the dancing master. The stage darkens. The dream ends with Sganarelle sleeping, as he was at the beginning.

From the opening prologue of act one spoken by Sganarelle before the curtain:

Kind Friends,
We fear *you* fear to see upon the stage
A Molière play in this impatient age
When nothing's bearable unless its new;
Well, we are scared to death, the same
    as you.
Yet, if solemnity's what you're afraid of,
That isn't what this offering is made of . . .

to Parker Stewart's behind-the-scenes Parisian streetsong opening:

Some like sober men, some like dandies;
Some like lollypops, some like candies;
Who'll buy my sweetmeats, who'll buy my sugarplums and
    sweetmeats—

it was a joy every night to listen to the play and watch it unfold: Mr. Rickett's adaptations of old French airs so felicitous, Rameau's music for the ballet a delight, Mr. Langner's incidental effects of thunder and lightning, the dancing bear, the appearance of Athênée, the magician's sleight-of-hand wonders, the bravos duelling in the street. The best dancing was the moonlit Columbine and Harlequin duet (Doris and Charles) in the second act, done with elegant sophistication.

The set had two houses, one on each side, both with sliding panel windows which permitted interiors to be seen. Step levels in the center led to a terrace upstage, behind it a painted Renaissance perspective of more houses lining a street. Since the play had been tried out in Westport the summer before, we opened cold at the Empire in October. José's opening night telegram, "Thinking of you between gasps good luck and love," reflected the different kinds of torrid dance demanded of him, Letitia and the others taking part in "Having a Heat Wave," the song-hit with Ethel Waters in *As Thousands Cheer*, a few blocks north on Broadway. Though I still felt unnatural in ballet slippers and weighted down with the corsetted tonnelet, I did not envy the other half of the group at all, and felt it was a grateful exercise in style to have to be artificial, wear a wig, curtsy, and move with polish.

But the reviews justified Sganarelle's intimation that modern audiences with their passion for everything new would look askance at something old. Atkinson of the *Times* recognized that Perkins, "crisp and marvellously adroit, bears an astonishing resemblance to old prints of Molière." But the dancing was "self-consciously literary," even "precious." John Mason Brown termed it "a dead play." To Burns Mantle it was "a thing of beauty and joy for sixty minutes. The second hour is a little less thrilling." John Anderson found it lacking in variety and suspension: "From its foreword to the end of the first act it seemed clear delight, mischievous, clever and ingratiating, done slyly and gracefully. The ballet interlude became tedious and over-elaborate and the third act was never able to recapture the fervent animation of the first."

Gilbert Gabriel appreciated:

Just about the time the middle-aged Jean Baptiste Poquelin, alias Molière, was contemplating marrying a very young lady, he eased his conscience by writing this "School for Husbands." Or by borrowing the best part of it, anyway, from an equally pert old Roman named Terence. One of the loveliest presentations ever seen in New York this revival does have . . . occasionally a Dresden-china bore, but forgiveably so.

John Erskine, looking ahead to the ideal blending of theatre elements, felt Langner was on the right track:

If you doubt there is beauty in this much-troubled world, go to see the Theatre Guild's new play . . . and forget the world is sometimes messy. The most modern theorists of opera talk of a coming form in which dance and pantomime will be the foundation, with only as much language as is needed to fill out the meaning, and only as much music as will assist the language and precipitate the mood.

. . . The theorists of musical comedy have talked a lot about an ideal show which would have in it all the elements of vaudeville, but blended in one plot and one artistic whole. I think Mr. Langner and Mr. Guiterman have achieved this ideal also. You have comedy and farce and sleight of hand, dancing, clowning and music, but nothing seems interpolated; every element is essential to the whole.

Joseph Wood Krutch, not meeting a midnight deadline for *The Nation*, thoughtfully found its

graceful gravity, that lightness of touch which remains, nevertheless, the very reverse of frivolity, is Molière, and is often the thing which the present version succeeds so often in preserving. It has a delightful neatness of pattern and a soul-satisfying finish of utterance quite impossible for any writer in the realistic manner to achieve.

There is one kind of pleasure to be derived from hearing people talk more or less as they actually do, but there is another and perhaps more acute pleasure in hearing them express themselves with a fullness, an eloquence, a pointedness, or a wit which is superhuman, and therefore artificial. It is that pleasure, plus the pleasure of an actor whose neat perfection is like Mozart's music, which makes some old plays potentially the source of a kind of delight we have almost forgotten. Molière's verse . . . is clipped enough to become tripping rather than stately and is therefore the perfect vehicle for the expression of a temperament to which the dictates of moderation and decorum presented themselves not as part of the pompous official philosophy of a solemn court but as the good-humored common sense of the citizens.

If modern audiences accepted the artificiality of *The Three Little Pigs,* Walt Disney's animated cartoon, why could they not take Molière without condescension, he asked.

Perkins's comic-pathetic acting was so risible that one night during the Egyptian mumming I broke up, laughing at him. Charles, watching in the wings, scolded, "Never do that again. If you laugh, the audience won't." It took tremendous concentration not to betray my enjoyment and amusement at the fantastically adroit Perkins, but I learned my lesson.

Arthur Guiterman, the poet whose adaptation of Molière was so successful, was such a small, retiring presence that we never knew when he was in the theatre. Having just been reprimanded about my unprofessionalism, it was balm to the spirit to meet the shy author of the play backstage at the bottom of the stairs and be complimented by him on my performance. Evidently he had missed my gaffe.

Mr. Martin thoroughly appreciated that "whatever the production possesses of the style of Molière and the French theatre of the seventeenth century is due to the labors of Miss Humphrey and Mr. Weidman." Quoting Bernadetto Croce's current article in the *Theatre Arts Monthly* on the commedia dell' arte, in his discussion of Molière:

. . . in him alone, there live the flowerings of invention and fantasy of the Italian Commedia dell' Arte. Buffoonery as they were, these (Commedia) performances did not have their vital nucleus in poetry or literature, but in plastic expression and in mimicry: hence the overwhelming importance of the grotesque, the mask, the attitude, the gesturings, and all the other things which are comprised in the technical word lazzi.

It is true that Molière has come to grief in our theatre largely because the style of his theatre has been generally submerged; the plastic expression and mimicry, the attitudes, the gesticulations, the lazzi, or action are made to play second fiddle to the words which should serve merely as a useful and charming accompaniment.

. . . in the ballet of Miss Humphrey and Mr. Weidman we are allowed to see, as through a knothole in a wall, something of the spirit of Molière's theatre. Miss Humphrey is as captivating and as decorative as the great Isabella herself, and there is more Molière in one move and gesture by Charles Weidman than in hours of spoken verse.

He quibbled that Doris had turned out our toes farther than historically necessary, but that overall "an excellent job has been charmingly done, and one more step taken restoring the theatre to its full estate."

This was the fall season when Doris, the baby, Leo when in port, Pauline, Charles and José became a "ménage à six," all moving to the third floor of an elevator apartment at 31 West 10th Street; Miss Hein, the baby's nurse, lived there too for a while. Unknown to them, the German Miss Hein had Nazi sympathies. When she called Humphrey "Putzi," they thought she was saying "Pussy." "Pussy" became the infant's name, to distinguish him from "Baby," the buff-colored long-haired cat. It was a strange household, inexorably bound by economic and artistic ties—Charles and Pauline taking to the child, Charles in fact seeing more of him than his own father could; Pauline continuing to cook, costume, accompany classes and rehearsals, as well as baby-sitting when necessary.

Our close-knit company, dancing in seventeenth century style nightly at the Empire and being paid for it, lived in a world removed from the national distress. But this bright idyllic sphere changed in December when Michael Meyerberg succeeded in persuading Charles and Doris that, since Prohibition had just been repealed, now was the moment for modern dance to penetrate to Broadway night clubs. The Palais Royal at Broadway and 47th Street, bought and refurbished by Ben Marden, was about to open with Emil Coleman's band, the singing Boswell Sisters, the singing Yacht Club Boys and Fred Keating as the M.C.

No doubt remembering their near-starving recent past, our directors succumbed. Unasked, we were signed to appear at the Palais Royal's dinner and supper shows, in between the hours of the Theatre Guild show. Charles created a new Gay Nineties *Cotillion*, a ballroom dance suitable for a night club. His *Piccoli Soldati* was also appropriate. Perhaps because of the architecture of the place, with two spiral staircases descending from the upper stage onto the oval floor below, Doris, insisting that one of her concert works be included

Humphrey-Weidman Group in Cotillion, *at the Palais Royal.*

in our night club debut on Broadway, chose, of all unsuitable works, the *Life of the Bee*. Theoretically, bees swarming up and down those steps might be fine; we were all dismayed at the choice.

Earlier in the summer, José had selected Bizet's *Andalouse* for a duet with me, for which Pauline concocted a romantically beautiful long dress of aquamarine organza with a white organdy pouf graduated from shoulder to hem; José, for once, got out of his basic blacks to wear white trousers. This was one of the dances auditioned for Broadway producers in the studio in the summer. Weeks later Charles confided that Hazzard Short had particularly liked my dancing and my "Tilly Losch" face, and wanted to take me to England for his next revue. "He couldn't have you," said Charles. "You're Humphrey-Weidman."

Though the *Andalouse* had never been performed outside of the studio, it was retitled *Tango* and selected to open the show at the Palais with Jack Cole dancing José's part. Jack habitually looked down or away, avoiding one's eye, because of a cruel accident in his childhood. Someone had thrown a stick at his face, resulting in a permanent cast in one eye. With his acute sensitivity, Jack often compensated for this misfortune by being intolerantly sarcastic. The change of partners meant that I had to dance with my knees bent all the time, for Jack was not as tall as José. Charles thought Jack's indirect focus made the dance more sexy. José himself was doubly employed, now choreographing the dances for *Roberta*, another Broadway show. It was a job he did not particularly relish, but with the money he made he bought a small organ on which he could practice Bach and Chopin to his heart's content.

The opening at the Palais was traumatic for both dancers and audience. When I heard Keating, new at his M.C. post, announce that Jack Cole and I had just been married that morning and hadn't had a chance to be alone until then, I wanted to sink through the floor. To speed up the show, *Tango* was dropped the next night. A front page story in the December 26, 1933 *Variety* reviewed us:

A night club troupe without a smile among them—but more astounding yet, simply covered with clothes. Opaque clothes too. And not to make their torso tossing more insistent either, because, incredible though it may seem, there was no torso tossing. The girls at the tables figured it must be the Rebellion. They were terribly impressed.

The second article described:

Room is a cross between square and oblong, with its floor brimmed by two rows of balconied tables. . . . Keating, whose material can be improved and most likely will, was a trifle stiff Friday night. Boswells are spotted too close, working around a piano on a little stage behind the band. A Tango dance team, Eleanor King and Jack Cole, provides the dance-flavor along with routines by the ensemble, all of which run to the modernistic and in both creation and execution provide a smart touch in keeping with the big-time atmosphere the Palais Royal strives for. Bee number is an ingeniously conceived routine, to which the Emil Coleman orchestra provides a unique accompaniment. Dances were created by Doris Humphrey and Charles Weidman. Coleman band, for both the show and the dancing patrons, is about the last word.

. . . Premiere night Friday, with arc lights outside making it look like a Hollywood film opening, drew a capacity crowd of 800. . . . Park Avenue came westward to Broadway for a change.

Everyone was overworked and irritable. At this time, when the Guild scheduled additional holiday matinees for *The School For Husbands,* we performed at the Empire at 2:30, went to the Palais for the 7:00 dinner show, back to the Empire for the 8:30 performance, returned to the Palais for the supper show at 11:00, repeated at 12:30 or 1:00. Sometimes, if there were enough customers in the house, the management asked us to do a third floor show at 2:00. At one of the *Cotillion* rehearsals I began to cry from fatigue and had to lie down. Jack, who had developed knee trouble, asked if he could be excused from rehearsing the second position balance in the *Bees* with others standing on his legs. Doris flatly said no: "No rehearse, no perform."

We traveled to and fro in taxis, getting as horizontal as possible, and when we weren't dancing on our legs we lay prone. To save time I moved into the Wellington Hotel. Unfortunately another Eleanor King had just checked out, and her friends didn't know that; my phone rang all hours of the night for someone else.

After a few of these seemingly endless nights at the Palais, the group in the dressing room petitioned Doris to meet with us to clarify what was in the night club contracts, which we had never seen. Doris left Meyerberg's table downstairs and came to see what the summons was about. She was surprised and hurt. We were acting like hysterical school girls; Denishawn dancers had done five-a-day in vaudeville year round and had never complained. She and Charles signed the contracts to protect us from all the bother of business details.

Strangely, Doris, a creator of the revolution in dance which had become such a strong, dynamic expression, had forgotten what a low level of energy Denishawn plastiques required, where the ensemble was largely a decorative adjunct to the stars.

Frankie Reed and Hyla Rubin, our outspoken leaders, requested that group members be informed before contracts were signed, and that we be given fair, not excessively demanding, treatment. No one minded doing five shows a day, but when it came to six and seven, it was physically impossible. When the management requested a third show, could we say it was not in the contract? Doris's exit from the dressing room was haughty. Our near-mutinous threat evaporated soon after, for the inescapable fact was that Broadway audiences were not clamoring for modern dance at all. At the end of the second week, the contract was cancelled by both parties. The resentment of the press continued when the succeeding show at the Palais was reviewed by the *World Telegram:*

On an extra excursion to the Palais Royal, it was our reward to learn that the Charles Weidman-Doris Humphrey bumble bees are out. Malice doesn't harden our heart against their profound terpsichore, but certainly the dinner and supper trade will understand our coldness toward a bevy of two-footed bees buzzing about our two-by-two table. Which managed to remain upright by the merest chance anyway, and especially when the bees were almost fully clothed. The new show isn't eyeblinding either, but at least it isn't Art.

The same critic was still rejoicing a month later:

The flowery show is out of the Palais Royal, and the floor show is in . . . is no longer consecrated to the genteel art of interpretive dancing but it was reformed as a big and biff-bang cabaret—which is just what it should have been from the start. Where a bevy of queen bees once dallied under the wands of Doris Humphrey and Charles Weidman the Feminine Form now struts about in sensible disarray. And there are Ethel Waters, whose singing is black magic; Caperton and Biddle, society swanks; the Loomis sisters who harmonize; Oliver Wakefield, a muddled monologuist; Emil Coleman, the world's dead ringer for Otto Soglow's "Little King" and a good many others who don't give their names.
    All in all, Mr. Marden has been wise in not martyring himself off to Art; the ladies are all lovely and lackadaisical, and its just as well they don't have to go off chasing honey. The show is livelier and flashier and the Palais Royal now belongs among the showy emporiums of Broadway along with the Casino de Paree, the Hollywood and the Paradise.

Backstage at the Palais one night, Jack, who often visited Harlem to study the extraordinary style of Negro dancing, drew some of us aside and offered us an experimental taste of a reefer supposed to have marijuana in it. I took a gingerly puff without any effect. Jack admitted some reefers were sold that had no marijuana in them.

The final night of the year, Meyerberg sent champagne up to our dressing room, then asked us to go as we were in our Gay Nineties *Cotillion* costumes over to the Waldorf to perform at a special party. We were bundled into taxis and sped to the ballroom, where the waiters balancing their trays walked right through our dance, endlessly interrupting the patterns. As in all night clubs, it didn't matter one bit; the guests were already so high they couldn't have seen clearly what anyone was doing. At dawn, when Broadway was a ghastly gray desert, I fell into bed at the Wellington. By then I had had too much champagne and was trying to hold onto my head, which seemed to have swelled up to 59th Street while my feet seemed to be somewhere around 42nd Street. This horrible disembodiment was enough to make me vow not to have more than two drinks of anything after that.

It was a great relief when the night club contract expired and we could be in our Molière world uninterrupted. I hated the whole night club atmosphere, the polluted air dyed blue with tobacco smoke which burned my eyes and nostrils and choked my lungs, especially during the Queen Bee role—having to make my entrance on the upper stage, descend the steps onto the floor, battle with Cleo, do her in, and lead the swarm up the other staircase, taking those great thoracic breaths with every step. The customers couldn't have cared less; they hardly noticed anything on the floor. We were competing with food, drink and titillation. The boys complained they were goosed with celery sticks by drunken customers if they got close to tables. We were so close that odors of food and remarks of the diners were inescapable.

Why Doris thought this was worth doing at all was a mystery. We knew how she felt about show business in general. Compromise was hardly a word in her vocabulary. She had accepted the Guild contract eagerly perhaps because the Guild, representing America's one outstanding art theatre, was a valuable liaison and she hoped that association with them or under their aegis might one day lead to the American Dance Theatre of everyone's dream.

After Christmas, we found a closing notice backstage at the Empire. The show would end in New York in January but tour to Pittsburgh, Philadelphia, Washington and Boston, for a week each. At last! We would be on the road, a goal I had long cherished. It seemed to me no one could be called professional who hadn't been on the road. New York was all very well, but out there was the rest of America, which I longed to see and explore. I was eager to experience this. Our Chorus Equity contracts, which we signed individually, were to be raised from thirty to forty dollars a week to cover our living expenses on the tour.

What a roller-coaster year for all of us! With Franklin D. Roosevelt taking office in January 1933, the country for the first time since the crash seemed to take hope, though to get started America went off the gold standard and there was a ten-day bank holiday.

Congress passed the National Recovery Act (voided two years later by the Supreme Court) and the Federal Relief Act and launched the Tennessee Valley Authority and the Civilian Conservation Corps, sound social programs as they proved to be, but all of them bitterly resisted by conservatives who equated these measures with the dreaded word socialism, in turn equated with even more fearful communism. Although economically the country was improving, the political picture was deeply shadowed. Ironically, while Roosevelt was stepping into office to become one of the great presidents of the United States, a man named Adolf Hitler was becoming Chancellor of the Third Reich in Germany.

For Doris, this was a truly eventful year. Her fulfillment as a mother had been realized. Artistically she had been able to fulfill the contracts with the prestigious New York and Philadelphia symphony orchestras. For Charles, after the debacle of his innovative full-length *Candide,* there was the welcome demand for his choreography in as many shows as he could handle. For the first time all the group members were employed either with the Guild or in a Broadway show, which was both good and bad.

Because of Doris's motherhood, I had had a marvelously rich year of growth and more responsibility with the solo in the experimental program at Yale, the lead of Cunegonde in *Candide* at the Booth, the center part opposite Charles in the Roussel *Suite* with the symphony orchestras, the Queen Bee (Doris's part) at the Palais, as well as the duet of the Egyptians with Sganarelle in *The School for Husbands* and the short-lived *Tango* duet with Jack at the Palais. The Guild was to stand out as our happiest theatre experience; the Palais Royal as our worst. Modern dance might theoretically be good and healthy for Broadway, but Broadway was demoralizing to the group and to the dance as art. Temporarily solvent, we had begun to feel in truth the corrupt taste of commercial success.

CHAPTER SEVEN:1934

Touring

LIKE THE EMPIRE IN NEW YORK, the Nixon Theatre in Pittsburgh was full of history. It was here that Duse gave her last performance. Having waited outside the locked stage door in the wind and rain, she developed a chill, which led to pneumonia and her untimely death in the Smoky City.

The backstage area was enormous and fascinating. Dressing rooms on the second floor opened onto side balconies which had rear views of the stage, so we were aware of the play's progress all the time. Having passed the test of New York, we were welcomed with open arms on the road. The Guild complimented Pittsburgh by sending them Molière, one critic said. We were received warmly and with delight. Performing there was relaxing.

In Pittsburgh, June Walker took painting lessons from Marcus, who asked me to pose for a portrait study. I loved June's voice quality and did not mind sitting still as long as they talked, for Marcus's aesthetic perception was an education. I was surprised to hear him tell June to use a lot of green when painting my hair. I thought it was simply mouse blonde with some red lights.

Traveling on the Pennsylvania Railroad from Pittsburgh to Philadelphia, we entertained ourselves with the written game of Guggenheim or the guessing game of Acting in the Manner of the Adverb. The old Chestnut Street Opera House was our next stop, another ancient playhouse with a fine tradition. At the back of the house a row of baroque mirrors in gilt frames reflected to us on stage

174

the lights of the show and our shadowy figures as we moved about. We enjoyed turtle soup at one of the famous restaurants, and happened to be there when Walter Huston (a great favorite), then playing in *Dodsworth*, was also dining there.

The group celebrated my birthday with a party. Doris and Charles gave me a charming antique silver-mounted carnelian locket; Marcus produced a poem and a pastel drawing; Jack Cole a glass bowl of water with a live goldfish. In honor of the Egyptians in the ballet, we named the fish Ptolemy, later adding a companion fish, Ptoleminna. Katey (my roommate) and I took turns giving Ptolemy ocean-size swims in the big hotel bathtub. As we continued touring, the cold-blooded pet actually made traveling simpler, if wetter, for me. All the hand-bags, tipping and tickets fell to Katey, leaving me to balance the bowl with both hands while ascending or descending into elevators, taxis and trains.

The houses were fine and suitably enthusiastic in Philadelphia, but we reached Washington in time for the coldest February in years. Blizzards and subzero temperatures decimated the houses at the National. In the hotel we slept under ten cotton blankets with our winter coats on top, windows sealed shut, and were chilled to the bone. Under these circumstances, the hope of an extended visit to Boston died. *The School for Husbands* finished out the week, then permanently closed.

Back in New York, rehearsals went forward for two Sunday night concerts in April at the Guild. The long-term view was encouraging, for we were now under NBC management (Artists Service). Michael Meyerberg was still personal representative for Doris and Charles. That long-envisioned goal of a tour of America was now in the planning stage for the winter of 1935. One day in March, before rehearsal started, I was startled to see Doris crying, a sight I had never seen before and never saw again. Later we learned that her father had died. Doris's relation to her father was much closer than to her mother.

Julia Humphrey had dictated Doris's early life and had held her to the career of a dance teacher by which she supported both parents to the end of their days. But Julia's possessiveness had been a trial on the Denishawn Orient tour. Rather than share her daughter with Pauline and Charles, Mother Humphrey returned alone to America. Doris had disciplined herself not to display or indulge in emotion; at least outwardly she transcended her griefs. Later, three years after she buried her mother, she composed that hymn to life, celebrating the continuity of family generations and man's need to devote himself to work, in *Day on Earth*.

Six new pieces were prepared for the Guild, two duets for the principals, the *Rudepoema,* music by Heitor Villa-Lobos, and the *Alcina Suite* of Handel; the important *Kinetic Pantomime,* a solo for Charles; a solo, *Pleasures of Counterpoint,* for Doris. For the first time, José joined Doris and Charles in a frothy trio entertainment, *Exhibition Piece,* music by Slonimsky. Charles's suite *Memorials: To the Trivial,* a comic solo for himself; *To the Connubial,* a period piece for the girls costumed nineteenth-century-New England style, weeping willow widows; and *To the Colossal,* a heroic march for the men. The old works were the *Two Ecstatic Themes, Dionysiaques, Studies in Conflict* and *Shakers.*

Rudepoema was curiously disappointing, for all its intriguing title. Dance to the Gods—Love Dance—Play Dance, offered good duet opportunities, but Doris's lyrical style seemed utterly at variance with the music; the svelte costume of purple and green luxurious instead of primitive. It was a dance Graham with her angular strength could have performed naturally. The *Alcina* came off much better with "taste, spirit and graciousness particularly in the first minuet, the dancers played delicately with the traditional design, informing their choreography with a wit that poked gentle fun at formalism, yet without a suggestion of burlesque. In costume and conception this is one of the happiest creations these dancers have offered here." Doris's costume was similar to my *Gagliarda,* with a neck ruff and a slit circular skirt. The metallic copper material had a regal Elizabethan look most becoming to her.

The group now numbered twenty-four, fourteen girls and ten men. For these, our first concerts in two years, "stunning audiences packed the Guild to the doors." Martin wrote:

The program involved . . . was rich and racy and the artists involved grace their world with extraordinary distinction. With two such leading dancers, who happen to be also brilliant composers, and such a superb ensemble, one can only wonder why there is any agitation for the establishment of an American Ballet. Here is certainly the finished article.
. . . the second half of the evening ran too much to lightness and humor . . . a fault of arrangement rather than quality. But "Memorials" had at least one movement that was a masterpiece of comic design.

Other reviewers were less enthusiastic. The social consciousness critics felt "Humphrey-Weidman had scurried back to the past for material . . . most of their offerings were concerned with hopefully witty recreations of other periods"—serious charges against modern dancers.

While we were working on the concerts, Charles also worked at

Doris Humphrey and Charles Weidman in Alcina Suite.

auditions for the group. Most peculiar was an audition in the Capitol Theatre dance studio where mirrors on four walls completely threw us off—we couldn't orient ourselves to one center focus and the spacing went to pieces. The only job that materialized was one for Charles, José, and Letitia (who didn't need one) at Radio City, where they danced to Satie's music for two weeks.

At this time with more theatre jobs in view and with some classes of my own which I had begun to teach—the students were my oldest sister and some of her friends—I graduated from living at home to sharing an apartment with Cleo on the second floor of one of the old brownstones in the West Fifties. At last I was on my own. We enjoyed our big high-ceilinged room, the walls painted in pastel colors, the woodwork cut on consoling bias lines or curves in keeping with the philosophical-vegetarian tenants of the Rudolph Steiner cult, which operated a restaurant downstairs.

Marcus, who loved the world of the dance but never felt he was cut out to be a dancer, devoted more and more of his spare time to the practice of photography. Soon he was busy photographing everyone, with pleasing soft-focus and typical Blechman makeup which he applied to all sitters. One day Marcus phoned that he was about to photograph Ruth St. Denis for the first time. Would I like to come and meet her and assist with the sitting? "She has the most beautiful arm movement you ever dreamed of," he said. "She knows more about camera than I do." I had never met Miss Ruth until she emerged from the dressing room, marvelously made up, clothed in yards and yards of white. After careful study in a mirror, she arranged herself on the platform. Two minutes after being introduced, she forgot my name. "Nice Person," she addressed me.

She commanded Nice Person to take up the strings whose other ends were safety-pinned every few inches around the bottom of her skirt, to twine the ends, as many as possible, around my fingers and thumbs and grip the remainder in my teeth, thus metamorphosing Nice Person into a twine-handed and twine-headed monster. Backing away from her, on orders, with teeth bared and fingers radiating, I lifted my hands until the skirt folds rayed outward from her body. "Ready," she cried, standing perfectly still on one leg, the other leg floating in the air. Marcus pressed the shutter, capturing the image of a rapidly turning dancer. Possibly La Loie Fuller had stumbled on this secret of the illusion of motion years before. In any case, Miss Ruth knew exactly what effect she wanted and she contrived the means to achieve it.

The next time I met Ruth St. Denis was through Jack Cole. He proposed bringing her to Cleo's and my place for dinner one night. We were honored, but equally dismayed. How did one entertain, let alone feed, such a personage? "No trouble," said Jack. "She doesn't touch alcohol, so no drinks. She loves Irish stew. Give her Irish stew, she'll be happy."

To our surprise, Miss Ruth accepted the invitation. She settled down on the studio couch by the window, we put simple fare before her, and at first all went well. Then I mentioned that the most vital and extraordinary dancing going on in New York these days was up at the Savoy in Harlem. Had she seen it? Miss Ruth stiffened. "Africa," she pronounced, "has never contributed anything to world culture. Egypt, of course, gave us great temples; Greece, great sculpture; Rome, architecture. But Africa? Nothing." Coolness descended over the atmosphere; the lady left soon after.

Came the John Murray Anderson revue with Bert Lahr and Ray Bolger, *Life Begins at 8:40*, and Charles asked me to assist him with the dances. I was glad of the job, but felt like a fish out of water the whole time. Cleo was later to be similarly engaged in helping with the ensembles for Joe Cook's *Hold Your Horses*.

Esther Junger was chosen to be the featured dancer, a performer with awesome intensity, no humor, and a formidable ego. Josephine Schwarz, from Dayton, Ohio, was Pomona, the lead in a charming Watteau pastoral scene, the boys with sickles, the girls with sheaves, and Jo sitting in a swing. John Murray Anderson, with his clipped, often outrageous British remarks, directed with scathing sarcasm, especially taking it out on the poor show girls. "Now, you, who have no earthly justification for existence, move over to the right," he would tell them. "The custom of using you on the stage went out with the bustle. Now walk to stage left, if you can."

Everyone was branded with a nickname. George Bockman, a favorite of his, became "Star." My task of trying to make the show girls bend in the middle was hopeless. One of them, a *Vogue* model, a typical photogenic slab of blondeness, protested, "Why, I can't do that. If I did I'd break in two." John Murray Anderson's label for me was "Mad Annie." Mad Annie mostly sat out front watching for errors, a tiresome, difficult process, for I was never good at detail, whether because of my anisometropia (unequal vision) or laziness, I don't know. Once the concept of an idea was achieved the process of working out details was always less fascinating to me.

During the trial rehearsals in Boston, before the opening, Charles left me in charge one day when he had to be in New York. As I watched the "Shoein' the Mare" number, a Cuban dance around

Esther, things looked messy and inaccurate. When I went backstage the group complained that their spacing was off because Esther had so threatened any one of them who got into the same spotlight with her, that no one dared to take the chance.

Among the boys dancing was Willem Van Loon, Hendrik Willem Van Loon's son. Papa, a histrionic character himself, did not condone his son's liking for show business, and Willem, who adored his father, was disturbed by that. What was invariably relaxing and restorative was the comedy of Bert Lahr. With his great moon-face he bawled out that travesty of all tenor solos, "On the Road to Mandalay," renamed "Things." He also appeared with stiff-upper-lip-ishness in the "Six O'clock, Must Dress" skit about the proper Englishman who, when informed by his Mater that he is "not legitimate," goes on buttoning his cufflinks and muttering to the bitter end, "Six o'clock, must dress." Ray Bolger, an effortless, prodigious dancer with a rubber body, clowned with Lahr perfectly.

The rehearsal period, hot steamy August in the Winter Garden in New York, was bizarre, a kind of limbo removed from reality. While the comedians had the theatre stage, the dancers were banished upstairs to the floor of a dusty old nightclub. The ceiling up there had the puffed satin contours of a declassée inverted bed. We rehearsed in the steaming odors from a chop suey restuarant below.

While eight, nine or ten hours a day were spent in this savory atmosphere, my real attention was on two new dances. John Glenn's friend, the pianist Thomas McNally, had tried out for *The School for Husbands*, and then played for us when he was not taking classes. He found Eugene Goosens' arrangement of the old English sheep-shearing song; immediately I knew I had to dance it. I felt only distaste and irritation for the *Life Begins at 8:40* type of theatre. My yearning went into everything that was just the opposite: simple, peaceful, natural, positive.

From Breughel's "Reapers" I borrowed the opening stance, legs apart, body bent over, arms stretched out and downward. The lyrical-ly sustained dance continued on my solo programs for three decades. It *was* simple. "Only you could get away with it," was Doris's one comment. The costume of sky and earth tones had a long-sleeved blue jersey top, a skirt of Belgian linen hanging from the hips, fringed at the bottom in umber-dyed red, and a scarf of the same material.

At the same time, John Glenn dreamed of a suite of contrasting madonnas, to *Die Passionen*, Hermann Reutter's piano piece. Reutter was a young German composer killed in World War I. The music's passionate flowing speech-rhythms, urgent, staccato, were magnifi-cent. John choreographed a *Madonna of Vengeance* for Ernestine, who, dressed in red, gave a vehement performance. Katey Manning, in gold, danced *Altar Figure*. John wanted me to be intense, sharp, wrenched, anguished in the *Madonna of Tears*. He sketched the first theme and asked me to improvise for the second contrast. Whatever I did, it was right. These two solos together, *The Song of Earth* and *Mother of Tears*—life and death dances—restored my equilibrium. As Doris often said, it takes irritation to produce a pearl.

The Broadway show-business fish-out-of-water felt only relief when *Life Begins at 8:40* settled down in New York, and I was relieved of the responsibility of checking the show. I never felt I had the flash, the quickness, the hardboiled approach necessary for show business, and assisting the choreographer, even gifted Charles, seemed like drudgery to me.

Optimism prevailed at the studio. Doris had written her mother in May, "Our careers are careening at top speed. I now have an offer to train the dancing in modern opera in Philadelphia next winter. Also, Lawrence Langner's play, *America Dances,* is getting underway and will go on the end of August in Westport."[40] The top-speed success, unfortunately, spelled ultimate disintegration for the group.

Doris arranged that for the usual three-week Teachers Summer Course we would do three concerts in Carnegie Hall Studio 61 for the teachers, including our original works and the *Oresteia*. Sol Hurok was very moved by *Oresteia* and congratulated Ernestine and me. We still clung to the hope that he, or someone else, would produce it. Curiously, though Hurok declared in his biography, years later, that we were the best of the modern dance groups, he never did anything to promote us. Was it his European chauvinism? He had introduced Mary Wigman, the German modern dancer, to this country. Did he feel that artists had to be European to be sold to the American public? After my new dances, John Glenn came to me and said, "You're a soloist, not a group dancer. When are you going to leave Doris?" "Not until my ideas are bigger than hers," I replied, astonished at his idea.

The chance to hear *Oresteia's* entire score did not come until two decades later when Dimitri Mitropoulos conducted the Philharmonic at Carnegie Hall in the only complete New York performance of Milhaud's work, with Milhaud's daughter singing the solo part. Happening to be in New York, I got tickets for Doris and myself. I could only afford balcony seats. It was an ordeal for her to manage to

Eleanor King in Song of Earth.

get up stairs, even with the elevator, and I knew she was uncomfortable where we were sitting. We were both overwhelmed by the magnificence, the dramatic power of the whole work, with fascinating percussion effects, like snakes hissing, and the French speech rhythms the most exciting I had ever heard. In the intermission Doris turned to me and said, "You had as much intensity as that."

Yet ever since the Palais Royal debacle, we had all been feeling dissatisfaction. That initial wave of selfless devotion to a cause which was greater than we were, that happiness of complete dedication to an ideal which had buoyed us up and helped us surmount all obstacles since the inception of the group in 1928, that original wave of creativity had obviously passed its crest; we were in a long trough, waiting for the next new wave of inspiration. The group members had matured, become individual artists, thanks to the creative method employed by the teachers. But the increasing demands on our time for Broadway junkets, the splitting up of the group, some soon to go on to Chicago in *As Thousands Cheer* left a splintered remnant in New York, not too happy with the way things were going.

The general malaise led to group meetings; various plans were voted on as measures to protect the welfare of the company. We wanted to stay together, to be solvent, to continue to have technical training. As Helen Savery put it later, we were used, not trained. To remedy this situation we scheduled self-led technique classes. Finally, we pledged to tax ourselves 2½ percent of whatever we as individuals earned through association with the group, thus creating an emergency fund that would take care of those who were most in need.

Protest meetings were going on everywhere around us—we were just four blocks from Union Square, that hotbed of radicalism. I dreamed of masses of people marching with banners around Union Square. It was an oppressive dream; the banners and the masses all were black.

With great daring, in whispers like conspirators, we decided to go beyond the scheme of economic taxation of the group. We would petition Doris and Charles to meet with us to discuss procedures which would give company members a vote in determining artistic policies. Along with taxation we wanted some say in the way people were chosen or rejected for jobs, and even some say in the choice of material which was to be programmed for concerts—taxation with representation! Either we were to go on being treated as employees subject to their judgment, or we could become a true cooperative in every respect.

While waiting for the members to assemble, John Glenn, José, Katey, Marcus and I would produce eight-handed Bach on the two upright pianos in the studio, making the little preludes and two-part inventions sound like a symphony orchestra, half of us only using the right hand, but all of us playing fortissimo to let off steam.

In July, the confrontation took place. Doris and Charles listened calmly to the first part of our demands. When we came to the group's share with representation on the governing board, Doris replied that as far as she knew, works of art had never been produced by committees. Art was by nature aristocratic, the accomplishment of an individual. But the concept of self-taxation for economic support was fine. She would be glad to help with our fund-raising project. We decided to start the fund with a studio bazaar, then to try to interest outside supporters in the idea. Cleo was elected president; José, vice-president; Gene Martel, secretary; Katey Manning and John Glenn, treasurers, I was to represent the group, calling on possible donors.

Studio concerts with admissions charged brought in a few starting dollars; the bazaar did well. Doris read palms, a talent she had picked up years ago, perhaps in the theatrical hotel managed by her father or from the vaudeville tours. She read all our hands. Looking at mine, she said, "You're lucky: your head and your heart lines are equal. You have the longest career line here."

One day Doris traveled with me to solicit funds from a movie producer up in Queens. In an old empty movie studio I presented the purpose of the visit to the producer, who agreed the plan was good. John Martin had thought so, and one Sunday in the *Times* he had devoted a column and a half to our endeavor. Doris surprisingly interjected, "But I don't think it will work." At the end of the interview he sided with her, contributing nothing; the meeting was a failure. The bazaar netted $126.

A year later the fund was several hundred dollars richer. Then José had a hernia attack. Restoring him to health cleaned out the fund; that was the end of it.

Doris wrote her mother on August 25th:

About "America Dances." It was indefinitely postponed because Langner lost money on his Westport season and couldn't produce it. We're looking for a backer and that's the last I know. The operas in Philadelphia have resolved themselves into one evening of ballet February 1, 2, 5, and "Iphigenia" by Gluck later the same month. It seems very likely that they will take "Orestes," and also Rainer wants us to do a Bartok fairy tale, and the Fire Bird in the same program.[41]

Despite all the unrest in the group, including discontent with the kinds of things we were dancing about, what held me to the company was the lure of the American tour coming up and the possibility, of course, that *Orestes* would see the light of production with the Philadelphia Orchestra. Doris wrote jubilantly to her mother on September 4:

It looks as though we were set for our heart's desires to be fulfilled this season. Fritz Reiner . . . has agreed to do three ballets, the "Fire Bird" of Stravinsky, "Orestes," Milhaud and a new one of Charles, "Paul Bunyan" by a composer to be selected. Pretty grand. Also "Iphigenia" of Gluck all in Philadelphia with the orchestra and opera chorus. We're getting to work on this pretty soon.[42]

Instead of starting to work on the dances for the Gluck opera, however, and despite the fact that she deplored the amount of time Charles spent doing Broadway shows, she herself signed with Arch Selwyn and Harold Franklin to choreograph dances for a Broadway production of *Revenge with Music,* based on *The Three Cornered Hat.* Cleo, now helping with *Hold Your Horses* and scheduled to do most of the teaching at the studio, was not in it. Nor was Katey, who was teaching at Bennington. But Ernestine, Ada, Frankie, Hyla, Paula and I were, along with Marguerite de Anguera, Marion Lawrence and Bianca Volland, plus Marcus, William Elliott, Raoul Fernandez, Tom Long, Gene Martel, Paul Mathis, Harry Pick and Herman Weiner.

Cleo and I moved from our apartment to a smaller, better situated one on the second floor of a brownstone between Sixth and Seventh Avenues on 58th Street. Kenny Bostock and Herbert Gubelman were renting the whole floor of the adjoining brownstone, subletting the rear of it to Josephine and Hermine Schwarz and Regina Beck, dancers in *Life Begins.*

Would *Revenge with Music* be another grand exercise of style, like *School for Husbands?* The scene was Spain, of the Napoleonic period. Doris composed the first act court dance with as much ballet as Spanish flavor, for Spain in the Empire period took its fashions from Paris. As soon as it was sketched out, we performed for Howard Dietz and Arthur Schwartz, the librettist and composer of the show, who seemed very pleased. Just at this time Doris was busy starting her fall schedule of classes in various schools, so she absented herself for a week from theatre rehearsals, telling us, "Go ahead and improvise that wedding dance in act two till I return. You all improvise so well now."

Improvise we did, along with a group of real gypsy flamenco dancers, a covey of dwarfs, a whole zoo of livestock including a gaggle of geese, donkeys, and an actual water mill that spilled water on a revolving stage. The principals were Edward Winninger, Libby Holman, Ilka Chase and Rex O'Malley. A far cry from Massine's taut ballet *The Three Cornered Hat,* to music by Manuel de Falla and decor by Picasso, this was to be a Broadway extravaganza.

At the end of the second week, when the producers were having the usual case of second-week jitters, we went on stage for rehearsal one night to be informed by Dietz and Schwartz that the famous Russian director Theodore Kommisarjevsky, newly arrived from London, would now take over the direction of the show. I understood them to say since Mr. K. preferred to work with men choreographers, he had chosen his old Moscow friend Mikhail Mordkin (see Appendix K) to replace Miss Humphrey. They begged the Humphrey dancers to remain and cooperate with the new ballet director.

Kommisarjevsky, a stocky shrewd-eyed man with the nose of a fox, asked to see the court dance. Then he came on stage and proceeded to inject minute pantomimic details among the courtiers and singing ensemble—distractions, it seemed to me, which would nullify the dance movement. Then Mordkin appeared. His costume consisted of a huge bathtowel draped around his neck, a bulky sweatshirt, trousers and tennis shoes. Never having done a Broadway show before, the poor man was frightened at the responsibility of demonstrating the Spanish fire that the producers were demanding.

Shouting in French and Russian, singing snatches of Tchaikovsky, Chopin and the "Volga Boatmen," he waved his arms and stamped his feet until the dust rose from the floor boards. "Dance wiz me," he shouted, grabbing my arm and pulling me through some movements, "vis-à-vis!" He gathered up one of the smaller boys, crushed him in his arms, kissed him, and dropped him. The next minute he was running on all fours, barking like a dog, miaowing like a cat; he ran in circles, then rubbed himself up against the proscenium.

Trying to stifle my laughter at this amazing display only made it worse. I fled from the stage laughing and crying together. (Broadway rumor later had it that Humphrey girls were so overpowered by Mordkin that they fainted.) Mr. Dietz came to me saying everything was going to work out all right, please stick with the show.

We consulted Doris, who was very angry indeed, but she also urged us to stay with the contracts and put up with the situation. Rehearsals from then on were a strange nightmare. Mordkin's two young assistant dancers assured us that the man was not really mad, that he acted this way only because he believed this was the way Americans expected Russians to act. It was a fantastic situation. Arriving at rehearsal, Mordkin would draw up a chair downstage and turn his back on us. As soon as the pianist began to play, he pantomimed playing all the instruments of an orchestra, interminably singing aloud and enjoying himself immensely. Since he didn't direct us, among ourselves we concocted the form of the remaining dances: on this measure we would start to circle, on this phrase let opposite couples cross. The organization and steps came from us out of the music.

When we had donned the black velvet wigs, the lace mantillas, and the silver and copper court dresses for the dress parade, Mordkin observed us. Slapping his forehead he crowed, "Now I know positively what the style of zis production should be: positively it must be Anna Pavlova's *Dying Swan!*" and he sang Tschaikovsky's air again. The only comment Mordkin repeatedly made which had connection to a Broadway show was his phrase, "Giff sonshine!" He wanted us to turn our faces to the front and smile as broadly as possible, "giffing rays of sonshine."

Madeleine Gutman (former Mordkin student and a past chairman of the American Dance Guild) wrote me in 1973 of this *Revenge with Music* episode involving the famous Russian ballet dancer.[43] In 1937 Mordkin, with the support of Lucia Chase, one of his students, organized the Mordkin Ballet Company which became the nucleus of Ballet Theatre. Mordkin died in 1944. Madeleine Gutman's illuminating comments provide insight into his behavior at the time:

As a teacher he could be inspiring, and he really cared about art—but he was a displaced person in many ways—psychologically in terms of his generation, culturally and geographically. . . . His erratic behavior continued and I am convinced that it was the reason that although Ballet Theatre was a direct outgrowth of the Mordkin Company, his relationship to Ballet Theatre was terminated before the end of the first season.[44]

This was the era, she reminds us, of Eddie Cantor's stooge, the Mad Russian.

The producers, more uncertain than ever, decided that what the show needed for salvation was a good hot rumba number. I do not recall who staged it, since I was reluctant to take part in this application of modernity to the Spain of 1804. Fortunately, no pressure was applied.

Kommisarjevsky picked Ernestine for a solo spot, to walk across the stage in a flirtatious manner when the act curtain was down for a scene change. Ernestine asked to have me do it with her. After one rehearsal Kommy chose another girl, a more flirtatious type.

We packed up for the opening in the Forrest Theatre in Philadelphia, where the physical problems were staggering for the scenery and for the cast too. Albert Johnson's sets had been scaled to the New Amsterdam stage in New York, which has the greatest height and depth of any Broadway house. The sets did not fit the Forrest, which was too small. Some scenery couldn't be hung at all; the turntable didn't work smoothly; at the opening performance flats and sandbags were falling all over the stage—one missed my head by inches.

Experienced troupers never drank the local water but always used bottled water; those who didn't wished they had.

In the dressing room every girl in the group received a gardenia from Kommy; Ernestine's box contained orchids. An unsigned telegram from Chicago, "Hope your revenge is sweet," came from the others, who were touring in *As Thousands Cheer*. And Doris's letter read:

Just a little note to wish you all success, you and the group on the opening. That is, I hope you will all be a credit to yourselves and me, and show to all concerned how good modern dancers can be, and how accomplished ours are in particular. At the same time do please remember that you are fit for higher and finer work in your art and that this is only a necessary fling with the left hand. When you come back we can go on with our real work, none the worse, I hope, for this encounter with pestilence and trial—til then with affection,[45]

In Philadelphia the directors perceived that they had a costly failure on their hands. To remedy this Kommisarjevsky left and Worthington Minor was brought in from New York to redirect the show. For two weeks, while playing the old version, we rehearsed the new one every day and after the evening show. Then we went to New York. Mr. Winninger, who was fond of the bottle, unsteadily got too close to the watermill one night, slipped in a puddle, fell, and broke his ankle. Because of his star status, and an ego to go with it, the show closed for four weeks in December. Thus at least a hundred people were put out of work—during the Depression—because he would not permit the perfectly capable understudy to take over while he recuperated. Like Esther Junger, Winninger's spotlight was sacred to his person; he cursed anyone who ever came near it.

Libby Holman, who was nearsighted, had a bodyguard with a flashlight to help her on and off the sets. A good performer, she had to memorize the number of steps she could take on stage because she really was half blind. When the show paused at Winninger's insistance, I left it happily, never to return.

In the first week of November Doris wrote Julia: "Charles and I both being deserted or freed from our group are turning attention to our own dancing which is highly salubrious."[46] The second week she wrote:

We've been busying ourselves for the last two weeks in making out a plan for the group for next year which will keep them out of shows and working together on concerts. We've just sent it out and we're waiting to hear whether they will come in or not. It demands considerable sacrifice in money and time. Most of them will be taxed 15% per week to provide a fund to carry them through next winter, so we'll see whether they want money or art most. If the majority come in we will replace the others and go on with the plan.[47]

The fourth week:

Our group plan has caused a furor, more like a fury I should say—they don't agree with each other about it and very few with us either and the whole thing is at sword's points.[48]

Two weeks later:

We had a long session with the group and went over the whole plan in detail, changing some of it with the result that we got a "yes" from each one. We still think, though, that if we ask any of the Revenge people to leave their jobs they will refuse. That has to be worked out very soon, we and they must know who is going on the tour.

We went over the expenses and probable income from the tour with Levine, the manager at NBC, and found that there will be just enough to pay the company the minimum Equity and the railroad fare with nothing for Charles or me—that means we have to lay out the money for our expenses. Facing this we can't get extra musicians for big theatres or anything extra however much we'd like to.[49]

The original plan submitted to the group in three and a half typed pages outlined the aim of a series of concerts from September 1935 to March 1936 in New York City, then a festival at the end of the season, with the final aim a Dance Theatre and permanent subsidy. The schedule called for a twenty-four-week season, with four Sunday night concerts at the Guild or a similar theatre, a festival week in the spring, and a minimum of a three-week tour under NBC management. During performance weeks, group members would be paid ten dollars a performance for Guild concerts. For any week in which there were three concerts or more they would receive the minimum Equity rate.

To pay the group for the remaining seventeen weeks, taxation of the group members was proposed at the rate of 15 percent whether remunerative work would be artistic work or not. Understudy group members would pay a 2½ percent tax to the group fund when they secured remunerative work from the directors or the group. The first money collected in excess of $3,000 would be devoted half to accident and illness insurance for the group and half to the festival productions.

Railroad fares out of town would be paid by the directors and, in case of an out-of-town day's rehearsal before performance, reasonable living expenses also.

Remuneration for teaching assistantships, helping Miss Humphrey or Mr. Weidman, was at the rate of $2 an hour; coaching for them, $2; $3.50 for teaching a class in the absence of the director; $5 for a class which was entirely the responsibility of the assistant. Group members teaching on their own would charge not less than $1.85 an hour, or half the price paid to Miss Humphrey and Mr. Weidman—whatever that enormous sum was—nor less than half the above price to their assistants.

Training for the technique of dancing, teaching, composing and demonstrations would be given by the directors when any of the group was available and the directors' schedules permitted. Miss Lawrence would give music training. A small paragraph under Privileges and Duties of the Directors on page two partially conceded the point we were hoping for:

Miss Humphrey and Mr. Weidman retain the privilege of directing the artistic policy; of being two of a committee of five which also includes Miss Lawrence (the other two to be chosen by the Group), to decide on programs for the twenty-four week season, and to consider procedure in the case of delinquencies by members.

One of the meetings was scheduled at the Brandwens' home (Mr. Brandwen was Doris's lawyer; his wife, Adele, was the painter). He had helped with the plan. I don't recall what modifications were made, but in the end we all accepted it without a written contract. Just which members of the group were voted onto the policy committee I have no recollection. Perhaps content with the general scheme which promised a modicum of support for a part of the year, the pressure relaxed.

Doris's fond dream of a dance theatre came too soon. Today dozens of modern dance companies tour the land with National Endowment for the Arts support, yet modern dance still does not have a permanent dance theatre.

1934 was the year of another utopian dream: the Townsend Plan. Originating in Long Beach, California, it proposed that every American over sixty receive $200 a month, which would have to be spent immediately and would therefore, the sponsors thought, get the economy rolling again. Social Security on that scale didn't have a chance. As if the Depression were not sufficient, nature struck a blow at the Middle West. Wind storms swept the overgrazed land, blowing away the topsoil, leaving desolation, sending farmers by the hundred in migratory waves to California—the land and the people uprooted.

Artistically the most intriguing accomplishment of the year was the production of *Four Saints in Three Acts* by the Friends and Enemies of Modern Music. Virgil Thomson set Gertrude Stein's text to music in oratorio-opera form. According to Carl Van Vechten, after Virgil Thomson saw *Run Little Chillun* with the Hall Johnson Choir, he decided to have an all-Negro cast.

Four Saints had a small ballet interlude for three couples, set by Frederick Ashton; Florine Stettheimer created the costumes and blue cellophane decor. The surrealism of the words, in themselves abstractions, the music with its familiar use of blues, Negro spirituals, folk songs and oratorio-style recitatives were as endearing as the visual effect of the baroque costumes and the cool heavenly blue sky setting off the warm skins of the brown saints. John Martin found it the most interesting and enlightening experiment in many seasons. *Four Saints* started in Hartford, moved to the Forty-Fourth Street Theatre, and ended up, as John Houseman describes it, "at that place which was everyone's favorite New York theatre with its glamorous and perfectly proportioned house, the Empire."[50]

Virgil Thomson had told Van Vechten, "I am going to have *Four Saints* played by Negroes. They alone possess the dignity and the poise, the lack of self-consciousness that proper interpretation demands. And they are not ashamed of words." He also told him, "I don't really want them to act. I want them to be moved." This concept, like a Japanese Noh play, succeeded in giving the hieratic spiritual level to the scenes. Alexander Smallens was musical director; Feder did the lighting. In the 1973 revival at Lincoln Center's Beaumont Theatre, choreographed by Alvin Ailey, the whole opera seemed fresh, timeless, and even more enchanting than before.

The other theatre offerings in that worst winter of the Depression included *Ah, Wilderness* (O'Neill's play of youthful romance), *Dodsworth* with Walter Huston, *Mary of Scotland, Men in White, Tobacco Road* (that thoroughly depressing picture of southern proverty and degradation), *Richard of Bordeaux* and *They Shall Not Die.*

In December, Doris was invited to choreograph Bach's *Christmas Oratorio* for one performance, at midnight Christmas Eve, at the Forty-Fourth Street Theatre. It was produced by Delos Chappell, with Macklin Morrow conducting members of the Philharmonic Symphony; with Rose Bampton, Jeanette Vreeland, Wilbur Evans and Frederick Jagel as soloists; and with a chorus of voices. Doris arranged a nativity scene with tableaux, processions, groupings and dances for angels. The cast included Gabriel (Charles Weidman), an Angel of the Lord (Kenneth Bostock), the Heavenly Host (Cleo, Ernestine, Dorothy Lathrop and me), Four Acolytes (Gene Ashley, William Augustine, John Glenn, Willem Van Loon), the Mary (Lillian Gish), Joseph (George Bockman), the Shepherds (Ben Caruso, Marcus Blechman, Tom Draper, Michael Logan, Milton Scher), and the Three Kings (Jack Carr, Frederick Curtis, Lewis Martin). Donald Oenslager did the setting and Millia Davenport the costumes; the lighting was by George Scheff.

Both Lillian Gish and Kenny Bostock were playing in Sean O'Casey's *Within the Gates,* she in the symbolic role of youthful love, Kenny dancing in the park scene folk dance set by Elsa Findlay. We loved working with La Gish, who was always first to arrive at rehearsals and last to leave. She shared some of her treasured books of Renaissance paintings with us so that we could feast on the images which the great painters loved to paint. How modestly she said she wished she could move as we dancers did, and would we help her with the positions she had to assume, as if she were not already beautifully formed and endowed with an inner grace in everything she did!

Since there were long stretches of arias and chorales where our phrases were not with the melody but by action, Doris stood in the wings counting cues for us to hear on stage. Shattered by the overwhelmingly beautiful sounds of the orchestra and the choruses combined, we were almost rooted to the spot, unable to breathe. This heavenly dancing was a benefit for the Henry Street Settlement.

The following year Macklin Morrow tried to follow up with another performance, to make it an annual event. Doris, who was out on the road, wired me to start rehearsals until she got back to New York. By the time she arrived, Mr. Morrow had regretfully canceled the plan. Again, no money. The performance, according to a *Times* Reviewer, "had the atmosphere of old miracle plays and the fundamental purity and directness of the theme itself, overlaid with a richness of color that expressed the rejoicing of those who believed."

It was essential to come to this spectacle in faith and humility. For those whose vision is narrow or sophisticated, it would have been difficult to be moved by the unostentatious approach: the chorus group on either side of the stage in front, the narrator and the singers standing close to the wings and moving off when they had done their share, the acolytes carrying the properties and bits of scenery into the middle of the stage, the principals enacting the deathless tale with economy of gesture and literalness of detail. And for each group the costuming was unexceptional—severe white for chorus and singers, white with silver ornaments for the angels, gold for the heavenly host, and gorgeous raiment of red and blue and then pure white for the Virgin. Mr. Morrow, who reduced the score with skill and sensitivity and conducted the orchestra with comprehension and authority, deserves special mention. It was in part his idea that was brought to realization. Miss Gish, who came an hour before from a mundane role, was a lovely Madonna, and Mr. Weidman and Kenneth Bostock as an Angel of the Lord achieved the largest parts for dancers with consummate ease. The sponsors hope to make this an annual event. This morning's experience was sufficient evidence that an interpretation of this kind can not only bring the arts together in joyful union, but can also be an enriching experience.

On this note of harmony the year drew to its close. I could not foresee then that it was the last Christmas I would be in the group. The company tour was to start in January. We would dance again with the Philadelphia Orchestra (in opera this time), perhaps *Orestes* would be staged; who knew what next? In this haze of uncertain dreams 1934 came to an end.

Dangerous Corner

Free of the *Revenge with Music* atmosphere, it was a relief to concentrate on rehearsals for the imminent Humphrey-Weidman tour. Before that got underway on January 6 at the Guild Theatre Doris and Charles appeared for the first time in New York without the group, each offering new solos, and together the premiere of *Duo-Drama*, Vivian Fine was at the piano, and the Gordon String Quartet played Roy Harris's *Concerto for String Quartet, Clarinet and Piano*. Doris's *Credo* was a lyrical statement, performed in a long dress with sleeves, a flower at her bosom; Charles's *Affirmations*, to a new score by Vivian Fine, was rhythmically incisive, a strong abstraction. *Duo-Drama*—in abstract form representing the struggle for supremacy between man and woman—had three sections: Unison and Divergence, Phantasm, and Integration. Pauline's stunning costumes for the first part (which had some of the close-knit design of the Scriabin duet) were made of felt, with monumental sculptural effect; for the last section Doris wore a sophisticated "moderne" shiny black oilcloth skirt. In the beginning the two figures were connected, then they broke away, at the end reconciled, to weave parallel but individual rhythms moving off together.

I admired *Duo-Drama* and was surprised at the bad press which the concert received. Evidently, Humphrey-Weidman, who theretofore could do no wrong, were now on the wrong side of the critics. "A self-indulgence to both dancers. Certainly no effort at communica-

Doris Humphrey and Charles Weidman in Duo-Drama.

tion had been attempted . . . they are the last standard bearers of the pure dance, which is to say dance of sheer movement signifying nothing beyond the manipulation of the body and the colorful occupation of space," one of them scolded.

Though Mr. Martin had good things to say about the solos, he thought the Harris music defeated the dance, since it wasn't theatre music in the first place.

Another reviewer's opinion was that "the American dance will go on purposively despite Miss Humphrey's appallingly meaningless credo . . . [and] Mr. Weidman's 'Affirmations' of complete artistic vacuity."

These excoriations came from a climate where the arts had to possess social significance or they were parasitic wastes of effort in the pressured maelstrom of the period. Perhaps it was because Doris strove self-consciously to make a positive statement—here am I, Doris Humphrey, and this is what I believe movement should be, flowing, lyrical, gracious, womanly, although half of me is now being torn by the spirit of the age and I feel I should do more dissident, distorted things—that it failed to move the audience. Audiences were now looking for statements with increasingly active red flag waving. The proletarian audience, quick to appreciate the use of modern dance for explicit propaganda, was irritated and embarrassed by dance which did not descend to the literal level.

That Friday some of us appeared at the New School for Social Research's continuing weekly lecture-demonstrations of modern dance. Katey, Ernestine and I appeared in John Glenn's visualization of the Madonnas: the gold Altar Figure; the red Madonna of Vengeance; the black Tears. *Song of Earth* also appeared on that program.

The tour began the following night, uptown at Columbia University's McMillin Theatre. We opened with the Prelude from the Roussel *Suite in F,* followed by Doris's *Two Ecstatic Themes* and Charles's *Studies in Conflict* with José, Kenneth Bostock, John Glenn, Gene Martel and Bill Matons. The men performed *Dance of Work, Dance of Sport.* After the *Rudepoema,* Charles's *Kinetic Pantomine* solo, then the *Dionysiaques* and the *Alcina Suite.* In addition to the five men, the girls were Cleo, Ernestine, Letitia, myself, Ada Korvin, Dorothy Lathrop, Katherine Manning, Frances Reed, Hyla Rubin, Helen Strumlauf Bach and Paula (formerly Rose) Yasgour.

After Rochester, at the Eastman Theatre, we traveled toward Toronto. Just before the Canadian border the train stopped to pick up immigration officials who, passing down the aisles, checked on birth certificates. Among the twenty of us, José with his strong Mexican-

Humphrey-Weidman Group just prior to the first tour.

Indian features (he was part Yaqui) stood out distinctly. The inspectors were interested. "And where were *you* born?" they asked politely. José lifted his head and chest, and answered proudly, "In Mexico." In his busy life, the one thing José had neglected to do was secure the birth certificate which we had all been warned about. Mr. Limón was promptly removed from the train. We proceeded without knowing his fate. Could he have been shipped back to Mexico and barred from re-entry into the States? Was he in jail? Just how NBC managed to connect with José's father in Los Angeles remained a mystery. (When José was seven, the Limóns had moved to Arizona from Mexico, settling in Los Angeles a few years later.) When José eventually caught up with us in Chicago, Pauline refused to speak to him for a week.

In Toronto we danced in a theatre on the top floor of a department store. Flurried by the necessity of re-setting and re-rehearsing all the dances, with Charles taking José's place where possible, we were not at our best. Before the curtain rose, as we took our places for the Prelude, nerves on edge, we were startled to hear orchestra strains of "God Save The King," with the audience joining in. The stagehands, dropping everything to stand at attention, burned baleful looks on us as we continued to warm up. The Canadians, having their first taste of modern dance, were polite but evidently baffled.

Over the snowy frozen wastes from Toronto to Chicago the train ride seemed long in the winter light, but I devoured the miles with my eyes, seeing it for the first time. It would have seemed even longer but for John Glenn. John carried along an extra long woolen scarf he was knitting in all the colors, as his therapy-on-the-road. When he tired of knitting, he opened a book he also carried along with him and read to us. The book was *Beasts and Saints,* Helen Waddell's translations from the Latin myths and fables of the early Christian fathers, with woodcuts by George Giddings. From the first paragraph about the Unsociable Lion, I was enchanted. Later I bought the book and synthesized the two similar fables of Saints Gerome and Gerasimus to make a pantomime comedy for an abbott, four monks, a wicked camel-driver, a lion and a donkey, titled *Beasts and Saints.*

I was indebted to both John and his friend Tom McNall for much. We attended concerts of Povla Frisch and Maggie Teyte together, and they taught me appreciation, the niceties of interpretation and the subtleties of style in performance. Mercurial Tom, and John with his sardonic streak, both of them bubbling with Irish wit and humor, were delightful companions. They called me "the Duse dancer" and helped me with choices of music.

In Chicago the opera-size auditorium was half-filled for our concert. Doris was publicized as a Chicago girl (she was born in Oak Park), and Charles as a Nebraska boy; loyal Middle Westerners responded warmly with an ovation. But Doris, writing to Leo on the Texas Special, had to report that the house was so bad the management paid only half the contracted sum.[51] We did a demonstration at the Congress Hotel and had time for a rewarding trip through the Chicago Art Institute. I bought a short-sleeved blouse, anticipating on my first southern journey that Texas would be tropical. When we arrived in Dallas the morning of January 23 the thermometer stood at 10° above zero.

Doris, tactfully the pioneer, spoke to the student audience at Southern Methodist University before the curtain to introduce the strange ways of the new dance. Again the house was small. On the returning northbound train, Doris, Charles and Pauline kept to themselves, as they had done before. Gossiping among ourselves, wandering up and down the aisles, or with noses pressed against frosted windows, we tried to absorb the passing landscape. In winter desolation, how bleak it seemed: the barren, treeless ground, the impoverished soil, the rickety little wooden houses set on a few bricks above the level of the earth—a land that God forgot. We talked about having a swim at the Y in Kansas City between trains, but were too numb from sitting to do it. In Detroit on the 25th we danced at Orchestra Hall. In Ann Arbor at the University we appeared on a stage with a concrete cyclorama, the first we had seen. By the 28th we were back home in New York.

What were the broadening effects of this 5,000 mile expedition through darkest middle America? Most of our audiences, seeing nonverbal art for the first time, were nonplussed, baffled. Teachers and students from physical education departments were enthusiastic. The small houses, the astonished admiration of a few, was a small resonance from the efforts we exerted. Aesthetically, the inspiring moments came from the too short visits to the big city museums. To stand in the presence of the great modern masters in Chicago and the Master of the Madonna of the Rose Garden in Detroit, were high plateaus for the spirit.

In a letter to Leo from Chicago, Doris wrote:

But another cross to bear is the fact that all attention in the press and social functions is riveted on the Shakers and Water Study. It's just as though Charles and I hadn't danced at all. My big healthy children are beclouding me.[52]

She wrote Julia a week later:

We've been home almost a week but a very long one. At first we were pretty
much knocked out by the tour, but couldn't think of that much as it was
necessary to begin at once on Iphigenia. Our old friend Bel Geddes is doing
the sets and costumes which will be lovely in spite of limited funds. There is a
good bit of dancing in it and numerous pantomimic scenes all of which are up
to us. I love to work at it just because I love to compose better than anything in
spite of the fact that I would never choose a Gluck opera if left to my own
devices. Charles is having even more trouble with his boys than I did with the
girls. He needs six in this thing. The two he wants in addition to the four on
the road will not leave their jobs in "Revenge" and there are no other good
ones among the understudies out of jobs. I've often thought how much better
off we'd be as sculptors or painters—the struggle would be just as arduous
but we wouldn't depend on people so much. Added to this problem is that
José the cornerstone is in precarious physical condition or something like it.
And so we're taking blows all around sorry to relate. Criticism on the road
was on the whole bad and the home press too, but to offset that, audiences
everywhere are vociferous in appreciation. Possibly it comes from only a few
who shout and clap enough to seem like a whole crowd. What the Chicago
critics said is mild pap to the American Dance magazine man who declared it
was all a deadly bore and trite to nausea. You can't help listening to them and
wondering, because these same people make comments on other dancers
which seem exactly right. So we wonder, watch everything with a sharp eye,
tighten the belt and say on with the dance.[53]

In Chicago, the Americanism of the dance was hailed by the critic
Glenn Dillard Gunn:

. . . history seems about to repeat itself insofar as it may record the origins of
new impulses and directions in this interesting and sometimes eloquent art.
For it will be recalled that the modern interpretative dance originated with
Isadora Duncan, an American. If these dancers have artistic ancestors I
suspect Ruth St. Denis or Ted Shawn, in which case the children have
developed far beyond their parents.
    These artists and their assistants are also American, quite unmistakably so
. . . Miss Humphrey and most of the girls possessing that aquiline sharpness
and harshness of profile which Europeans are wont to ascribe to the true
Yankee . . . their technical training . . . betrays no trace of Russian or German influence. . . . While most of the program was made up of what might be
called dance abstractions . . . they sought a subject absolutely American for
the one brief example of the dance-drama offered . . . only the climax [of the
Shakers] was unconvincing, since the chief penitent raising a saint-like face to
heaven, at the same time executed a swift pirouette to send her skirts high
and exhibit a fine pair of legs, so that if she was saved above she doubtless
was damned below.

While he questioned the taste not only of that particular accent but the choice of religious subject matter in a manner that could invite derision, he nevertheless extolled the "amazing command of bodily agility and of expressive gesture." He hoped

. . . somewhere they may discover or invent an American ballet repertoire to challenge the color, the spirit, the amazing range of emotion, the thrilling drama that the Russians, who in no way are the technical superiors of these Americans, have brought to our stage. If they can do that, one house almost sold out will no longer be the measure of their appeal to the American public.

Detroit newspaper critics were more disturbed than edified. Russell McLaughlin wrote:

The Humphrey-Weidman idea has added a tenth muse to the immortal nine; a muse of modern dancing. It is a male muse. Its name is Euclid . . . it probes for the intrinsic beauty in the hypotenuse of a right-angled triangle and seeks the emotional meaning of Pi-R-square . . . on this basis of angularity and jerks it occasionally produces something crisp and hard and meaningful. It is, however, almost altogether without beauty. What can dancers achieve without this beauty? They can certainly achieve conflict . . . humor, of a dry and polished sort. They can excellently express much modern music, itself unbeautiful. These things are seen to satisfaction. . . . One thinks, however, that these nowhere fill the gap which beauty created when she winged away. They appear to leave out the romantic principle altogether.

Nevertheless, he found *The Shakers* a grand number and *Water Study* brilliant.

Ralph Holmes, another voice, was impressed because

. . . it is less as dancers than as a social symptom that the Humphrey-Weidman group are significant—because they have the courage to mock at tradition and because of the response which they awaken. If I were a person of entrenched wealth, living by the sweat of other people's brows, it is not the boys on the soap-boxes yapping economic platitudes they but half-understand, I would fear, it's those half-mad clairvoyant creatures, the artists. For they have the power to distill dangerous ideas into dangerous emotions. The real enemies of the Rousseaus, the Voltaires and the Marxists are the artists and that's why a Humphrey-Weidman recital has a deeper significance than perhaps even they themselves are aware of.

Mr. Holmes disagreed with Miss Humphrey's statement that these dances were typically American. Jazz, and refinement of the old country jig into "tap" dance, he declared, are the only "typical" American dance.

The dances Miss Humphrey and her associates gave us Friday night are profoundly international, products of a war that left a new generation without ideals or illusions, as willing to scorn an aristocratic art as to scoff at a bloodthirsty church or junk an immoral political system. . . . These modern dances are dances without joy, being the product of an unhappy world. Not once Friday evening did a dancer smile. . . . I personally don't think they represent an established form; they are merely an experimental technique with which the dances of the future will be fashioned. . . . The Humphreys and the Weidmans are very, very dangerous people. They make me shudder with fear. But this I do know—that the younger people in the audience responded to the tortured twistings, the hard groupings, the preoccupation with angles, thrusts, staccato movements, and that is what interested me.

In *The New York Times,* Mr. Martin examined the evidence, discerning that:

The vast majority of the audience comes not from the diamond tiara sector which turns out aglow with orchids for dance performances which have glamour to boast of, but from the colleges and the John Reed Clubs where there is manifest an eagerness to participate in vital contemporary activities and to retrieve the arts from the category of ostentatious sedatives. This is largely a balcony audience, but its potential numbers more than make up for its lack of wealth; obviously limited contact with dancing thus far, is aware of itself and capable of experiencing vigorous reactions without demanding hearts and flowers, symphony orchestras and scenic effects. Ultimately it is *the* dance audience whether in New York or on the road.

At Teachers College, Columbia University, with Vivian Fine at the piano, on February 16 the company performed the opening Roussel *Prelude, Shakers* and *Counterpoint No. 1;* the men danced *Work and Sport* and *Studies in Conflict;* Doris's only solo was the *Two Ecstatic Themes.* She and Charles danced *Rudepoema.*

At the studio we were in the throes of preparing for the Philadelphia premiere of Gluck's *Iphigenia,* working with a piano reduction of the score. Unfortunately, the task of choreographing nine dances in three weeks—shared by the two choreographers—was more demanding than expected. Ten days before the opening we went to Philadelphia with much still to be composed. We worked hectically in hotel ballrooms, in the opera house lobby, wherever there was space, usually on cold marble or stone floors, in drafty cold places, and we worked from morning until night.

Because of the pressure, Doris's patience wore thin; she was overtired to begin with. Her attitude seemed disparaging—why did she have to waste her time with eighteenth century dances when what she wanted to do was creative modern dance?

Finally, the diverse elements of the opera assembled on the stage for a series of runthroughs, each one more chaotic than the last. Alexander Smallens, the good, faithful dance conductor since Anna

Doris Humphrey and Group in Iphigenia in Aulis.

Pavlova's days, was in charge. When short, red-haired Bel Geddes bellowed over the orchestra to his electricians: "Bring up your pink spot on column six and kill number eight," Smallens turned on him, enraged at that trumpeted intrusion on the dulcet strings of the orchestra. "The Philadelphia Orchestra has never needed and does not now need this hubbub about lights." Bel Geddes, using purple language, went right on shouting commands.

Entering for the opening Air Gai group dance, we found ourselves surrounded by swarms of singers, making a shambles of their introductory chorus because, they protested, they couldn't see the assistant conductor's lighted baton over the heads of the dancers in front of them. The dancers, nervous as horses at the starting line and squeezed for space, took the tempo faster than before. Smallens lowered his baton. "What *is* the tempo you are trying to dance? Can't you count?" he demanded of Charles. When Cyrena Van Gordon (Clytemnestra) arrived late for her aria, she sang in hurried confused gibberish. Smallens interrupted.

"Where were *you?* Why are YOU late?"

"There was no conductor in the wings to cue me. How can I come on in the dark?"

"Take it again, please, and not in a language never heard before on land or sea, but in *French.*"

The conductor was furious at the star. The star was furious at the conductor. The singers of the chorus were unable to sing because of the presence of dancers. The dancers were unable to move because of the chorus of singers. All this added up to bedlam. Not one thing went well until the performances (February 22, 23, 26), when miraculously everything fell into place.

Iphigenia was overwhelmingly beautiful. The exalting, pure, noble music thrilled me to my toes. Herbert Graf, the stage director, selected Letitia and me for Clytemnestra's handmaidens in the second act aria, when she mourns the coming sacrifice of Iphigenia (Ross Tetoni, for two performances; Alice Mock, for one). We were to restrain Clytemnestra from running after Iphigenia as she mounted the long ramp to the altar high above. Cyrena Van Gordon weighed close to two hundred pounds and had a vulnerable leg, caused when her heel caught on a step in an *Aida* performance the year before, with subsequent fractures to hip and ankle. As she sustained her motherly anguish for her child, we supported her on both sides. At the climax, leaning back on our arms while she addressed the last balcony with open mouth and throat, in an aside to me she murmured, "Lower your arm, dearie, my hair net," and on the next beat of the music she made the rafters ring again.

Eleanor King and Katherine Manning in Iphigenia in Aulis.

This *Iphigenia*, with Bailli de Rouellet's gilded ending adapted from Racine's version, was several times removed from the Euripides tragedy. It pleased eighteenth century French taste to appease the gods and to have Iphigenia not only saved from sacrifice by Achilles, but also married to him at the end. At the 1774 premiere in Act 3, when Achilles swears he will slay the priest upon the altar rather than permit the planned slaughter of his beloved, officers rose from their seats, swords drawn, ready to dash upon the stage to assist the hero. Unlike the Greek tragedy, *Iphigenia* à la française ends in a wedding dance. Doris created a processional dance for the girls, each holding a different musical instrument. She used clappers, Cleo and Dorothy held crotales, Katey and Tish harps, Ernestine a tambourine and I a drum.

Doris wrote her mother:

In this first breathing spell I seize the opportunity to tell you that the American premiere of Iphigenia seems to be a big success—especially the dancing. This is hardly deserved on our part because the dances were very far from being perfect—but there you are—we didn't realize what a big job it was and left only three weeks to compose and train nine dances. Consequently we worked like slaves late at night and early morning.[54]

The critics were enthusiastic not only in Philadelphia but in New York, where John Martin's Sunday feature article appealed to the Metropolitan Opera directorate to consider native talent in choosing a new ballet master for the Metropolitan Opera Ballet, citing the brilliant success of the dancing in *Iphigenia* first of all. According to one Philadelphia critic:

Palms were blistered by applause for the beautiful dancing of Doris Humphrey and Charles Weidman and their concert group. The most lively feature of the offering, they caused great enthusiasm and prolonged applause for their superb ensemble and solo dancing in the second act, which included some not-so-easy-gymnastics, while they graced the opening and closing acts also.

Another critic wrote:

The costuming of principals, chorus and ballet also is impressively done in classic style with a "modern" touch, in this manner also being the ballets, performed with remarkable vitality and skill by Miss Humphrey, Mr. Weidman and their dancers, supple, agile girls and well-formed young men who appear in the thrilling terpsichorean episode of the second act.

Two weeks later we were in Boston for two evenings at the Boston

Repertory Theatre. Charles's severe bronchitis limited him to his role in the Scriabin duet for the opening night, his other roles taken by José. He recovered sufficiently to perform the second night. The program was the familiar *Prelude* (Roussel), *Water Study, Shakers,* and the Gigue (Maypole Dance) from the *Suite in F.* The boys did *Dances of Sport* and *Ringside.* Duets were *Rudepoema,* the Scriabin *Poem No. 1* and *Etude No. 12.* Doris included her *Credo,* retitled *Lyric Theme, Sonatina.* Boston critics were still puzzled by the abstractions. Said Ann Ames, "much of it seems crude, obtuse and uninteresting. Its chief deficiency seems to be its lack of humor."

The Transcript critic wrote:

Bewildering though much of it may be, it is undeniably stimulating. The more difficult to grasp and the least enjoyed to the average spectator are the dances that may be described as abstractions. They seem mainly virtuoso displays of technique, awakening little emotional response. The widest appeal lies in the more pictorial compositions. "Water Study" and "The Shakers" though they are among the earlier studies of the group and to the initiate may be obvious are remarkably effective excursions into something that resembles American ballet.

Four nights later the company appeared at Pennsylvania State College. Charles was able to add his *Kinetic Pantomine; Dionysiaques* ended that—the last big concert of the year for the company.

At the end of March, Doris wrote her mother:

We've had two offers in our work this last week. One is to do the choreography for an American Ballet for the Monte Carlo people, and with their dancers—we can't think of a theme for that as yet that would seem to offer hopes for success. Then the YMHA at 92nd and Lexington has a new director [William Kolodney] who wants to make a dance center there. They have an enormous institution with lots and lots of space not being used. They have a theatre, four large studios, 20 practice studios, three gyms, a swimming pool, an amateur orchestra and chorus. The man asked Martha to be Chairman of a committee including Charles and me to participate in and direct the work. You see we're in between the high ups with money, Russian ballet and American ballet, and the low down like the many workers Dance League who also have money. So its something to have an offer to help us from somewhere. The Workers Dance Group here are something very powerful indeed, numbering nearly a thousand dancers—not being on the top or bottom makes it very difficult for us.[55]

Nothing ever came of this offer to modern choreographers to compose something for ballet-trained dancers, but for the next two and a half decades, the Dance Center at the YMHA was a continuing haven for modern dance. Neither Martha nor Charles figured in its organization; Louis Horst and Doris co-directed the activities, the classes for children and adults; most important, they acted as a selection committee, holding auditions and choosing dancers to appear on the Kaufmann Auditorium stage. At first it was open to the young and coming dancers, but the jury system, much criticized, became more and more restrictive as time went on.

The first rebellion in twentieth century dance had been against the ballet and for dance as the art of movement, following earlier revolutions in the other arts: painting was color; sculpture, shape; music, sound; and away with all connections to literature, to story-telling, to dependence on any other art. But now a new current swept the arts. The arts were to be weapons in the struggle against social and political forces. The modern movement in dance, initiated by Martha Graham in her recital of 1926, and by Doris and Charles in 1928, had now become the establishment. Suddenly there were Red Dancers, Rebel Dancers, Needle Trades, Office Union groups, the Workers Dance League.

Of the lot, the New Dance Group persists today, a professional school charging nominal prices for tuition, teaching all types of modern dance, ballet, tap and ethnic forms. The original performing company with Sophie Maslow, Jane Dudley and William Bales continued to be very active for two decades. These young rebels were as much against abstraction and mysticism in dance as they were against fascism, exploitation of the workers, and poverty. In trade union halls and workers' cultural centers they danced for huge audiences such themes as *Anti-War Cycle* (The Theatre Union Friends Dance Group); *Kinder, Kueche and Kirche* (Nature Friends Dance Group); *Scottsboro* and *Tom Mooney*. This was dance for the people on subjects the people could understand; it was "noncommercial mass production, the only profits accruing the spiritual benefits to the people about and for whom they danced," as Margaret Lloyd wrote.[56] She further noted that large scale as their activities were, they were exclusive; the enthusiasts were snobs for the working class. But dances with titles of *Eviction, Hunger, Unemployment, Homeless Girl, Barricades, Parasite* (Nadia Chilkovsky); *Well Fed, Demagogue, While Waiting for Relief* and *Letter to a Policeman in Kansas City* (Bill Maton's Experimental Group) came out of their own experience.

Both Charles and José gave studio talks and appeared on programs with them. Two entirely masculine evenings of Men in the Dance were given by the League that spring, the first at the Park Theatre, the second at the Majestic. By this time the League broadened its efforts enough to include William Dollar and Valya Valentinoff, ballet dancers.

Although folk forms were emphasized from the beginning, Margaret Lloyd noted in her *Borzoi Book of Modern Dance* that gradually the worker was replaced by a more general sense of humanity, the folk superseded the proletariat, and the rebels, so passionate about social injustice, learned that dance itself cannot right social wrongs, that politics is not the most suitable material for dance expression.[57] Over the years they softened their hammer blows of rage and became more subtle in tolerance and wisdom.

Programs at the New School for Social Research reflected these impulses. The week following our Penn State tour, young artists from the New Dance Group, the Dance Unit from the Graham Company, and Humphrey-Weidman collaborated. They presented *Van Der Lubbe's Head*, to the poem of Alfred Hayes; Miriam Blecher danced *Three Negro Poems* and *Woman* from the suite *Disinherited;* Nadia Chilkovsky danced *Homeless Girl* (Modoi). The Graham dancers— Bonnie Bird, Dorothy Bird, Ethel Butler, Sophie Maslow, May O'Donnell, Gertrude Schurr, Anna Sokolow and Lily Mehlman— offered the *Fifth Partita* (Bach). Cleo and John Glenn opened with Mompou's *Cancion y Danza;* Cleo, Helen Bach, John Glenn, Katey Manning and I danced Poulenc's *Three Spring Songs;* Helen Bach repeated her lovely *Prophet Bird* (Schumann), and Bill Matons his unaccompanied *Demagogue;* my contribution was *Song of Earth.*

On April 2 The Little Group appeared at Montclair State Teachers College. Katey Manning replaced Letitia, now touring as featured dancer in *Life Begins at 8:40* as replacement for Esther Junger, who didn't want to leave New York for the road. José opened with his very first composition, *Two Preludes* (DeKoven); Ernestine performed *Nocturnes* to Ravel and Schmitt; I danced the Stravinsky *Minuetto;* we three girls, *Dances for Saturday, Sunday, Monday;* José, his new *Cancion y Danza* (Mompou). After the four of us tripped through the Medtner *Funebre*, Ernestine danced a satiric new *Valse* (Lermanjat); then the *Three Madonnas Suite.* After *Song of Earth,* we all together concluded with the Stravinsky *Finale.* This was the last full concert of The Little Group.

The big group was to have one more performance with the Philadelphia Orchestra. But instead of the April 10 program at the Academy of Music containing the *Orestes,* the *Fire Bird* and a new Paul Bunyan opus, as hoped, we danced the only two possible symphonic numbers of the old repertoire, the Roussel *Suite in F* and Ravel's *La Valse*. For the first part of the program Josef Hofmann played Ruben-stein's *Piano Concerto in D Minor*. In between our two ensemble dances, Doris and Charles performed the *Alcina Suite*. The whole performance was a special benefit for the Robin Hood Dell summer symphony programs. Artists usually contributed their services on benefit programs.

Doris wrote to Julia in mid-April:

Our concert activities have put us in a hole. There were losses on the tour again, on the opera in Philadelphia, and then all that had to be put into railroad fares and company salaries in Boston where the money didn't begin to meet the expenses. Not only that, but the subsequent two dates, State College, Penn. and Great Neck, L. Is. had to be thrown into the balance in order to pay transportation which always comes first. I have a faint hope that my lawyer can collect something from "Revenge With Music"—but anyway the money situation is bad.[58]

A week later she confessed:

I have a strong impression of what it will be like when I take Pussy [Hum-phrey] two weeks in June when Miss Hein takes a vacation as I've just had him for a weekend at the farm. Of course he's lots of fun too, but I'm just not built to enjoy it and think of nothing else.[59]

Immediately after the Philadelphia performance, Doris with nine of her group—Cleo, Helen Bach, Ernestine, myself, Dorothy La-throp, Katey Manning, Edith Orcutt, Beatrice Seckler and Mildred Tanzer—journeyed to women's colleges in Virginia for a week. Mary Baldwin College, Randolph-Macon, Sweet Briar and Lynchburg heard Doris lecture briefly on Modern American Dance. We demon-strated movement in dance form, *Counterpoint No. 1*, *Shakers* and *Water Study*, with Doris performing her *Variations on a Theme of Handel* and the *Two Ecstatic Themes*. At Lynchburg there was consternation at first over the presentation of *Shakers*, the authorities fearful that the audience would take offense at the theatrical presentation of a sacred dance. After Doris spoke to the president, he gave in. The young southern ladies were astonished at our energy. "Wha, I could never do *that*," one of them drawled, "It would kill *me*."

The flowering Judas trees, the forsythia popping out, the red clay soil, the pines of Virginia were appealing, but the continual offerings of southern fried chicken, hot biscuits and dumplings didn't make us feel any lighter. We were by now tired of being on trains and on the road, static for long hours, then required to be in top form for a brief few hours, then more transportation to another new situation. With the first breath of spring softening the landscape, it was with peculiar sadness that we took the overnight cars north to New York, as I anticipated, with a sinking heart, the coming dissolution of the group.

Sitting together on the train, Ernestine confided to me that she was leaving to study with Kreutzberg at Salzburg in the summer; that she would first go to Switzerland to teach at a children's school in June, and then to Austria. She had just communicated this plan to Doris, sitting alone, up front. Frankie and Hyla had already withdrawn from the group, addressing their letter to Doris a few weeks before:

Since there is so much controversy about our position in the group, and realizing that next year we will be again faced with the same difficulties which prevent us from going on this tour, we feel that in all fairness to you and the group, we should tender our resignations now. After our last meeting with you, we can clearly understand that your future plans will require more of everyone's time. Consequently, this will make it practically impossible for anyone to arrange for a steady source of income from activities outside of the group. As the group has always been a vital part of us, it is regretable that economic reasons cause this action.

With best wishes for every success. Sincerely, Hyla-Frankie.

Please ask John to get in touch with us at the theatre for an accounting of the group fund money.[60]

To hold a dozen and more dancers together with the predictable hazard of low remuneration, and occasionally no funds at all, purely on the strength of the work's being artistically important and satisfying, was sheer triumph for Doris as a leader. But inevitably marriage and earning a living took their tolls: Sylvia Manning, Celia Rausch, Evelyn Fields left in 1932; Rose Crystal in 1933; Gail Savery in 1934, to take paying jobs. Now Hyla—the baby, who was only thirteen when she started and seventeen when she left—and Frankie were pulling out for the same reason. Hyla remembers "a feeble attempt" at organizing, and "someone suggesting (possibly me, fresh kid that I was) that all finances be shared equally, and that if they, Doris and Charles, expected us to starve in garrets, why then they should be prepared to do likewise (a highly impractical idea)."[61]

Hyla expresses a feeling that when Doris changed her original lyric, naturalistic style to the use of distortion, she may have lost some people by this shift of emphasis and technique.

From the original company of 1928, Cleo, Katey Manning, Dorothy Lathrop and I remained. Of Ada, Ernestine, and Letitia, who came in 1929, Ernestine was about to leave; Cleo and Dorothy would soon follow. The new replacements were Katherine Litz (1934) and Joan Levy, Miriam Krakovsky, Edith Orcutt, Beatrice Seckler and Sybil Shearer (1935).

With mixed emotions I made my way to where Doris sat alone, for I, too, was going to announce the break from the fold. How wan and fatigued she looked! "Doris, I have something to tell you. It's about this summer. I have a job teaching movement for actors at a summer theatre, and it's a job I can't refuse to take. I will continue to rehearse with the group until summer, then I'll be gone. In the fall I want to start working alone."

"Ernestine is leaving because she says she wants to dance for the people. Is that why you want to leave, too?"

"I want dance to be more than concert dance. I want it to be *theatre dance.*"

"I believe in that, too," said Doris.

"Well, perhaps we both have the same goal; only there may be different approaches to the same end," I concluded lamely. If she had asked me how I was going to go about achieving this theatre dance, I could not have told her. It was an impulse in the dark, as strong as it was blind, an instinct I had to obey.

The telegraph poles outside flattened themselves, declined, vanished. The train rushed on. For me it would be a future without my two artistic parents, without the group. I would no longer have guidance, nor would I have the companionship of the dancers with whom I had grown up as a professional. The past eight years, shared so deeply with talented men and women, had been my college, my university; they had taught me dance as an art, a philosophy, a way of life.

It was a wrenching moment, but not a surgical break. There were several weeks of studio rehearsals to come; there was no final goodbye; there never would be complete rejection of my artistic parents.

About the Virginia tour, Doris wrote Leo:

The college dates here are well enough but three days of women without men is already too much. No wonder women's colleges are peculiar one way or another. They make me feel super-normal with my *two* men. [62]

She waited until the end of May to confess to her mother the burdens under which she now labored:

You see everything is very bad for me now. I don't like to expatiate on it because you're not going to like it any more than I do, but I must so you will understand. It's so bad that I feel I have to go to a fresher place than

Eleanor King in Mother of Tears. *Photos by Edward Moeller.*

Dummerston [Vermont] for my only two weeks of freedom from the grind. I haven't any money, and it probably won't seem fair to you a bit for me to borrow it or get from my insurance (which I did) and use it for my own ends by going to Bermuda! I'm going to take Pussy who goes free—and take care of him myself.

The big trouble is that the group I trained and labored over so long is leaving me one-by-one, some for Communism, some for Broadway shows. This leaves me a very shaken understudy group and a fear in me that what I want to do is [not] in step with the times—I don't like shows or Communism—and moreover I haven't the money to offer my girls, which even the Communists have. I know that if I'm to get through this summer with any grip on myself, I must go somewhere, so I'm just seizing this trip which won't be so much in the way of rest or inspiration, but I am hoping it will do more for me than sitting in a little town in Vermont—I do hope you will understand something of the struggle and the desperate pass I get to once in awhile.[63]

My dream of theatre dance had nothing to do with show business; I was thinking of movement, poetry, music combined in abstract, nebulous ways. And my first experience with the Communists was dismaying. ACTION, a leftish organization, invited Ernestine and me to appear on April 25, at Mecca Temple (now City Center). The invisible judges sitting in the auditorium approved the two Madonnas of Vengeance and of Tears. Since "religion is the opiate of the masses," Katey's idolatrous Altar Figure was not even considered. And our titles would have to be changed.

I could not think of a substitute; neither could Ernestine. The judges put their heads together and suggested that if we would accept Mother instead of Madonna, with its sacred connotation, the dances would be in. I despised this Marxist limitation of censorship in principle; and despised myself, equally, for giving in simply because I, too, was an opportunist and couldn't resist the chance to dance. *Mother of Tears* was received respectfully, Ernestine's flaming *Mother of Vengeance* roused the audience to shouting.

On that program, Fe Alf danced her *Cycle of the City:* Girl in Conflict, Slavery, and Degradation; the Blanche Evans Amateur Group closed the first half with *Unite Against War and Fascism.* Dance Players presented *Protest.* After another intermission, Jane Dudley danced *Call* and *The Dream Ends;* I danced *Song of Earth* in between. Ernestine performed Action from *Patterns of Protest;* Bill Matons' *Demagogue,* then Ernestine's satirical *Valse,* and the New Dance Group closed with *We Remember.*

Edna Ocko, dance critic for the *Daily Worker,* reviewed the Mecca Temple solo recital:

On the basis of a broader program against war, fascism and censorship, dancers were invited to present their works, for the most part when no affiliation of active participation in the League's program was contemplated . . . the dances presented disarm the reviewer; he cannot criticize the dances for their lack of specific or conscious revolutionary content, since these dances were never originally created to contain them.

This audience instinctively showed where their sympathies lay. . . . They enjoyed the fleeting but pointed satire on bourgeois refinement in Ernestine Henoch's Waltz, they supported with lusty appreciative applause her dramatic intensity in Mother of Vengeance, and her brief but dynamic Action.

Eleanor King's Mother of Tears, while less brilliant, and her Song of Earth, introspective and lyrical, were nonetheless sensitive and beautiful performances which present this young dancer as a performer of promise and sincerity.

To encourage the dancers, Miss Ocko exhorted them:

. . . to consider their audience, an audience that demands ideological and emotional explicitness in dances; let them consider the revivifying support that a revolutionary audience can give its artists. This support cannot be minimized, and it is only given to those who consider and understand the profound convictions of huge masses of people.

Ernestine departed for Europe after that. The final New School for Social Research modern dance concert on April 24 consisted of dances by Gertrude Prokosch, The Little Group minus Ernestine, and the New Dance Group.

Gertrude Prokosch's solos were stark and impressively beautiful. Doris had invited her to perform privately at the 18th Street studio for the group one afternoon. Her integrity, her majestic body, nude to the waist in her unaccompanied *Earth Mother*, performed in seated position, made a deep impression. Gertrude's second work at the New School was accompanied by poems of Iris Tree, read by Phoebe Guthrie; her last piece, *Chromatic Variations* (musicless), had three sections: March, Dirge, Valse.

The Little Group, now down to Katey Manning, Helen Bach, José and myself, repeated dances from the Montclair program, with Tom McNally as pianist. New Dance Group members who appeared in *We Remember* were Miriam Blecher, Jane Dudley, Frances Bardine, Mildred Gold, Janet Janov, Edith Lange, Selma Mazan, Clara Nezin. This was the last appearance of The Little Group, which had served its purpose by giving us a chance to compose and perform on our own for four years.

Family pressure at home—a skeptical father, an indifferent

mother, five brothers and sisters who thought I was crazy to be a dancer—had intensified. Going on stage at the New School for *Song of Earth,* I felt this was probably the last time I would ever be able to perform that dance, a recurring emotion which was the normal expectation during the trial solo years. Each time I entered a stage I thought it was the last time ever, the very last time. I was continually dancing my farewell to the dance as well as the *Song of Earth.*

Sophia Delza had organized the young dancers series at the New School, with an auditions board of Paul Boepple, Martha Hill, Mary Wood Hinman, Louis Horst and Paul Neumann. Mr. Martin reviewed the season as encouraging, if not always entertaining:

Probably in the entire series there was no finer performance, judged simply as movement, than that of José Limón. His dances were neither new nor significant, but as a dancer he proved again, as he has often done before, that he belongs among the elect. Another first rate talent on the masculine side is Jerome Andrews. He is equipped with an admirably serviceable technique, although it is too obviously eclectic to make any sort of unified style possible. He has also the gifts of the theatre, with their corresponding penalties. Louise Kloepper presented one of the best numbers of the series "Idyll," Lucretia Barzun, Lydia Balsam, Elizabeth Waters and Nancy McKnight all offered dances of merit, uneven in excellence but characterized by a common fundamental seriousness of approach.

Ray Moses, though still in a sense a shadow of Martha Graham, has a distinct gift for group composition as well as solo performance. Merle Marchovsky, of Miss Graham's group and also the Dance Unit, contributed a stunning "Agitation." Hilda Hoppe, of Elsa Findlay's group, presented a most promising set of "Three Jewish Songs." Eleanor King, of the Humphrey-Weidman group, exhibited again her beautiful lyricism of movement which deepens into tragedy in her excellent "Mother of Tears." John Glenn, also of the Humphrey-Weidman group, revealed a charming if extremely tenuous sense of comedy in his "Three Spring Songs."

Among all the Agit-Prop dances demonstrating immediate political and social protest, none of them has endured as Charles Weidman's brilliant *Traditions* has done. It survives because it is in the best sense an abstraction—a distillation of an essence of experience with implications beyond any specific crisis. The dance, a trio for men, began with a movement pattern initiated by Charles, imitated by José and Bill, repeated enough to become firmly established. When one of them breaks away a bit from the mold, the new design in turn is imitated until it too becomes tradition.

In May, Congress approved the Works Progress Administration, authorizing five million dollars to provide twenty million Americans with work relief within their own skills and trades. Less than one percent of this was allocated to the arts, providing for the Federal

Doris Humphrey and Charles Weidman in New Dance.

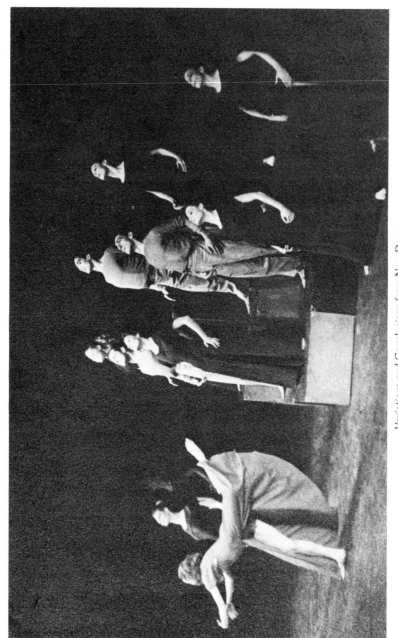

Variations and Conclusions from New Dance.

Artists and Writers Projects, as well as for a Theatre Project, of which dance and music were units, which began to function in the fall of the year. In the representational style of Thomas Hart Benton, post offices and official buildings bloomed with mural paintings; enduring state guides came from the writers.

The Dance Project, administered by Don Oscar Becque, had a staff consisting of Tamiris, Felicia Sorel, Gluck-Sandor, Doris and Charles. Hallie Flanagan's Theatre Project achieved extraordinary successes, especially with the Orson Welles-John Houseman Negro Theatre in Harlem; Tamiris's *How Long, Brethren* and Charles's *Candide* saw the light of a Broadway production just before Congress, frightened by the bogy of socialism and communism, wiped out the entire project in 1939.

1935 was the year of Sinclair Lewis's *It Can't Happen Here;* Thomas Wolfe's *Of Time and the River;* Clifford Odets's *Awake and Sing;* and *Dead End.* Helen Hayes triumphed in *Victoria Regina* and the Lunts in *Taming of the Shrew;* Garbo in *Anna Karenina,* and Fred Astaire in *Top Hat,* memorable movies. Lincoln's Gettysburg address, spoken by Charles Laughton in *Ruggles of Red Gap,* was a heartening sound in a world where Hitler had repudiated the Versailles Treaty to call up a German army, and where Fascist Italy had invaded defenseless Ethiopia.

At this tag end of the season, when the original animating spirit had left the group, Doris, who had been reading the critics about the dancers who never once smiled during the whole performance, gave us a lecture on "the look of a dancer"—something to be cultivated from the outside, a matter of holding the head up, widening the eyes. Sad now to think it must be achieved mechanically. Until time to leave for New London, I rehearsed with the group on *New Dance,* impressed with the rhythms Doris worked out for her concept, not as yet fully sketched out. The accomplished work, when it finally came to New York, deeply moved and exhilarated me. After its Bennington premiere, Doris, in an abyssal artistic and financial depression, with half her dependable dancers gone and needled by the vociferous left groups, took a long look at the good life and responded with a symphonic poem to the best hopes of democracy, a worthy affirmation to the protestations of the workers. Perhaps, like Renan's judgment of Turgenev, "born essentially impersonal, with the conscious of a people," Doris could rise above the smaller issues, in praise of what was noblest and best in each individual. The symphonic ending of *New Dance,* with each member of the group contributing to the ensemble rhythm, was a masterpiece of eloquent simple design. How affirmative it was!

I wrote Ernestine in Paris:

. . . when I saw Doris after her last concert she took my hands and said they needed me, that the last dance (Theme and Variations) needed my particular quality and it would be a much better dance if I were there! to which I demurred that it was too late now, the dance was all composed. She said "Oh no, it's not." Then she put her head on one side and deprecated a bit: "You would have your little run after the theatre, now you see . . ." "But I'm still running after it, Doris, I just haven't achieved it yet."

(I could not say the words that would mean a return to the group.)

Then McNally stuck his head in between, singing "Bring back my bonnie to me, to me" whereupon we all laughed, but when he went on: "Is it true Doris, you plan to do the *Orestes* this summer?" She said Yes, she was hoping to do it at Bennington, and quickly turned away.[64]

Whether the music rights were not available, or her impulse to do something new was stronger, I can't be sure. In any case, instead of *Orestes* she produced *With My Red Fires* at Bennington in 1936.

I would carry the indelible Humphrey-Weidman stamp with me and look back on eight years with them as a golden age shared with a remarkable family: José with his tremendous dynamic power and innate Spanish-Yaqui reserve; Letitia, the sculptor's dream, the pair of them matched in breathtaking physical beauty; Ernestine's vivacity, Katey's musical sense and humor, Ada's mystery and fatalism, cherubic Hyla, Cleo's flair, perceptive Frankie, debonair Kenneth, George's eagerness, Jack Cole's sense of style, Mad Matons' excesses, John Glenn's ironic detachment . . . these people and their gifts had helped to mold me into a professional.

Now I would progress alone, without these stimulating presences. The director of the New London, New Hampshire, Summer Theatre, Mrs. Josephine Holmes of the Curry School of Expression in Boston, had seen *Orestes* at Columbia University. She hired me to teach movement to her actors and apprentices, and to stage the pantomime scene in Pinero's *The Enchanted Cottage*.

New London was a sleepy New Hampshire village with an elm-lined main street, a post office, a general store, the barn theatre and typical New England green-shuttered white houses. In one of them, owned by an elderly widow whose face was potato-white from lack of sun, I had a room. Sitting in her starched gingham dress, rocking in her porch rocking-chair, she confessed envy of my being a dancer, something she had always dreamed of being, which her father would never allow.

New Hampshire had its quota of eccentrics. A romantic figure of a woman, always covered with a veiled garden hat, daily pottered about among the roses in her garden. Passers-by could overhear her reciting Shakespeare. One of the Russell sisters (famous nineteenth century actresses), when she saw anyone interested and listening, would lean over the hedge to announce in stentorian tones, "*I* am the *only* woman Otis Skinner *really* loved."

The New London Theatre scheduled *Pygmalion, The Crime at Blossoms,* and *Enter Madame* besides the Pinero. I was terrified at the idea of being responsible for movement within a play, until I saw the company of young players and realized how simple everything would have to be for these actors, most of them with bodies stiff as boards. I breathed more easily.

We moved the morning exercise class from the dusty, dark barn out to the lawn. In the afternoon, walking down the street, I would see the village children imitating the movements they'd been watching earlier.

Peter Joray, assistant director, was the bright spot of the summer. Peter, born in Amenia, New York, had the verbal grace and wit of a true comedian. He had acted in Theatre Guild plays and with Jane Cowl in several of her productions. Once at a dinner party he tied his dinner napkin around his face, acting Queen Victoria with such success that he developed a whole program of "Royalties of the Past," all in pantomime, including Catherine of Russia and Frederick the Great. Beatrice Lillie was so delighted with his Victoria that she took Joray along with her to Hollywood. Everything Peter said was droll; he was a delight to the mind. Peter wanted to do his mimes; I wanted to try some new dances; together we gave a double bill at the Barn Theatre. As contrast to the Puritan *Summons to Sabbath,* for which David Diamond wrote a score, premieres included a Witches' *Summons to Sabbath* (De Falla) and a lyrical *Summer Song,* also to De Falla. *Catherine of Russia Dictates a Letter to George III of England; Louis XIV Dining Before His People,* and *Queen Victoria* Peter sandwiched in between the *Antique Suite* (Gagliarda, Siciliana, Minuetto), *Song of Earth, Mother of Tears* and *Festivals.*

Kenny Bostock was with the Keene Summer Theatre not far away and we attended a fine production of *Pelleas and Melisande* there, directed by Herbert Gellendré. Kenneth Bisbee, Margaret Mower, Stiano Braggiotti, Royal Beal and Virginia Stevens were leading players. I liked the use of masks and the artistry of the production. At the end of summer, we were invited to contribute to the Keene Theatre's Farewell Program. Kenny danced *Parade* (Milhaud), *Fanat-*

icism (Doris Dennison), and *Danza* (Soro), with Doris Dennison as accompanist. Herbert Gubelman sang two groups of songs; Peter gave *Victoria*, I danced *Minuetto, Summons to Sabbath, Song of Earth* and *Festivals.*

Peter invited me to drive New York-ward with him and his friend DeWitt Peters (brother of Rollo, the actor) and to stop at his "Upsandowns" country place near Albany. DeWitt, a painter, went to Haiti later and was instrumental in organizing the native art school there. No letdown was possible in the presence of these two beguiling conversationalists. Best of all, Peter drove us to New Albany's Shaker settlement, where we found two old ladies and one old gentleman, the last of the New Lebanon Shakers. Sister Sarah Collins, outgoing, gentle and sweet, gave me her photograph, together with an eighteenth century book on the trial and imprisonment of Mother Ann Lee at Harvard, Massachusetts. She even danced and sang for me, one of the little childlike pieces, "Here we go, to and fro, tap the toe, lines just so." I notated the song and the steps, putting it inside the rare little book; later both treasures disappeared, alas, from my Seattle library.

Cleo having made other plans, we gave up the apartment we'd been sharing, and I moved alone to the next brownstone, 158 West 58th Street, into what was originally a first floor dining room with a butler's pantry, converted to a single apartment. The dining room, which had a fireplace and a big bay window facing the back, became my bedroom-studio; the pantry, with a dumbwaiter, was the bathroom. Pauline Lawrence had given me her studio bed; I bought unpainted pine chests, and put rag-rugs on the floor made out of old costumes and silk stockings. Upstairs Kenny Bostock and Herbert Gubelman had taken the whole floor, renting the back room to Josephine and Hermine Schwarz and Reginia Beck, all dancers. In between the two large high-ceilinged rooms, Herbert arranged a cooking area in the bathroom, where Herbert, a good chef, cooked delicious meals to which the six of us individually contributed two dollars a week. We dined off Chinese rice bowls, and luxuriated in the spacious rooms, which Herbert (graduate of a university around-the-world cruise) decorated with Chinese ancestor portraits and Chinese lacquered tables and chairs.

Kenny, with Alice Dudley as partner, was dancing in night clubs; Herbert studied singing; the three girls were in *Life Begins at 8:40;* I taught a few pupils, and earned the rent at the Leighton Rollins Studio for Acting in Beekman Towers, teaching movement for actors. Social Register names graced Mr. Rollins's list of patrons and patronesses; big name people of the theatre were "advisers." Laura Elliott taught acting; Helen Lanfer, a great delight, who played for my classes, taught rhythm. Classes were in the ballroom of Beekman Towers. Mr. Rollins's interest in hiring me was the fact that I had been on the experimental light program at Yale, though he had no theatre or place for lighting where this experience could be helpful. He was largely invisible.

Katherine Bard and Arthur Little were outstanding students. In exchange for living quarters, Arthur acted as secretary to Madame Ouspenskya of the Moscow Art Theatre. Like me, he had started with Clare Tree Major, but whereas I was a beginner in her school, he toured with the Children's Theatre. From there he later went to the Barter Theatre in Virginia, then became director of a Little Theatre in Georgia. A conscientious objector during the war, he met the president of Earlham (Quaker) College and was invited to develop the drama department at Earlham. In the sixties, with a foundation grant assisting middle western colleges in Asian studies, Arthur would teach at Tokyo's Waseda University and study the form of Noh, before writing *Saint Francis,* the first Noh play in English. We had been close friends for years; Arthur commissioned me to choreograph the 1970 production of his Noh play at the college.

John Martin once characterized the new dance of the thirties as a dance of "divine undiscipline." My eight years with Humphrey-Weidman, equivalents of college and graduate work, were my university and diploma in the art. Here I was, a late starter, with weak ankles, anisometropia, and no leg extension. Furthermore, as Pauline once said, looking hard at me from her place at the piano, "There's something awkward about both José and Eleanor" and "There's nothing you can do with hair like that." Still the fact was that I had grown up with Doris's off-balance suspensions, her fall-and-recovery dynamics, her emphasis on breath rhythm which became second nature, with Charles's pointed satire and unique pantomime to balance the "pure" dance. After four years of growth, The Little Group outlived itself, though at one point Doris warned, "You have to choose between your dates and ours, whichever is most important to you." Hoping for the crowning experience of touring with the company, I had opted to stay. The big group's immediate prestige and growing success carried the germ of its demise as Broadway shows splintered us apart, left little time for new works, and pulled many of the group in the opposite direction from the concert field.

With the exception of the Theatre Guild experience, I knew I did not want any more of Broadway show business. The conflict over my

untrained body had, to a certain extent, been won; the conflict between "we" and "they" had been solved in their favor until now;
there was no conflict in my mind between show business and dance
as art. The time for the plunge of independence had come. As
Mother's baby book recorded—as if it were remarkable—"Eleanor
has a will of her own." And wherever it was going to lead, I had to
find my own path from now on.

CHAPTER NINE : 1936

Shadows; 'Icaro'

DARK CLOUDS OF FACSISM cast long shadows of censorship from Europe to America. Hitler marched his armies unopposed into the demilitarized Rhineland. Equally unopposed, violating the Locarno Pact, Mussolini took over Addis Ababa. Germany, Italy and Japan signed the Axis agreement, to conquer and divide the world between them. Civil war carried Franco to power in Spain. The day Mussolini forbade Jews to travel in Italy, Elsa Herrmann, Jane's mother, was in tears. "Where in Europe can we go?" she lamented.

We knew what Doris thought of war—"a dirty trick which men play on each other." Glamorized homicide is rewarded with acclaim and gratitude while single murder is condemned with society's heaviest penalty, the double standard pointed out by Ruth Benedict in her brilliant essay, "Natural History of War." When the first skywriters began blowing advertisements across the heavens, Doris called it "the rape of the sky." When television arrived, she said, "Now men will learn they have nothing to say about each other." To a certain extent a female chauvinist, often murmuring about "the male ego," she, like all artists, understood the need for freedom. Later *With My Red Fires* expressed her feelings about the female ego of possessive mothers; *Corybantic* would be her diatribe against war.

Once, at dinner with José in a Spanish restaurant, the exotic food was secondary to the vehemence with which he dwelt on the condition of Spain and his loathing of Franco; a disturbing meal. Decades later, after José's death, when the Limón company was just back from

227

Russia and appearing in Paris at the Théâtre de la Ville, a French publicity release quoted José: "I despise Richard Nixon and all his works," a testimony to his hatred of dictatorship.

I was myself to stand in a small shadow of Italian fascism. One day in the 42nd Street Library I came across Ruth Draper's translation of Lauro de Bosis's *Icaro*, the Italian verse on one page, her prose opposite.[65] I realized with joy that my search for a theme for a dance-drama had found its goal.

The companion volume, *The Story of My Death*,[66] explained why I had not heard from Lauro again, after the talk about choreographing his *Oedipus*. For Lauro, my poet acquaintance, had gone to his death on October 3, 1931, when he flew alone over the city of Rome, scattering pamphlets addressed to the King and the Roman people, advising them to resist fascism. He made the flight in his monoplane, which he had learned to fly for that mission. He was pursued and overtaken by the Italian Air Force and driven from the skies to an unknown end.

The same passion for freedom which consumed him burns symbolically in the text of his classically set *Icaro*. The complete work, five acts with five choruses and a prologue, I realized was beyond my reach. Somehow, I felt, the choruses legitimately could and should be danced. Just how to do this was obscure; the compulsion to dance this theme was irresistible.

Before starting work on it, I had to hear the verse read in Italian, for English prose was out. My friend Jane, who had introduced me to Lauro, no longer lived in New York; she was now married and living in London. I thought of the Casa Italiana at Columbia, where Lauro had planned one day to stage the *Oedipus*. A letter to Prezzolini, head of the Casa, brought a telephone request for a meeting the next day. When Prezzolini entered the reception room—a yellow-faced old Cicero—he abruptly stated that he had sent for me to tell me there was nothing the Casa Italiana could do in connection with the production I had in mind of Lauro de Bosis's *Icaro*; the Casa had no resources whatever.

"Oh, you misunderstand. I am not asking for a production here. All I am asking is for some Italian voices to read the verse-drama for us."

Silence. "Were you born in England, Miss King?" "I am American." Head angled, he asked, "Do you mean to say that you consider this work of De Bosis has some artistic value?"

"Unfortunately I can't judge the original Italian, but in English it is the most inspiring theme I can find; its classic style is simple and clear, and the modern implication makes it pertinent for today."

He gestured, then gruffed: "It is not art at all; it's full of bombast. What we call D'Annunzioism. Words—propaganda; propaganda—not art. Just bombast. Nothing to do with art." He hesitated, then went on: "Of course, I was responsible for his winning the prize [the Olympic prize for poetry, 1928] a few years ago. But everyone knew, Lauro himself knew, that it had no merit whatever. Why, I wrote Lauro that. I told him that we were giving it to him because we wanted an Italian to have it, not because it had merit. It's just propaganda."

The gloomy room, the yellow old man, the effect of his words oppressed me. I made a last effort: Were there no available Italian actors or people with choral experience whom he could suggest as possibilities? Reluctantly, he offered, "A Mr. Sterni has a theatre on Broadway. It's not art what they do, either." I took the address he wrote out for me, and hurried from the massive Florentine stones, the grilled windows, feeling I had escaped a prison.

Tucked away in a misty corridor of the Longacre Theatre building, a week later, I found the office of Commendatore Sterni, where a secretary had instructions to get more information from the signorina: Who were the backers? Who was the producer? Who was the director?

I explained there were neither producers nor backers; it was just an experimental idea, not yet even begun, pending the search for Italian voices.

The secretary smiled politely. Unfortunately their professional actors were so busy with their week of playing, then a week of rehearsing, and appearing on radio. In short, it was out of the question to expect professionals to give their few free hours to work for nothing on an experiment.

I persisted. Didn't she know of any Italians anywhere who could read the verse for us?

Perhaps if I got in touch with Mr. Fioroni, secretary of the Dante Alighieri Society, he could put me in touch with some; he would know all the Italians in the city, and their choral clubs. She wished the signorina good luck.

A week later I walked down Fifth Avenue to Rockefeller Center, past the Prometheus fountain to the Palazzo Italiano, and upstairs to the Dante Alighieri Society's office—Venetian blinds, Renaissance furniture, and on a high pedestal a bust of Dante himself. Mr. Fioroni, a smiling, handsome young man, extended his hand. "Ah, yes, Miss King? Let us sit here on the sofa." We were alone in the room. "So you knew Lauro de Bosis?"

"Not well. I only met him a few times."

"Did you have any communication with him?"

"I never heard from him after he left for Europe." He repeated the same questions; I repeated that I knew him only briefly socially.

"Lauro de Bosis," he murmured softly. "You know, I knew him too. In fact he was one of my best friends. I think sometimes there can have been no finer mind in all the world than his. But—" his voice changed—"do you not know? You do not know how he deceived everyone. Even his friends. He did not tell anyone what he was doing, what he was up to. All the time he was deceiving us!"

I smiled to myself, thinking, he had to deceive you if he was going to undeceive his country. Mr. Fioroni went on: "You understand I cannot have anything to do with his name. Yet, I don't know why, I would like to help you. I shouldn't do it. But I will do you this favor. Then perhaps sometime you will do a favor for me. You might dance for one of our entertainments sometime? I have had all the singers from the Metropolitan Opera House so many times, we have the same thing over and over."

"Of course, I would be glad to dance, perhaps the *Gagliarda* and *Siciliana* to Respighi's music. But how soon may I meet some of the Italians in your choral society?"

"What is that? Is there such a rush?"

"Mr. Fioroni, I have been searching for a month. It seems so difficult. Prezzolini thought I was some kind of a spy. Mr. Sterni's company is too professional. All I want are a few good Italian voices to read the verse, out of sight, unseen."

"No, no, I see. You are just an artist. I will help you but you must not mention my name. You may come when we have society meetings. I will pick out the people who have the purest Tuscan speech; you can hear them; if you like any of them, you can arrange what you like with them. But you will not mention me. I must have nothing to do with it."

"Of course, Mr. Fioroni, I understand. When may I come?"

"If you are in such a hurry," a shrug of the shoulders, "a Tuesday or Friday at eight."

"Splendid. I'll be here next Tuesday, then."

"Let me show you the auditorium we have here in the Palazzo before you leave. I helped to design it myself." He escorted me to a corridor so full of packing cases and consulate records that it was impossible to get through. Instead of seeing the auditorium, he gave me another quick handshake, and showed me the elevator.

Fortified with the presence of George Bockman, who was interested in the idea of *Icaro's* dancing choruses—for which he wanted to design the production—the two of us entered the Dante Alighieri Society office the next Tuesday. Two old men, a few students, some young girls among them, were in the room. Mr. Fioroni arrived, disappearing quickly into an inner office. After the secretary took my name, I was invited to go in. Sitting behind a desk, a distinguished gentleman, introduced by Mr. Fioroni as Baron So and So, rose; to my astonishment he delivered the Fascist salute in my face. Mr. Fioroni's smile was perfection. "Yes? And how are you, Miss King? How is everything? And just what is it again?" He had never expected me to return.

Without mentioning De Bosis, I requested the help of some readers to read Italian verse for a dance project. Would there be people here tonight who might be available?

"I don't know. I will take a look and pick out the best voices here tonight."

He returned in a few minutes with a rosy-cheeked Miss Camera, American born of Tuscan parents. Camera's eyes were bright, she looked pleased and interested, answering questions put by the Baron, so I could catch the purity of her Tuscan. Mr. Fioroni indicated I could make further arrangements with the girl if I wished. Outside of the office, George and I made an appointment with Miss Camera for Thursday evening.

"Yes, indeed, I would like to come. My sister, a doctor of philosophy, teaches at Brooklyn College; I myself paint during the light hours. But please, just what is it about? It is not clear to me."

I mentioned De Bosis's *Icaro,* how we hoped to work on the choruses. She said she would like to come and would be there Thursday.

Just then, Mr. Fioroni reappeared, closing the door behind him.

"Now, Miss King, what is this poem that you want to do?"

"*Icaro* by Lauro de Bosis."

"De Bosis, the elder or the younger?"

"The young man."

"Are you sure?" He was trying to help me out of it. "If that is the case, we can have nothing to do with it, in any way. That name is tabu."

Was this a twentieth century office building or a primitive jungle of unholy spirits and vicious magic? He turned to Miss Camera and in a torrent of Italian told her the story: airplane, propaganda, credo, Mediterranean. Her face changed.

"Oh, I see," she said hurriedly. "I can have nothing to do with it. It's out of the question."

A few more bursts of Italian between them and she faded away; Fioroni faced us with embarrassment.

"I'm so sorry. I should never have spoken to those people. But you see, it is impossible. But couldn't you use some other poem? We have thousands and thousands of beautiful poems. Like the *Divine Comedy*, or Dante's *Inferno*."

"Unfortunately that is the one poem we wish to do."

"But you see, the man played the government a dirty trick, all the time he was here on government salary he was playing a dirty trick. No one here can have anything to do with anything that concerns Lauro de Bosis. If it were anyone else . . ." A shrug.

We were ready to go, but the Baron, who had joined the society members, started to read Italian poems aloud. Fascinated by the liquid cadence of tone, we listened until the reading was over. As we left, Fioroni, who had been watching George and me all the time, said nothing more about my dancing for them. As we shook hands he said sternly, "Please forget all about it entirely. Assume this has never happened."

Assume it had never happened? Lauro de Bosis had sacrificed his promising young life so that freedom of thought and action could again belong to his people, who no longer had those freedoms. The transcendent vision of one of the world's great heroes could not be ignored or dismissed with silence. I was more determined than ever to do it. Official Italy could not speak his name. Where to go next?

When I appealed by letter to Ruth Draper—an artist whom I revered—her reply was discouraging. She hoped nothing would be done with *Icaro* as a production at this time. Permission would have to be secured from his family in Italy, who were hoping that some day a great composer would make an opera of it. At this moment, for the sake of his family, she hoped nothing whatever would be attempted. She could not understand how we were going to use the poem. I should have gone to see her, but somehow I felt she was inimical. She had given copies of *Icaro* and *Story of My Death* to the libraries where anyone could read them; they were available to the public.

A group of poor dancers working on his poem in America with no hope of "production" of any kind seemed justification to me for my negligence. I was thirty years old, here was the golden apple on the tree of art within reach. Blind with the desire to go ahead with it, I admit to utter ruthlessness. I would not write the De Bosis family to tell them what we wished to do; it would only upset them; no one warned me I could be sued by the De Bosis family. To the Italian government, the work was tabu. I was taking a risk of annoying the fascist officials in America. As far as I know, there were no repercussions in Italy later, nor on culpable me for illegally using the work without permission.

Not long after, at a meeting in the New Dance League's downtown studio, a notice on the bulletin board about Italian lessons caught my eye. Sol Rosenfield, a young Bronx scholar just back from a two-year scholarship in Italy, offered lessons. What a relief to talk to someone who was not afraid of the De Bosis name! Sol himself was agreeable and volunteered to find additional voices for me.

With Sol's tenor voice and Anna Maria Errante and Gwendolyn Mannes in the soprano and alto range, at last we heard the singing Italian lines and I could work on the first strophe:

> L'Universo sfavilla di miracoli;
> ma niun ve n'e che come L'uomo solenda!
> diritto ei marcia tra infiniti ostacolo,
> bello e regale, e niuno sa ove tenda.

> *The universe sparkles with miracles;*
> *but none among them shines like man!*
> *Erect he marches through infinite obstacles,*
> *beautiful and regal—whither, no one knows.*

The first chorus of twelve quatrains had three strophe and three antistrophe. We were going to dance to speech rhythms first; later music would be added for introductions and to bridge the choruses. But the choruses without the actions they summarized were not enough. Two pantomimic scenes would be essential, with music supporting instead of speech. I had much work to do.

> I was born in this century of flying the year one,
> It began as a humming of voices, a soaring, a kind of song.

Thus Seldon Rodman in his poem, "The Airman," describes Lauro de Bosis, who grew up in the century of the air, child of an American mother and a Roman poet father.

Becoming aware of fascism in his native country, De Bosis joined with friends in a secret anti-fascist movement. While he was temporarily living in America, his friends were discovered, sentenced to fifteen years, imprisoned and tortured. One of them received so many facial blows he was permanently deafened. Lauro resolved to return to Rome, to scatter from the air four hundred thousand letters, which he wrote and had printed himself.

As reported in *The Story of My Death*, in a letter written to a French

Eleanor King in Peace, An Allegory. *Photo by Marcus Blechman.*

friend and mailed just before he took off for Rome, Lauro wrote: "The sky of Rome had never been flown by enemy aeroplanes. I shall be the first—I said to myself—and I began at once to prepare the expedition." So in exile Lauro, who couldn't even drive a motorcycle, took flying lessons; word of his first solo flight reached the ears of the fascists. He had to disappear, emerging in England with another name. On the second flight from France, he had an accident with the plane and had to abandon it in a field. Again, he went into hiding. The third attempt on October 31, 1931, succeeded. For half an hour at sunset he flew over the crowded streets of Rome. Four hundred fascist pursuit planes, flying at twice his speed, took after him. The rest is silence. No one knews where he went down, whether like Icarus into the waves or elsewhere. He was thirty years old.

Lauro had translated Aeschylus, Sophocles, and the abridged Frazer's *Golden Bough*, and he had written the introduction to the *Golden Book of Italian Poetry*. *Icaro* received the Olympic Prize for Poetry in Amsterdam in 1928, five years before the poet's act.

Leonard Bacon said of *Icaro* that it was

poetry and not drama—it states simplicities with passion. It is clear. It is anything but the attitudinizing, theoretical, neurotic music to which the times have grown accustomed. And it is full of burning fire. Implicit in every syllable is the sincerity which became a flaming act. De Bosis was himself one of the unified, integrated men to whom he pays tribute in his essay on Italian poetry, whose nature is their art, whose art is their nature.

Though the poem is alive with sharp thought, wisdom beyond the poet's age, and lovely imagery, its virtue and glory is a kind of heroic intensity, which I am convinced circumstance has *not* compelled me to read into it. . . . It was two hundred and eighty-nine years before a statue rose to Giordano Bruno in the square where they burned him. It may take generations, but there will be yet another statue in Italy . . . to courage at least as great as the philosopher Friar's.

Soon after finding my "voices," a bout with the flu laid me up for ten days. Convalescing, I read Tolstoi's *War and Peace*. As soon as I was on my feet, I began restlessly trying to do a dance on this enormous subject. I postured and gestured and felt defeated by the magnitude of the subject, so much vaster than any single individual's symbolic statement. As I labored it came to me that the serious solo form was completely inadequate. Perhaps there was a way of treating the serious subject lightly, to make a point as satire.

Peace, An Allegory comes alive in a silent pantomime: the dancer enters on her toes with tiny fast bourrées, costumed in Greco-Roman style, a padded bosom, a pink chiton, a long blue silver-striped wool

Portrait of Eleanor King by Edward Moeller.

mantle trailing on the ground, a spray of laurel leaves a little too long projecting from the crown of her head. The majestic bosomy lady glides lightly, swiftly about the stage, trying to find a quiet resting place. She lowers her heels, stretches out an arm, mimes playing a harp, enjoying sweet sounds, which are interrupted by disturbances in the distance. She waits for silence, but there is none. She moves to another spot, trying again to produce harmony with her plucking. The third attempt is interrupted so violently she is tossed from side to side by the explosions around her. Moving front, she places index fingers on her mouth to make shushing gesture, and dances to the sad melody and halting rhythm of a Scarlatti sonata with enormous legato gestures, an appeal to the audience to be peaceful. World violence ultimately blows the Lady of the Branch off stage.

George Bockman designed the very successful costume and *Peace, An Allegory* had its premiere at the New School on March 11. George also designed the linen dress, with a wide-rolled collar meant to suggest the stocks, for the Puritan *Summons to Sabbath*. Keith Coppage danced in *Lyric Poetry* (Debussy); *Bravado* (Bach); *Pastorale* (Mozart); *Adolescence* (Debussy) and *Memoranda for Midnight* (Wilckens). Ann Agin danced *Invocation* (percussion) and *De Glory Road* with Edda Hiller.

My first full-length solo recital, with Helen Lanfer accompanying, was for the Westerly (Providence, Rhode Island) Music Club on March 2. The facilities of the library auditorium kept lighting problems to a minimum, fortunately, for I was trying light effects of my own for the first time. "Miss King held her audience and everyone seemed to feel the very definite mood she created in well contrasted dances," was critical help. With this notice and others, I had enough comment to have a publicity folder, with photos by Edward Moeller, printed in brown ink on cream stock. Father paid the thirty-five dollar cost for me, the first financial encouragement from the family.

When my Studio of Acting salary check did not arrive the first week of March, I was embarrassed about not paying the rent. Day after day I put off the morose caretakers of the brownstone, a white-faced couple who looked as if they had always lived underground. I wrote, I telegraphed, but nothing came from Mr. Rollins's office except the report that he had gone to Florida. I returned from stage rehearsal at the Vanderbilt Theatre one Saturday afternoon to find the apartment door chain-locked on the outside. My costumes and make-up, needed for the next day's matinee (sponsored by the Dance Guild), were within. I crept upstairs to Kenny and Herbert who plotted that I should sleep in their living room that night. Herbert would force the key early Sunday morning and I would be able to appear at the theatre.

A very nervous dancer on stage kept looking into the wings dreading to see policemen with a summons and a paddy wagon waiting to take me to jail. The check finally arrived, with no apology. The Studio of Acting director was a smooth talker and always in financial straits. He went on to start a summer theatre in Bar Harbor, Maine, at the end of the season driving rapidly away leaving behind thousands of dollars in debts.

The Dance Guild matinee program offered Miriam Blecher in *Letter to the President* (Moross) and *Official* (Debussy); Blanche Evans in *Resentment, Awareness, Into Action* (a suite, music by Howe); Jane Dudley's *The Dream Ends* (Eisler); *Four Portraits, Swivel Chair Hero* (Honegger), and *Liberal* (Prokofiev); Mary Radin performed *Three Dances of Frustration* (Wilckens-Koss), *Rebel Woman* (Koss), and *War Fragments; Lament* (Shostakovitch), *Widows Waltz* (Hindemith), *Dead Man's March* (Prokofiev).

Mr. Martin, reviewing the concert, found *Peace, an Allegory* a burlesque, genuinely funny low comedy dancing, and *Summons to Sabbath* "equally excellent but in a diametrically opposite key." *Dance Observer*, a monthly edited by Louis Horst as a vehicle for Martha Graham, listed my four dances—the other two being *Earth* and *Tears*—as high points.

Perhaps my defection from the group still rankled with Doris, for when she came to speak on dance and drama to an audience of theatre people and students at the Beekman Towers—a series of lectures sponsored by Mr. Rollins—she was in a bad mood. Arriving twenty minutes before the hour, Doris walked through the ballroom, set up with several hundred chairs. In the powder room she scolded: "You shouldn't invite America's greatest dancer to appear without guaranteeing an audience." Fortunately the room filled up. When Doris spoke, it was to demolish the idea that there could be any connection between dance and drama. To her thinking these were separate entities and never the twain could meet. This was the direction I was groping toward but I could not refute her, not yet having a clear conception of how this could be achieved. Not knowing it had already been perfected in the classical Japanese theatre, which is based on dance.

Paul Love, manager of the New School dance recitals, and variously dance editor for the *World Telegram, Theatre Guild Magazine, Modern Music Quarterly* and *New Theatre Magazine* (to which he also contributed elegant line drawings of such artists as Mei Lan Fang) was interested in the recording and notation of dance. While he lectured on this subject at the New School, I demonstrated for him as he chalked the various styles of notation on a blackboard. Collaborating further, with the assistance of Helen Lanfer, we three train-traveled to Chicago, sitting up all the way there and back, to do one combined lecture-demonstration-recital of modern dance. The fee covered travel, with ten dollars left over for each of us.

Intrada in 6/8 Time, for which Alma Lissow wrote a piano score, was a new opening dance. After the Puritan *Summons to Sabbath,* Paul talked on the background and principles of modern dance innovations which he found in movement (not spectacle as in ballet), in metakinesis (the overtones of movement), in thought and relationships expressed in dynamics or elements of conflict, and in form, which I demonstrated. After intermission, I repeated the *Intrada,* concluding with *Earth, Tears,* and *Peace, An Allegory.* Ann Schumann (Later Halprin), attending her first modern dance concert at the Goodman, said she was terrified by the *Sabbath.*

In June, Elizabeth Timmerman, an actress friend of Kenny's and Herbert's, invited me to do *Peace, An Allegory* at the tryout of a new politico-social revue, *Pins and Needles,* on the Labor Stage. Just a decade before I had started studying for the stage in the Princess Theatre. Now, its baroque velvet elegance replaced by sterner stuff, it had become streamlined, a functional stage painted utilitarian black to accommodate the strivings of the new owners, the richest union in New York, the International Ladies Garment Workers Union.

At the tryout I didn't feel I performed well. My balance was thrown by the 1,000-watt follow-spot that blinded me, filling my eyes with tears when I had to project to the front, which was most of the time. The show itself was delightful, lively, with clever music and lyrics by Harold (Heckie) Rome: "Not Cricket to Picket," "Nobody Makes a Pass at Me," "Sing Me a Song of Social Significance," and "Peace Quartet." Geordie Graham (Martha's sister) acted in the skits and choreographed one of the group dances. The sketches satirized the Boss, the Union Man, Mr. Hearst, Father Coughlin, Al Smith, and J. P. Morgan; the Supreme Court was lampooned. "Mother, Let Freedom Wring!," "Men Awake," "No Time to Sing a Gay Song", testified to the earnestness behind the foolery. Syrjala designed the production, and the young company, including Elizabeth Timmerman as actress and dancer, was full of zeal and enthusiasm. A *Times* man reported of the tryout:

. . . it makes excellent fun of the heavy-handed conventions of the radical

Tempera of Eleanor King by a 10-year-old at Perry Mansfield Theatre and Dance Camp, Steamboat Springs.

stage. It is a little disconcerting, after that, when the show falls into some of
the errors it has just been kidding—when it lapses into the equivalent of a
sentimental torch-song, an awake-and-sing mass chant, or one of those
dynamic group dances which Fanny Brice was supposed to have invalided
forever. But the company will probably get over that.

The strongest propaganda piece on the show was the "Peace Quartet," which featured Eden, Mussolini, Hitler and a Japanese officer.
My *Peace* solo preceded the Quartet, taking some edge off it. When, as
immediately happened, *Pins and Needles* proved a success and moved
to a Broadway theatre for a very long run, *Peace, an Allegory* was
dropped.

Just as well. My summer was to be eventful; Portia Mansfield
invited me to Perry-Mansfield Theatre-Dance Camp in Steamboat
Springs, Colorado, to teach modern dance, where I could try out the
choric movement for *Icaro*. Mr. and Mrs. Love (Ora) were going too.

To Ernestine I wrote:

. . . my dream of going West is coming true. I wrote Portia Mansfield about
my dance project which would require more than three weeks. D. H. was
weekending with her when my letter came; she advised Portia it would be
better if I taught them The Little Group dances like the *Capriole Suite* instead
of working on a long project! But when I saw Portia I convinced her to the
contrary so I have the zestful pleasure feeling I am accomplishing what I
please and not what D. H. thinks I should do. I'm tremendously interested in
choreography now, did I tell you? and can't wait to do this [*Icaro*] Chorus
there. I want to start a school of my own next fall so have to make concert
dates this summer.

My first trip West! What an air of freedom, what exhilaration in the
mountains! The Loves drove out in their little Chevrolet; I made the
trip by bus, sitting tortured and numb through the slums and waste-
land of the Industrial East until we got to Chicago. To uncurl my legs
and recover, I spent two days breathing the fresher air of the Windy
City. Already I was delighting in the openness of the people, feeling a
difference between East and West. From Chicago onward, the horizon opened up more and more; the vast ocean of wheat through
Kansas; the miraculous snow-peaked Rockies, and at last the Colorado road to Steamboat, on the western slope of the Great Divide. I
had only a few days to adjust to the altitude before Paul and I drove
down to Boulder to repeat our lecture-demonstration at the university. Breathing was difficult, but I got through it.

Perry-Mansfield was a rugged but stimulating experience in magnificent Rocky Mountain country. Three fascinating Smith girls ran
it—Portia Mansfield, director of the dance and riding departments

(the camp was a ranch, and horses were popular too); Charlotte Perry, who directed plays and the drama classes; and Helen Smith, a woman of extraordinary perception and sensitivity to people. In addition, notables that summer were Gustav Eckstein, Mrs. Eckstein, who taught Dalcroze, and Alix Young-Maruchess. Everyone in camp began the day with Portia's "body mechanics" exercises to warm up. At 6,000 feet, mornings and evenings were frigid. I taught two classes in the morning and took acting class with Kingo—as Miss Perry was called—getting my first dose of the Stanislavski method. (Kingo had studied in New York with Ouspenskaya of the Moscow Art Theatre.) Afternoons, having only girls to work with, I sketched the Chorus to Glory from *Icaro*. This was presented in the theatre with twelve dancers, four readers speaking in Italian, and incidental music arranged by Alix Young-Maruchess for zither, gong and cymbals.

At the end of the course, Joey Luckie, one of the bright young beginning students, invited me to Santa Fe for ten days of private lessons. Santa Fe was enchantment, the air bouyant, clear and dry so that I skipped with joy instead of walked and wanted to pat every rounded adobe house we passed. The Luckie family sent Joey, her sister and me on excursion to the Indian cliff dwellings at Frijoles Cañon in Bandelier National Park.

On the way purple thunder clouds alternated with black washes of rain and gold swatches of sunshine, with three rainbows visible at once in the sky. At Frijoles the rain caught up with us and we reversed our drive. A flash flood in an arroyo caught our Fred Harvey driver unawares; we drove right into it and sank down until the water reached the door of the car. "What do we do now?" I asked. "Get out," said he. The thick brown current came up to our waists as we waded ashore. A roadside cafe providentially offered haven, towels and hot drinks; then a busload of Indians brought us back to Santa Fe before evening. To feel the earth turn destructive in a liquid way is as alarming as an earthquake.

At the end of ten glorious days in Santa Fe, I climbed into the Loves' car with a kitten they'd adopted, and after five days of driving we reached New York.

Letter to Ernestine, still in Paris:

Domestically after the first of October we (Kenny, Herbert and I) will be all set for *real* studio life at 5 West 12th Street in the most ideal studio I've seen yet in New York. Tamiris and Grace Cornell each had it once. Big living room with fireplace, walk down three steps into studio with skylight, go down trap door to basement with another fireplace—a real old fashioned brick one—plus kitchen, frigidaire, tiled bath etc.

I wish you could be here for the project we are working on now—an independent theatre group with dance as a basis—to embrace pure (concert variety), dramatic dance and the revue form. John Martin has a revue he wants to put on with us. We are studying voice and acting and I've started my verse drama with them. It's exciting to work with all these accomplished dancers—we have Jack and Duds, Tish—(she's married, did you know?)—Ada, Beatrice, Sybil, George, Kenny, Katey and Katherine Litz (now Leeds), twenty altogether; all good workers and fine dancers, something I doubly appreciate after having to stop to teach people how to move all summer.

The idea is that everyone in the organization should be willing and able to direct or choreograph, and call on outside directors if wanted. Doris and Charles are supposed to be intrigued with the idea of dance-theatre, but skeptical. Of course you are one of the people who should be here—but I've talked enough and now its your turn.

Jo and Hermine Schwarz, with Regina Beck, were leaving to go on the road with *Life Begins at 8:40*. John Colman's sister Betty, whose quick wit and radiance added to our joy in life, arrived from England, where she had been with the Jooss Ballet at Dartington Hall. She later became the fourth of the Kenny-Herbert, King-Colman menage. The delightful ground floor apartment on 12th Street had French doors opening onto a spot of garden at the rear. The basement was not supposed to be used for cooking or living quarters, so we quickly threw a rug over the trap door whenever the fire inspectors called. In this studio I devoted a year to *Icaro*, one of the most challenging happy-in-work years of my life.

This year Eugene O'Neill won the Nobel Prize for literature. People were reading Carl Sandburg's *The People, Yes; Gone with the Wind, Listen to a Lonesome Drum* by Carl Carmer, Dale Carnegie's *How to Win Friends and Influence People, Not so Deep as a Well* (Dorothy Parker) and Van Wyck Brooks's *The Flowering of New England*. The Federal Theater project set up its centers from sea to sea: in Atlanta, Boston, Chicago, Denver, Los Angeles, New Orleans, New York, Philadelphia, San Francisco, Seattle.

Gielgud's Hamlet, supported by Lillian Gish as Ophelia and Judith Anderson as the Queen, was the finest *Hamlet* we were to see ever. Robert Sherwood's *Idiot's Delight; You Can't Take It With You; Stage Door; The Women; Tovarich; On Your Toes*, with Balanchine choreography; *The Show Is On* and *Red Hot and Blue* enlivened Broadway. Most significant was Chaplin's film *Modern Times*, an inspired, only too prophetic satire on the mechanization of life.

Stokowski appeared in *One Hundred Men and a Girl* with Deanna Durbin; Hollywood produced *Romeo and Juliet*, with dances by Agnes de Mille, Leslie Howard an intellectual Romeo, and Norma Shearer (Juliet), Basil Rathbone (Tybalt), Edna May Oliver (the Nurse), and

CHAPTER TEN : 1937

Wings; The Theatre Dance Company

L AURO DE B OSIS'S LIFE AND ART, incandescently parallel, drew idealistic youth to the *Icaro* project. Eight dance soloists and seventeen others for the choruses, with musicians and readers—in all thirty people—worked for months for the satisfaction of participating in a work we all believed in. The dancers supplemented the readers' voices with their cries of "Oh," "Ee," "Ai," "Ah," echoed occasional words, and shouted "Nikê! Nikê!" (Victory!) They had to memorize cues, move to Italian speech, feel the rhythmic transitions, sometimes silent, more often with music bridging the verses. It was not easy.

Progress was slow, but from the beginning everyone took to the task with enthusiasm, so that progress was itself a kind of celebration of something that was bigger than we were. I ate, slept, dreamed *Icaro* for nine months, sometimes waking up in the middle of the night to try out the motions I had just dreamed in my sleep. There were occasional low periods when Betty and I subsisted on peanut butter sandwiches for a week at a time. I remember once walking the streets in a euphoric state, having had nothing to eat all day. Of course, I could always go home to Brooklyn for a meal, but I preferred not to.

Grant Code offered us a chance to perform at the Brooklyn Museum Dance Center. Code, editor of the *Brooklyn Museum Magazine* and director of the Dance Center (one of the first in the country to sponsor performing as well as static arts) had been one of the Harvard "Eight" poets. A dance enthusiast himself, he asked me to teach classes and direct a workshop for students there. Then he became interested in *Icaro* and offered us rehearsal performance space. The Museum furnished elegantly printed programs and covered our fifty-dollar musical expense. David Diamond composed a score for piano, percussion and trumpet; Franzisca Boas gave us wonderful rhythms on her drums. The publicity release from the Museum found "some subtle and brilliant effects achieved by a fusion of poetic and dance rhythms and emotional and dramatic effects to which both dance and poetry contribute, a difficult and notable accomplishment."

Icaro opened with the Processional Chorus, "The universe sparkles with miracles," led by four chorus leaders, followed by a Chorus to Glory: Invocation, Celebration (Icaro and the chorus). A mime scene prepared the way for the Chorus to Nikê: Dance of Triumph, Theatre of War, Prophecy and March (leaders and the chorus). Another mime scene was the approach of Theseus of Athens, coming to Crete with the body of Icaro, which the Athenians had seen encircled with lightning as it fell into the sea. The conclusion was a Paeon for Heroes with solos for Irigone, Daedalus, Theseus and Ariadne accompanied by the chorus.

The marble columns of the Sculpture Court were our scenery; the dancers wore black practice clothes, Jack wore white. For symbols of wings, I found some eight-feet by two-inch aluminum molding material, which flashed and rippled when Jack wielded them in the air. The Brooklyn Museum Dance Center's programs, free to the public, began at 10:30 in the morning. Several thousand people filled the place on April 10, 1937.

The soloists, in addition to Jack Cole (Icaro), were Kenneth Bostock (Daedalus), William Bales (Minos), Alice Dudley (Phaedra), George Bockman (Theseus), Ada Korvin (Irigone, Mother of Icaro) and William Miller (the Herald). Sybil Shearer, Katherine Litz and Letitia Ide were splendid Chorus Leaders; Elizabeth Colman, Gloria Garcia, Mary Schultz, Millicent Ellis and Janet Whitemore were the chief choric dancers; and Hugh Chain, William Miller, Louise Allen, Margaret Jones, Virginia Miller, Frances Reed, Eleanor Stauffer, Betty Schlauffer and Ruth White were Athenians.

The experience of no longer directing the choreography, but simply observing it from the farthest corner of the enormous room, was strange, sometimes exciting, but too microscopic to be satisfying. The trumpet theme exalted, Franzisca's percussion gave excellent support, the readers' voices blurred, but even seeing the movement as if

George Bockman as Theseus, with Betty Colman in Icaro. *Photo by Marcus Blechman.*

from the wrong end of a telescope, I was proud of my dancers. A two-page letter came from Doris soon after:

What an enormous undertaking you set for yourself! I've heard about the difficulties [Louise Allen, Bill Bales, George Bockman, Katherine Litz, and Sybil Shearer were in the Humphrey-Weidman Company, whose concert and touring schedule made many conflicts with Icaro rehearsals] and so can appreciate the courage and the purpose it took to pull your "Icaro" together for Saturday. There were lots of parts in it that I found both exciting and satisfying—especially the conclusion and exit in the first part, and the sort of fugue near the beginning of the second part—and there were exceptionally good solo parts. Of course, I realize that was a horrible place to give anything in—especially with voices—but the important thing is that the idea of the form is such a rich one for the theatre (not that I did not know this) and has been given such a fine impetus through your will-to-do. In the group I would especially like to congratulate Alice Dudley both for choreography and expressiveness. I must say I missed your own heroic style though. Things I didn't like so well were the Italian words for the dramatic gestures—I think you really have to understand the meaning of the words to make it clear—unless you want the Italian to function as music. Also I thought the choreography on the whole rather scattered—I would like groups more massive and the phrases longer—I hope you will take this in good part from one who believes in you as a fine artist.

Miss Ruth penciled a note to Jack Cole:

I am fearfully tired from last night—so forgive me for running. You were simply superb! The scene with you and the others Duds [Alice Dudley] was marvelous! Both in feeling as well as technique. As for the composition as a whole, please tell Miss King that her variety and dynamics of pattern are superlatively clever—and her courage in tackling a work of this kind is to *put her in the debt* of all people who are watching the progress of the American dance with real interest. It was splendid from many points of view!
    Later you and I will talk about it in detail—I am glad I came!

On May 2, *Icaro*'s second performance ("We have to dance it more than once," everyone said) had better acoustics in Studio 61, Carnegie Hall. Instead of a thousand people, we had a hundred. The ripples of response were mostly positive, though Maria Theresa Duncan said, "It was not *Greek.*" (We had tried to be pre-Hellenic.) *Dance Magazine*, initiating awards that spring for choreography, ranked Tamiris's *How Long Brethren* and Lily Mehlman's *Harvest Song* as winners, with honorable mention for *Icaro*. Joseph Arnold Kaye wrote:

So ambitious a venture came as a surprise. This is a long dance drama based on an Italian play in verse by the late Lauro de Bosis; it deals with the flight of Icaro in the wings invented by his father Daedalus, and of his fall into the seas

Letitia Ide, Alice Dudley, Ada Korvin, Jack Cole in Icaro. Photo by Marcus Blechman.

Eleanor King in Hornpipe. *Photo by Robert McAfee.*

"encircled by lightning." The conclusion invokes glory to him who dares, a paeon for heroes. Through this creation Miss King raised herself to a high rank among those from whom fine things can be expected. That she realized her aim only in part can well be forgiven. She undertook a large work and it is to her great credit that many portions of it were poignant and exciting . . . the choreographer was faced with the problem of reconciling her modern dance techniques with the antique Greek period. In some of the movements she used the Greek style, but chiefly she worked in her own idiom. The fusion appeared satisfactory because of the common denominator between the free movement of the modern dance and the free movement of the ancient Greek dance . . . both Jack Cole and Alice Dudley approached their new task with what appeared to be devotional respect. The other dancers gave understanding interpretations, particularly William Miller in a small role. Miss King herself did not dance.

The second positive result from that group experience was the emergence of a new Theatre Dance Company. I had declared on leaving Doris that I wanted to work alone, but who wants to dance alone all the time? Dance and theatre, dependent on people, are always experiences to be shared. Ten of the *Icaro* group were enthusiastic about sharing; we formed a cooperative. We would have a training school and a performing company, and each would take turn-about at being choreographer. We had already begun to augment our various theatre-dance backgrounds with classes in diction (taught by Barna Ostertag) and in acting (Mrs. John Martin). We planned to study all the dance styles we hadn't had. Our Advisory Board consisted of Remo Bufano, Grant Code, Agnes de Mille, Louise Martin, Stanley McCandless, and, later, Curt Sachs. John Colman agreed to be our musical director and to give us Dalcroze when he could fit it in.

The ten cooperating members were Bill Bales, George Bockman, Kenneth Bostock, William Miller, Alice Dudley, Fe Alf, Louise Allen, Betty Colman, Sybil Shearer and myself. With ten five-dollar contributions a month, we rented a loft on the fourth floor of 5 East 19th Street. We installed a ballet barre and a floor cloth to cover the rough wood, and George designed and hung aquamarine curtains at the back. With two spotlights we were able to have studio performances. Out of necessity we took to wearing soft ballet slippers.

During the *Icaro* gestation period, we were daily having one-hour diction lessons with Barna, followed by two hours every day with Louise Martin. This generous woman provided us with a technical background in the realm of feeling and acting which proved of inestimable value later on.

I spent the summer at Surry, Maine (where Betty Colman had taught the summer before) working with the Surry Players on movement and choreographing the end dance for *As You Like It*. Most of the actors were unwilling early morning risers—only Shepperd Strudwick and Ann Revere really seriously trained—so I had time to produce a solo concert with some new works: *Warning; March; Lament;* a stark suite to other sections of Reutter's *Die Passionen;* and what turned out to be a slight little piece but far more durable, *Young America Hornpipe*. The program was divided into Old World and New World Dances; *Hornpipe* was the gay conclusion.

Hornpipe was the happy result of my first trip West. I saw the Colorado mountaineers barn dance of a Saturday night when Portia Mansfield took us to Hahns Peak to participate. The character-lined faces, their iron-hard arms and hands, the incredible zest in the ankles of the stalwart mountain people, all amazed me. Back in New York, in three weeks I set the design for the movement, all springy, starting from the image of a ship's figurehead tilted forward, a rather wooden body entering on a zigzag tack, to a Victor recording of hornpipes—"Young America" and "Soldiers Joy." The former was the name of a famous clipper ship which broke the record sailing around the Horn from New York to California. To the alternating lilting and gay melodies, I crisscrossed the stage using folk steps and ideas such as Boxing the Compass, Look Up the Mast, and Blow the Man Down, ending with a series of tilts and runs, a sailor hat lifted and waved for the end runoff.

Alan Handley, sophisticated actor-director, designed the delightful costume: a gathered blue cotton skirt over a red-white striped string petticoat over an unbleached petticoat, and a blue short-sleeved blouse with white sailor collar. I found a round straw hat in Bangor, dyed it black, and added long black ribbons for an enchanting accent. *Hornpipe,* two and a half minutes of continuous bounce, was great fun to do.

The Surry playbill opened with *Candida*—Ann Revere's warm and glowing performance—then *Youth at the Helm, The Nuremburg Egg* and *As You Like It*. The director, Sam Rosen, gave the cast an enlightening interpretation of Shakespeare, according to Karl Marx. Katherine Emery played Rosalind to Shepperd Strudwick's Orlando. The "Peace Ho! I come to bar confusion" lines—usually cut from the play—were given to me in the role of Hymen, for which George Bockman designed the costume in New York. I enjoyed the farcical tying up of knots, the excuse for the general country dance finale to "Rufty-Tufty."

Ann would go on to Hollywood, her career blocked by the House Un-American Activities Committee, organized the year before,

Eleanor King in Hornpipe. *Photo by Barbara Morgan.*

which was beginning to round up suspected Communist sym-
phathizers. Shep, a really fine actor, continued on Broadway with
increasing success. Wittner Bissel (Marchbanks), Norman Budd (Old
Adam), Peter Hobbs, Jabez Gray, Boyd Smith, Edwin Shaw and
Helen Wynne (Shep's wife, Betty Colman's cousin) were among the
players. They had several seasons in Maine and one on Broadway.
Then they, too, folded.

Back in New York, Eugene Goossens' piano music *Hurdy-Gurdy*
started me on a city piece, a contrast to the *Hornpipe*. The image of a
city child in between tenements, with no space to move, hearing a
hurdy-gurdy, trying to dance without knowing how, worked out
quickly. Then I chose "Camptown Races" to make a fast-moving,
city-style syncopated dance called *Hoe-Down*, influenced by the
currently popular Big Apple. With these added to the Hornpipe, I
had an American dance suite of nineteenth and twentieth century
rural and urban movements. On October 31 the YMHA gave the
chance to try it out on a program shared with Lil Liandré and Mary
Radin. Reviewing that concert, Joseph Arnold Kaye hailed it in *Dance
Magazine:*

A new American Folk Suite should be one of the outstanding compositions of
the season. It consists of Hornpipe, Hurdy-Gurdy, and Hoe-Down, music
for the first a traditional tune, and the other two by Goossens and Foster-
Nordhoff, respectively.
Miss King showed fine ability last year as choreographer for the ambitious
Icaro. In The American Folk Suite she was both choreographer and dancer. It
is a work deriving its inspiration from native life, and while preserving the
folk quality and good dance rhythms, is refined for concert purposes with
true artist's feeling and taste.
Prophecy is a risky business, but I want to wave the flag for Eleanor King
and predict that she will rise high as a creator of American dance.

The *Daily Worker's* critic, Margery Dana, thought:

Miss King's work showed the most consistent development. Her interest in
and approach to folk material (exemplified in the Hornpipe of her American
Suite) is engagingly direct and original, and her dances always move, even
though sometimes, in larger themes, such as "Renascence" a somewhat
mystical tint obscures the point.

A Theatre Dance Company! What a good idea we had! With Leon
Arkus's help we managed a sixteen-page brochure outlining our
purpose, which its pages said was twofold:

First, to adhere strictly to the highest principles of the dance, and second, to translate this artistic integrity into a vital form of popular entertainment.

Where the more conservative organizations of this sort have been inclined to ignore the drama, the THEATRE DANCE COMPANY is convinced that the dance form is most nearly itself when allied to the theatre. This, in fact, is the idea behind the very title of the group. Thus—since rhythmic sound, both vocal and instrumental, is one of the elements of the dance—the philosophy of the THEATRE DANCE COMPANY is a synthesis of music, the dance and the theatre. The revolutionary notion behind it all is attested by these comments of Mr. John Martin, the celebrated dance critic of the New York Times:

. . . Already we hear murmurings about something called "dance-drama." . . . If it can be captured and turned to dramatic uses, it will inevitably provide a new technique for the actor's art and a revolution in theatre tactics.

We would combine the techniques of dance and drama to produce a repertory of original works culminating in a resident theatre, a touring company and a permanent training school. Our purpose was to use the dance as a dramatic medium, at once artistic and entertaining to the general audience; to present ballets on historical, topical, imaginative subjects, the form and style of each determined by its content; the range of subject to be as comprehensive as possible and as diversified as the ideas of the ten artists.

The prospective repertoire listed thirteen ballets: *At the Fall of an Age* (William Miller's dance-drama based on Robinson Jeffers' poem concerning the legend of Helen's death on the island of Rhodes); *Devotional* (Alice Dudley), a cathedral mood for five dancers (Debussy); *A Fable* (Sybil Shearer), eight animal characters with an entertaining moral; *Folk Suite* (Eleanor King), traditional music (on accordion), Hornpipe, Hurdy-Gurdy, Hoe-Down; *Night Court* (Eleanor King); *Parade* (Kenneth Bostock); *Parodisms* (Elizabeth Colman) to Walton's *Facade Suite*, five dancers; *Relics* (Elizabeth Colman), a fantasy on present day economics, music by John Colman; and *Witches Sabbath* (Alice Dudley) to music by John Colman.

Of the plenitude of ideas, five were achieved before the advent of World War II aborted the rest.

Graduates of the three-year training course would become eligible for the professional company. The three-year curriculum was well planned. From the perspective of today, one essential I see lacking was the study of mime. In 1937 this concept of theatre was undeveloped. Except for Angna Enters, we had no mime in America. I did not see Marcel Marceau in Paris until 1952.

First-year students would have one hour of daily practice each in body technique and in ballet and dramatic improvisation, with one hour weekly of eurythmics, solfège, choral singing and national dance styles. In the spring term, dramatic improvisation would have two hours per week.

In the second year body technique and ballet continue; pre-classic dance styles replace national dance styles; eurythmics and solfège continue; and composition and make-up, one year each, are added.

In the third year body technique as basic continues; dance styles of the nineteenth and twentieth centuries replace ballet; choral singing, composition, and dramatic improvisation have two hours a week each.

The concept, the goals, the outline were promising. We looked for scholarship money to run the school, which would in turn subsidize the company. Betty's and John's Dartington connection provided entrée to Mrs. Leonard Elmhirst (through Mrs. Natalie Dana, secretary of the Whitney Foundation), who expressed interest; and Maurice Wertheim, one of the board directing the Theatre Guild, was known to be interested in advancing theatre affairs.

One day Betty and I, in our best clothes, armed with our beautiful prospectus, took the subway downtown to Wall Street and ascended one of the skyscrapers nearly to the top. We crossed marble floors to enter Mr. Wertheim's Renaissance law office with a breathtaking view of the harbor below. Mr. Wertheim sat behind a big desk. A mild-looking man, he gravely examined our literature; he heard our story and gave us hope.

We were asking for $12,650 as the first year's running expenses for the school, the company, the musical director, the management, the costumes, booking, mailing. The company member instructors would be paid $2 per hour for teaching. Full-time services of the dancers would be rewarded with $20 per week for fifty weeks. Three new ballets per year, one of which would be a large work, would be costumed for $400. Students taking classes would pay $1 per hour. Fifty-one students taking one class a week, or twenty-six taking two classes a week, would be enough to guarantee the studio and external company expenses.

Mr. Wertheim offered to give us a sum, provided Mrs. Elmhirst matched it, on condition that the Theatre Dance Company became incorporated as a nonprofit institution in the State of New York. All we needed was a lawyer to draw up the papers, a simple process taking a month to six weeks for approval from Albany, and fifty dollars.

How elated Betty and I, then the whole group, were! We had just given some studio performances of the ready repertory, and after one of these, Mr. Freidman, a lawyer friend of one of the boys, expressed interest in helping us on to "deserved fame and fortune." For the fifty-dollar fee, he would draw up the papers, we would be incorporated, then funded, and on our way. That month all the members scraped up an additional five dollars apiece to pay the man who was so impressed with our worth. We paid him. We never saw him again. He had found us, but we couldn't find him. Strangely, he seemed to have no address; there was no way of tracking him down. He left town with our precious money, taking our hopes with him.

Even if he had been honest and the incorporation had come through, it wouldn't have mattered. Fate determined that our plans were in advance of the times. Mrs. Elmhirst's funds were now tied up in Britain, and she could not help. Without her start, Mr. Wertheim would not contribute. Our dreams folded; we put them away. Three of the group, active members of the Humphrey-Weidman company, continued to tour and perform in concert with Doris and Charles. Alice and Kenny paired as a nightclub dance team; Louise Allen left for social work in Philadelphia; Bill Miller retired to a turkey farm; Fe ran her own studio. Betty and I were left with a few students, including Ellinor Westerling from Amsterdam, to teach.

This was the year the Big Apple, a modified square dance originating with Carolina students, became a national craze. Benny Goodman, King of Swing, drew frenzied youthful audiences, who danced in the aisle of the Paramount Theatre. The current slang was of jitterbugs, in the groove, boogie-woogie, jam sessions, killer-dillers. Gian Carlo Menotti composed his *Amelia Goes to the Ball*; Archibald MacLeish's *The Fall of The City*, a radio drama, had music by Bernard Herrmann. Ernest Hemingway published *To Have and Have Not*; John Steinbeck, *Of Mice and Men*; Elliot Paul, *Life and Death of a Spanish Town*; and John Marquand, *The Late George Apley*.

Orson Welles was a memorable Faustus in Marlowe's *Dr. Faustus*; Maurice Evans appeared in *Richard II*; and the Mercury Theatre easily transposed *Julius Caesar* into a fascist plot by using modern dress. *I'd Rather Be Right* tried to follow in the footsteps of *As Thousands Cheer*. *The Eternal Road* employed hundreds of dancers in an epic history of the Jews. Surprises of the year were *Pins and Needles* and Marc Blitzstein's *The Cradle Will Rock*, which, banned by the WPA Federal Theatre, moved from the Mercury to the Windsor Theatre. There, without scenery and with only piano accompaniment, it played 108 performances.

In films, we saw *The Good Earth* with Luise Rainer; *Lost Horizon,*

Bennington;
Ballet Intime

THE THIRD *ICARO* RESULT, a fellowship at Bennington, was one of three offered to Louise Kloepper, Marian Van Tuyl and myself. The year before, the Fellows were José, Anna Sokolow and Esther Junger. The fellowship meant full production of new choreography scheduled for opening night of the Bennington Dance Festival's fifth season, having the best of young dance students to choose from, costumes and music supplied, and Arch Lauterer to design a set.

Before going to Vermont, John Colman found and played music from the Brown University Collection of Early American Music. For a large group work, we decided on *The American Hero*—"A Sapphick Ode by Nathaniel Niles, A. M. Norwich, Connecticut 1775. This stark and splendid song was sung everywhere in camps, churches and public meetings; it summed up the hopes and fears of the rebellious colonies." John wrote an exciting prelude and planned three sung verses with the original score, thematic development to come between verses. I sketched a flying entrance of women distraught by war, running on in pairs, singles and trios, fugue form, and departed for Bennington with high hopes.

Bennington, that idyllic spot in the Vermont hills, in theory so liberating and inspiring, with all conditions met for creating dance, was divided that summer into armed camps. The big four—Martha Graham, Doris Humphrey, Charles Weidman, Hanya Holm—were all there working on big group works. As usual, Graham dancers were forbidden to speak to other dancers. Though the Holm dancers were friendly, cliquishness and factionalism prevailed. This was the fifth and final year of the Bennington Plan; the next season it would be transferred to Mills College. After the war it became the American Dance Festival at Connecticut College.

To start the day, I took morning technique classes with Hanya Holm, and otherwise spent the time composing and rehearsing with the delightful, spirited young dancers who opted for my project: Jean Aubry, Jane Forte, Wanda Graham, Mildred Rhea Shaw from New Orleans, Margot Harper, Gertrude Lippincott, Alice M. Mulcahy, Marian Ryder, Ann Schumann (Halprin), Marty Starks. John's brilliant improvisations, which he had promised to write and send, never arrived. Norman Lloyd came to the rescue and did what had to

John Colman.

be done, arranging the voice parts and adding percussion to tie it together.

Betty Joiner's costumes for the *Ode to Freedom* were splendid: black stripes painted on reds and grays of the individually different woolen tunics (supplied by Vermont sheep) on long side-slashed cotton skirts, with cylindrical bonnets open at the top from which pony tails hung out. Lauterer's skeletal set, a number of poles, outlined an abstract setting. With Norman Lloyd's completion of the music, and Ruth Lloyd among other singers, the *Ode* was moving to hear; at the first run-through, Martha Hill had tears in her eyes.

The second work I chose for Bennington was the *American Folk Suite*, expanded from solo to small group. Instead of the Hurdy-Gurdy, the "Bonja Song"—one of the oldest burnt-cork melodies (1820) written for the bonja or primitive banjo (Brown University Collection)—developed into a trio for Wanda Graham, Ann Schumann, and me. George Bockman designed big polka-dotted red skirts for the girls; Macy's supplied blue bellbottom trousers and striped T-shirts for the men. The folk music was played on two pianos by Norman and Ruth Lloyd.

The performances were advanced a week. Graham persisted in her recluse mystique. Two teachers from Hawaii who had to leave before the Festival were refused permission to attend a rehearsal of her new opus, whose very name was kept secret. Pauline encouraged me by reporting that my ten girls were enthusiastic, and I was proud of the way they danced. Alphabetically, my name was first on the initial program so the *Ode*, a heavy piece for the opening work, was in the wrong place; *Folk Suite* closed. In between, we heard the audience stamp their feet and beat a tattoo on the railings for their favorite, Louise Kloepper, an exquisite dancer whose solo, *Statement of Dissent* (Gregory Tucker), was a great success. Her other solo was *Romantic Theme* (Harvey Pollins); her group of nine dancers appeared in *Earth Saga*. Marian Van Tuyl from Chicago opened with a solo, *Directions: Flight, Indecision, Redirection* (Lopatnikoff), followed by *Out of One Happening* (Tucker); and, with a group of nine, *In the Clearing* (Tucker).

Reaction to the *Folk Suite* surprised me. At that purely abstract stage of modern dance, it was considered "unorthodox." Louis Horst was horrified at my use of traditional music. A year later Doris would do her *Square Dances;* four years later, Agnes de Mille, building on the identical experience in Colorado, would unite folk material with ballet to make *Rodeo* into an American institution. Though ruling opinion at Bennington was negative, Curt Sachs, who lectured to us

George Bockman and Ann Schumann (Halprin) in Hornpipe. Photo by Barbara Morgan.

on music and stayed for the Festival, said "the *Hornpipe* is really dancing." When the Festival was breaking up, Martha Graham told me she was very interested in the *Ode*. Doris said nothing at all to me, but to Bales and Bockman she said she should have done the *Ode to Freedom*.

Doris's big work that year was the monumental Bach *Passacaglia and Fugue*. One of her masterpieces of design, she was unmercifully criticized for going "Bach-ward," even though she was speaking of the good life in affirmative and noble terms on a level with Bach's music. In line with the political temper of the times, many people objected to art without immediate social significance. The choreography was so sculpturally designed I would like to have seen it without music, or even with another score written for it; it could stand alone.

Charles's zany *Opus 51*, a collection of abstractions of gesture based on mime, was hilarious, inventive, endlessly surprising. Hanya Holm's *Dance of Work and Play* was a typical space excursion, clean, usual; Graham was the most controversial. The secret opus turned out to be *American Document*, with a Mr. Interlocutor, quotations from the Declaration of Independence, words spoken by Chief Joseph (the Nez Percé Indian); Puritan Episode, a love duet with Erick Hawkins to selections from *The Song of Songs*, and a Cakewalk at the end. We were used to seeing Martha and Erick walk hand in hand over the meadows that summer; their marriage was announced at the end of the season, much to Louis Horst's disgust: affairs, yes; marriage for artists, no.

In the *Times*, Martin wrote:

Though as with most dance works whose program is dictated by a literary antecedent, it [*Ode*] is inclined to be obscure choreographically, it has some fine phrases of movement and some beautiful movements. At present the solo role dance by Miss King is underwritten, but the design of its relation to the group is excellent and rich in possibilities. Miss King also presented an "American Folk Suite" at the end of the evening, the intention of which was no doubt merely to bring the curtain down on a gay note. Of the three dances which comprise the suite, the last one, a Hornpipe, is much the best. All of them, however, though cute enough, are inconsequential and truth to tell, inclined to be a bit inexpert.

His summing up later, in the same vein:

"Ode to Freedom" was a distinguished piece of work and revealed not only the effect of several years of discipleship under Doris Humphrey but a marked personal gift for work in this medium. Miss King has made a fine and convincing number of it choreographically. It is based on a Revolutionary

Bennington performance of Ode to Freedom.

War hymn, the argument of which is that a man's life is a small thing to lose in so great a cause. Her "American Folk Suite" was not so distinguished, largely because it had at least one eye on the music hall.

Joseph Arnold Kaye, in *Dance Magazine,* found that the *Ode*

has a fine bold opening, but the development is not very clear and only moderately successful in its purely dance elements. The resolution at the finish is good, the marching formation giving one a hymnal sense of devotion to country, which is the theme of the poetry.

A second work, American Folk Suite, contained two dances presented by her a year ago and a new one, Bonja. The original suite was given honorable mention in this year's Dance awards for choreography, but as seen here, it still lacked the quality to make it a work of first class. The fault lay in the meagre development. The dances—Hoe-Down, Hornpipe, and Bonja—were little more than sketches. They proved to be attractive enough, and colorful, but too much like light vaudeville.

Margaret Lloyd, in the *Christian Science Monitor,* differed:

Contrary to surrounding comment, I did not find it (the folk suite) trivial in the least, but after an evening of watching the try-out of young wings in solemn parabolas, of listening to . . . ineffectual music, rejoiced in its light-ness and gaiety, its (in this environment) almost unorthodox steps and patterns, its music arranged from traditional sources. I relished too the compatible insouciance of George Bockman's dress designs.

Mary Jo Shelley was particularly delighted with the folk suite; at the closing party she commanded a *Hornpipe* performance. Martha Hill thought I was the white hope of American folk dance and urged me to apply for a Guggenheim research grant to pursue it. Katey Manning and I piled luggage into her car and left very sleepily the next morning. About mid-afternoon on the road, when both of us were dozing, the car hit another car. No one was injured, but we had to abandon the Manning car and continue by bus to Saddle River, where Katey's parents lived. When we recovered, we played four-handed Bach at the piano, our usual consoling diversion. After ten years with Doris, Katey went on to Chicago University that fall to teach in the dance department there.

Dance Magazine later featured an article by the composer Glenn Bacon, titled, "Look Homeward, Americans," illustrated with a pic-ture of Graham's *Frontier* and of Bales, Bockman, Ann Schumann and me in *Hoe-Down.* He urged dancers to consider native material:

Only now are dancers beginning to turn their attention to the real fabulous wealth of historic and contemporary material of this country. We have for so long been awed by the great historic pageantry of Europe that our own incredible backgrounds have not been given their proper place in artistic expressions.

Both American music and dance are far behind the other arts in the pioneering toward what will be, as nearly as possible, an American Expression.

This was the year when twenty-five bands played a Carnival of Swing at Randalls Island for 23,000 jitterbugs. The *Times* reported that the park officers and police had all they could do to protect the players "from destruction by admiration."

Thornton Wilder's *Our Town* won the Pulitzer Prize for drama. Robert Emmett Sherwood's *Abe Lincoln In Illinois, Knickerbocker Holiday*, an all-Negro *Mikado* in Chicago's WPA Theatre (changed to *The Hot Mikado* on Broadway), *The Boys from Syracuse, Hellzapoppin'* (a vaudeville with ducks and geese flapping up from orchestra seats), *Kiss the Boys Goodbye, Outward Bound, On Borrowed Time* and *I Married an Angel* were theatrical successes.

The Theatre Dance Company went to work composing, rehearsing, teaching and—a new departure for me—studying ballet and Jooss technique. Atty Van den Berg, a charming Dutch dancer now living in New York, gave us Jooss technique, with its Laban-based spatial emphasis and its balletically turned out feet. First Ruthanna Boris, then Margaret Sande, disciplined us with ballet at the barre and center floor. Boris in Russian style; Sande, a pupil of Luigi

Eleanor King and Mary Jo Shelley backstage at the Bennington Festival. Photo by Barbara Morgan.

Albertieri—himself a pupil of Enrico Cecchetti—gave us the Italian method. As a group, we began to dance better, with more finish. I regretted that I had not had ballet sooner; brilliant foot and leg work was never my forte. The *Bonja Song* would have been much better if I had known more ballet and something about tap dance too.

We prepared for a January YMHA Theatre Dance Company concert, reveling in *Parodisms,* a suite of seven dances to Walton's orchestration of the *Facade Suite.* Betty Colman had tried it out as a solo in London to Edith Sitwell's voice recording. Made into a dance for five acrobats, who bring on a clothes-tree hung with props and costumes (changed on stage), it was farcical relief from the somberness of *Icaro.* We opened with Fanfare, circus style; a Polka, with Colonel Dilly Dally (Bill Bales), Louise Allen and Betty as the Girls; Alpine Echoes, a travesty on William Tell and his son, who after father pulled the bow, quickly thrust an arrow pulled from his leotard into the apple on top of his head. The three girls twirled ruffled boas and parasols in Popular Song; the two boys contested in Scottish games in Highland Fling; Bill Miller as Manuel, reluctant to face his impassioned partner Rosita in Tango, crept away hiding behind his Spanish ball-fringed hat; the five of us waltzed together for the finale. Norma Fuller's costumes were apt; the clothes-tree setting dressed the stage and gave opportunities for some surreal humor.

Another light number was Sybil Shearer's *A Fable,* characterized with Mr. Cat, Mlle. Horse, Dame Lion, Mr. Ostrich, Widow Duck, Miss Chick and a pair of uninvited Mice (music by J. P. Sondheimer). Alice Dudley's *Devotional,* for five with Denishawn overtones; Sybil's and George's *Coronation* duet (Satie) were smaller works. The major piece was a cut version of *Icaro,* with Jack Cole again in the lead, plus Jennifer Chatfield, Gloria Garcia, Helene Hetzel, and Janet Whitmore to swell the chorus. The shallow YMHA stage restricted the chorus to fifteen instead of thirty. *Dance Observer* reported of the performance:

"Icaro"—ending before the tragic denouement with the Chorus to Nike, celebrating the first flight as a "new freedom, a victory of universal brotherhood," received six curtain calls. The first two sections, Processional and Chorus to Glory, seem the most effective. They fill the stage with color and movement. The measured tread and style of the dancers, the costumes and the sense of impending drama key the dance at a high pitch. And "Parodisms" won solid success, as a completely meritorious piece of "surrealist" humor.

In December, Klarna Pinska, who for years taught Denishawn children's classes, visited me one day at the studio, inviting me to choreograph *A Song About America,* written by Hoffman Hays, with

Eleanor King, William Miller, William Bales in Parodisms.

Eleanor King and William Miller in Parodisms.

music by Herbert Hauffreucht, to be given in Madison Square Garden in January. I could compose for a forty-foot square stage with steps leading up to it on four sides, with an audience of twenty-two thousand people. Seduced by her "You are the only one who has real feeling for folk material," by the promise of a group of ten men and ten women dancers to work with, and by the challenge of that open square stage, I was flattered into it, although the sponsors were the Communist Party and I was not a Communist. The work was to span 150 years of American history to show, in Lenin's words, that "America has a revolutionary tradition"; the date, January 23, fifteenth anniversary of the death of V. I. Lenin. The play would use 250 actors and orchestral and vocal music, everything for the dance would be provided. I would not be paid, except for the private satisfaction of testing my ability to handle large-scale folk material. The scenario began with immigrating men and women with shawls on their heads and carrying bundles, a diaspora, the cultivation of the land, and building the first railroad to the West. In a grubby studio downtown, I began rehearsing the dancers.

The strange year, which saw the House Un-American Activities Committee begin its work, brought Thomas Mann to America; Pearl Buck won the Nobel Prize for Literature; John Gould Fletcher's selected poems won the Pulitzer Prize, and the Orson Welles *War of the Worlds* radio broadcast was so realistic it caused public panic.

Vassar College provided the Theatre Dance Company's first touring date, January 14. Sidney Stark and Ellinor Westerling, our young Dutch student from Amsterdam, and Willem Van Loon joined the company for *Folk Suite*, *Fable*, *Ode To Freedom*, *Parodisms* and George's new ironic suite, *Biography of a Hero:* Adolescence, Reminiscence, Courtship, Celebration and Parade—"another opportunity for blind celebration."

Bonja was dropped from the *Folk Suite*; and Hurdy-Gurdy was made into a boy-girl duet of slum children for Kenny and me. The college paper noted "innovative new technique used: costumes, scenery, speech added to effect the dance"—a new attitude toward form joined with the use of current, pertinent matter:

Folk Suite was notable for the excellent technique of the dancers, who have a large repertoire of interesting and unusual movements, good floor patterns and delightful music.

The Ode . . . accompanied by a trio who sang a "Yankee War Hymn" [had] extraordinary delineation of individual character in the mass, and stimulating floor and movement patterns, with effective counterpointing. Both dancers and audience evidently enjoyed the last number, Parodisms, a burlesque of William Tell, a Highland Fling and a tempestuous Tango. Timing was perfect. Every opportunity for comedy-situation, pantomime, costume, exaggeration of movement—was cleverly used.

The dancing was uniformly well controlled and sensitive throughout. The use of theatrical technique, although still in the formative stage, has already evoked wide imitation. The company is young, intelligent, and up and coming in the dance world.

The next day, the company appeared at Mecca Temple on a big program including Benjamin Zemach and the Freiheit Gesang Verein; Juan Martinez with Antonita, José Limón with Katherine Litz, Demetrius Vilan, Anna Sokolow and Dance Unit, Miriam Blecher, and Bill Matons with Ailes Gilmour.

The *Billboard* of January 21 recognized the company as

the dance group that has been attracting attention because of its efforts to theatricalize and make more commercial the modern dance. The dancers are successfully getting away from the now heavily stylized modernistic movements and are doing a good job with both heavy dramatic and lighter comedy subjects. The program's highlight was Ode To Freedom . . . the finale was outstanding too. It was a group of special numbers that were snappy and understandable—a miracle for modern dancing.

Miss Dana of the *Daily Worker* previously hailed us as a "Dance Cooperative Going Places" before our series of studio concerts (subscription fifty cents) on November 3, 4, 6. We were "a cooperative in the best sense, a group with its feet on the ground, bodies full of the joy of living, and heads full of fresh ideas."

Now she found flaws:

. . . this company has unique gifts and a great deal in its favor. Yet the limited conception in approach to material—the weakness in "Biography of a Hero" was the emphasis upon attacking human frailty in a negative sense. Ode to Freedom . . . done with chorus and orchestra, and in an almost classic-tragic style which is also suggested by the costumes and indicated in the title. Yet it is based on American Revolutionary material. The approach here, while intentional, seems an arbitrary one; and its effect was further confused, unfortunately, by the fact that the orchestral accompaniment was too strong, the lyrics indistinguishable on the general din.

For the first time the *Ode* had full orchestral accompaniment, Arthur Mendel conducting the musicians with the Arthur Mendel Chorus, and with Gladys Lea, soprano. The age-old battle between words and action, as in opera, may have baffled the audience, but again as in opera, it is the emotional timbre which moves us, not the specific literal words. The text, unfortunately, was not printed in the program.

Sybil's solo suite after Breughel, *The Battle of Carnival and Lent* (in the street, game playing; in the church; in the street, dancing) had a "stunning costume inspired directly by the Breughel painting [which] added much to this dance."

Rehearsals for *Song About America* were more difficult than I had anticipated. Attendance of the dancers was erratic, especially the Negro boys from Harlem. One of the weakest dancers, who always wore pale lavender satin shirts to rehearse, caused trouble. The day before the final rehearsal, when we would move onto the Garden stage, I asked the group to go through it as they would in performance, without a pause. The Building the Railroad section required strenuous falls by the men—rolling over like logs, rising and falling again repeatedly: "Laying down the ties."

"Ah'm not goin to git mah clean shirt dirty on that floor," the lavender lily boy objected.

"Anyone who can't demonstrate that he knows his part now cannot perform," I said.

Since I was responsible for the dance I had to be certain at this last rehearsal that the dance was performance-ready. Still the boy refused. Klarna, who was watching, quickly stopped the rehearsal and called a conference with committee members outside.

The committee, agitated, did not want any hard feelings, especially with Negroes. I explained that it was not a matter of skin color, only of artistic responsibility. Either he could demonstrate he knew the dance or he couldn't dance it. The committee withdrew to consider the problem. At last, someone thought of a solution: a red carpet was brought in and rolled out on the floor. Even so, the boy, who had missed more than any of the others, did not turn up for the performance the next day after all.

John Cambridge in the *Daily Worker* reviewed the affair, admitting a few flaws:

The things that really mattered were the Boston Tea Party, the whooping Indians, the dispossession of the Negro farmers after the Civil War, and the beautiful dance to "Song About America," and the poignant and ingeniously stated Haymarket execution.

The next invitation to choreograph came from Wilson Williams, on the theme of Br'er Rabbit and de Tar Baby, for his all-Negro group from Harlem. I had grown up on Joel Chandler Harris as a child—except for *Tom Sawyer* and *Huckleberry Finn*, no book was more lov-

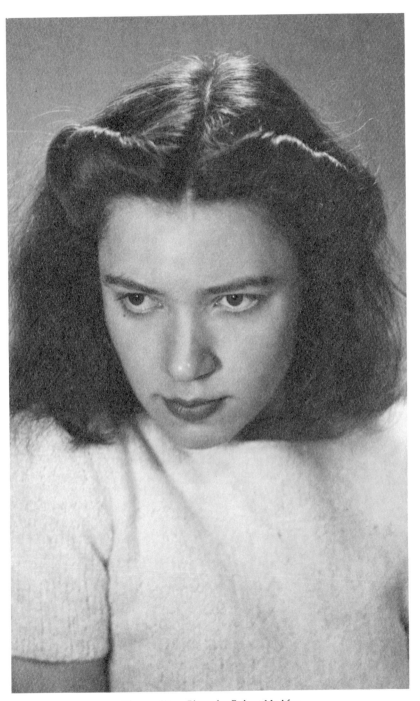

Eleanor King. Photo by Robert McAfee.

ingly read to pieces by all the King children. For three weeks Herbert Hauffreucht, commissioned to write the score, and I together sketched and outlined the ballet. Finally rehearsals, arranged at the Theatre Dance Company studio, began. If the dancers on call for the Communists were erratic and undependable, the Harlem dancers were even more evanescent. At first only two, later four or five showed up, always late. Worse, the movements I sketched out for them they couldn't retain. Or count. It was very frustrating.

After two weeks of this, Wilson Williams himself left town. He had talked of performance royalties; Herbert Hauffrecht was going full steam ahead on the score, but the ballet died before it was born. A terrible obstacle, Wilson said, was the matter of carfare from Harlem. Most of the time the members of the company didn't have it. But there was no rehearsal hall in Harlem to which I could have gone.

Later I realized my mistake, I should not have imposed my style on them, but should have built on their innate ease of movement and sense of rhythm and worked out the dance from there.

As soloist, I was invited to appear on March 17 at the Master Institute Theatre (the Roerich Museum) in a program presented by the American Dance Association, with Pauline Koner, Lillian Shapiro, Ailes Gilmour and Bill Matons. Margaret Purcell played accordion for *Hornpipe, Hurdy-Gurdy* and *Hoe-Down*, with John Colman at the piano for *Mother of Tears* and *Song of Earth*. Ailes Gilmour—the beautiful part-Japanese part-American girl, sister of Isamu Noguchi, the sculptor-designer—danced *Primitive Holiday* (Villa-Lobos) and *Word Day Dreams*, based on Sean O'Casey's story of a drudge, "The Star Jazzer." Bill Matons danced *Escape* (trapped, a young man turns to crime as a way out) to Kenneth Fearing's poem. Together they danced *American Rhapsody*, music by Clair Leonard, poetry by Fearing; and *Wally and Eddy*, a calypso satire on the importance of kings. In this, Bill, as Eddy, played with a yo-yo; Ailes danced as Wally, with a handkerchief.

Lillian Shapero, long a soloist in the Graham company, performed *Song of the Harvest* (Krennifokk); *Dance of the Steppe* (Weprik); *Young America Suite:* To Begin, March, Reverie, To End (Ray Green); and *Holiday* (Joseph Achron).

Pauline Koner presented *Two Soviet Songs:* "Lullaby to a Future Hero" (Myaskovsky, arranged by Harvey Brown) and "Harvest Festival" (Vasiliev-Buglai, arranged by Colman); *Among the Ruins* (Brant); *Yemenite Prayer* (folk song arranged by Brown); and a pas de deux from *Surrealist Sketches* (Chopin), a clever parody of ballet (Pauline's perfect technique came from her study with Fokine) in which she used gloved arms instead of legs.

Before the concert started, I happened to overhear a conversation between two unknown, unseen women of the audience who were anticipating the performance. The one who said, "King is the one who dances with a soul," helped to sustain my ego for many dreary months.

The thunder and lightning of war had begun: on March 13, Hitler marched into Austria; the Republic of Czechoslovakia was dissolved the next day; the Nazis were in Bohemia, Moravia, Memel. The Hungarians were in the Carpatho-Ukraine; the Japanese had seized Manchukuo. Germany and Italy had signed a ten-year military pact on May 22.

Ellinor Westerling spoke of returning to Holland for the summer. "There *can't* be a European war," she said hopefully. The Theatre Dance Company, so lovingly launched, was falling apart: Louise left for social work in Philadelphia, Betty was to marry William Snaith, a designer with Loewey, Inc.; Kenny and Alice were busy dancing in night spots; Bales, Bockman and Shearer were touring with Doris and Charles.

It is one thing to meet an artist socially, another to work with the person professionally. My previous meetings with Miss Ruth, social or semi-professional when helping with the Blechman photography, had been brief encounters. Now, thanks to Jack, I could appreciate her professionalism, having been given opportunity to dance with her at Adelphi College. Jack had just begun to make a name for himself on Broadway, performing classical Hindu to jazz music in a spectacular way at the Rainbow Room. A Denishawn product, he was naturally attracted to Oriental ritual. Miss Ruth had recently been appointed nominal head of a new dance department at Adelphi College, where Jack, Anna Austin or other Denishawn dancers did most of the teaching for her.

Yearning to do something more sacred and less secular, Jack saw a mystical vision of Miss Ruth as catalyst for blending rites of Osiris with the Passion of Christ. It was a large project involving two choruses, one of professional dancers, the other of college students. Jack asked me to be chorus leader. Sparing no expense, he hired a Broadway composer, union musicians and theatrically made costumes. The dancers performed for the privilege; we rehearsed weekends in the college gymnasium.

The opening processional started well, dancers appearing two by two, with Egyptian arms raised like ceremonial branches, wrists rotated inward, fingers stretched apart. Arriving at the step levels to the stage, we dropped the mudra-like homage to Osiris, bunching into small groups for the Christian zone with spoken texts selected from St. John of Revelations and other Evangelists. Originally Jack intended to have choric speaking from all the dancers but the mixture of accents defeated the plan. The only enunciators he could abide were Miss Ruth and me. Striding a few steps, standing still to deliver lines, I found myself alternating with her, sometimes the impersonal narrator, variously, more uncomfortably, as St. John, Angel Gabriel, Joseph, Mary, Pontius Pilate, Judas, St. Peter. Ultimately, it fell to Miss Ruth's lot to stretch out her arms in a T shape, to become Jesus Christ himself, crucified. Around her figure, I stalked in a circle, spitting and miming flagellation.

No one is more enthusiastic than I about dancers reversing age and sex roles as they do it in classical Kabuki in Japan. But where is the actress who can convince us aesthetically that she is Jesus Christ? Nevertheless Miss Ruth's "Lama sabachthana" was spoken so that no one laughed, however they may have felt about this casting of a white-haired woman in the Christian god role.

A week before the performance the musicians, the costumes, the dancers came together for the first time. Only one thing was lacking, and that was an ending to the composition. When we reached the stage after the processional at a new section in the music, Miss Ruth turned to Jack and said sweetly, "Jack dear, we have different ways of working, I know. You are a perfectionist who likes to proceed step by step; I like to have a clear concept of the whole before I begin to move. I have two questions, dear, so that I can perform my part better. Can you tell us how we are to speak with the solo instruments, do we come ahead of the oboe or the trumpet, or under it, or after it? And just what is the conclusion to be, so that we can gauge our tension in the work as a whole?"

The musicians stopped, the dancers stood still, everyone focused on the choreographer. Vulnerable Jack, who was straining every nerve nightly at the Rainbow Room and commuting to the college by day, was unprepared. His face flamed. He walked a perfect circle of rage, raised his shoulders, shouted: "I'm through with the whole thing!" and walked out.

My sympathies were with the star of the production, who was on a spot. Formal invitations had been sent out by the college, an audience was expected, and the work was unfinished. Among ourselves we set out to make some kind of recessional. In half an hour, some students rescued Jack from the empty railroad station and brought him back. I do not remember how Jack concluded it, I never read any review of this work, but my respect for St. Denis as a professional couldn't have been higher. She was a born performer, equal to any demand of voice or body, and her professionalism topped Jack's.

My next encounter with Miss Ruth was as a not too satisfactory landlady. After the dissolution of the Theatre Dance Company, Anna Austin phoned one day with good news: Miss Ruth, taking a studio at 55 Fifth Avenue, was making time available to special dancers. Anna showed me the empty space with a good parquet floor. At the first class session with students the studio seemed smaller; now two large candelabra occupied one end, large theatrical trunks reposed between them. As we moved about we discovered cracker crumbs underfoot, along with feathers and other souveinirs from Miss Ruth's parakeet, which was allowed the freedom of the place except at night, when it was caged.

In the middle of the third class a door opened and Miss Ruth made an entrance. "Pay no attention to me at all!" she called out cheerily, flourishing a long white arm. "Just go right ahead!" Keys rattled, lids banged, trunks squeaked as out tumbled Nautch skirts and tinkling bells. After some moments of searching and finding, Miss Ruth disappeared in clouds of colorful draperies.

When I arrived for the fourth session the studio was blue with smoke, freighted with the aroma of steak. The secretary came in, wringing her hands. Miss Ruth had forgotten the studio schedule and invited the president of Adelphi to dinner; it would be all right for the class to meet if we would please muffle the gong and keep the drum as quiet as possible. Thereafter I moved uptown to the Gertrude Hoffmann studio, a less exotic but more dependable place for work.

Jack's personal success was so great at the Rainbow Room that he was also booked to perform at Club Mañana. The Rainbow Room asked him for more shows, so he turned to Ernestine Day (former Denishawn dancer), Letitia, Fe Alf, George Bockman and me to make up a small *Ballet Intime* company for a six-week engagement at the Room.

He choreographed *Begin the Beguine, Pawnee Indian War Dance,* Ravel's *Bolero* and *Georgia Revival Meeting.* We opened on June 5. Raoul Pene du Bois designed the *Beguine* costumes, and Madame Karinska's seamstresses snatched the unfinished dresses from our shoulders the minute we got off the floor. Her detailed attention to lace-edged petticoat underseams had slowed the process. The Du Bois costumes were extravagantly beautiful; mine was an impossible ten pounds of flounces and a huge hat. For Jack, costuming was of

BALLET INTIME

Exotic dances directed by Jack Cole

AL DONAHUE and his celebrated society orchestra with Paula Kelly
EDDIE LE BARON and his tango rhumba band
NITA CAROL brilliant singer
EIGHT MEN OF MANHATTAN with melodies in modern rhythm

For reservations call Circle 6-4400

Rainbow Room
ROCKEFELLER CENTER
NEW YORK ★

The New Yorker *advertisement for Jack Cole's Ballet Intime: Eleanor King, Letitia Ide, Ernestine Day, George Bockman.*

prime importance: a beautiful fabric in itself was excuse enough for a dance. He ordered a black caracul Persian lamb coat made to his measure in Persia; theatrical substitute fabrics were not for him. But when it came to music, he compromised.

Ernestine Day, adopted "Princess" of an Oklahoma Indian tribe, had lived as a child on the reservation and knew the steps. She taught us the authentic Pawnee movement. Our twelve-piece costumes consisted of black wigs with two long braids, white fringed doeskin jackets, kilts, leggings, and enormous feather cartwheels attached to the back, plus armlets and anklets of feathers. Beating on our individual drums, we entered heel-toe, heel-toe in impressive fashion to drum beat. All this authenticity disappeared when Paula Kelly, soprano, sang a jazzed-up version of the "Indian Love Call," which Jack insisted was essential for a nightclub audience.

The girls alone danced the *Bolero*, costumed as "Penitentes in Seville in Holy Week." The dance, which progressed in additive form, first a solo, then duo, trio, quartet was one of continuous self-flagellation in three-four time. We beat ourselves with long cords from our waists. The dresses were princess style, black, with red-edged skirts, long red gloves, and red net snoods for our hair.

The dance which we all enjoyed and which was the real hit was the *Revival Meeting*, performed to "Swing Low Sweet Chariot," first played straight, then, inevitably, syncopated and jazzed up for an ecstatic ending. George had to slide across the floor on his knees, in a slant-back position—a Cole specialty—while we women shook our full ruffled skirts four times faster. One reviewer wrote: "This troup does an excellent job of expressing the dynamic frenziness of the body-shaking revivals. The number won an ovation, something unusual here." We were the "Most exciting moment of the evening," which featured Mary Martin, the Eight Men of Manhattan, a young Van Johnson, Paula Kelly, Al Donahue's Band and Eddie LeBaron's Latin American Band.

While the world was falling to pieces, we were booked for a return engagement at the Rainbow Room in August. On the 24th, Germany and the Soviet Union signed a ten-year nonaggression pact. On September 1, the war clouds burst: Hitler declared war on Poland; the Polish allies—England and France—declared war on Germany. The seven-year holocaust began on September 3. President Roosevelt declared a limited national emergency on September 8. To be dancing at all was incongruous. To be dancing nightly atop Radio City was to feel exposed and vulnerable, eerie, at that high level above the defenseless city. There it was spread out—the crossweb of streets and bridges, the ships moving in and out of the harbor, the beauty of the city lying open to the skies. Soon the bombs were falling on Europe. What but a whim of Hitler kept them from falling on New York?

If we were spared bombs, we were not spared currents of feeling, even in our insignificant little company of five dancers. Although Fe Alf wore a jeweled American flag pinned to her coat, her sympathies were with her native country. To her, America's democracy stank. What would make it a great country would be dictatorship. I asked her why, if she believed dictatorship was so superior, she didn't live in Germany. There was no reply. An abyss of divided feelings kept me silent in the dressing room. It was a difficult paradox to be united in the harmony of the dance with someone whose beliefs were inimical.

The second run at the Rainbow Room, descending to a wartime low, offered an Egyptian magician, Ali-Ali, a fakir who went from table to table pulling baby chickens out of his sleeve, "See little de chick-chick." Although *Billboard* picked Ballet Intime as a show possibility, we had a long winter without further work. I lived back home in Brooklyn.

This was the year when the D.A.R. barred Marian Anderson from singing at Constitution Hall, whereupon she sang for 75,000 people at the Lincoln Memorial, sponsored by Eleanor Roosevelt and Harold Ickes. John Steinbeck's *Grapes of Wrath*, William Saroyan's *Peace, It's Wonderful*, Thomas Wolfe's posthumous *The Web and the Rock* appeared. The House Un-American Activities Committee forced the Federal Theatre Project to close. *Life with Father* surpassed *Tobacco Road* and *Abie's Irish Rose* for a long run on Broadway. Dad enjoyed movies but hardly ever went to the theatre—he didn't have to; he could stay home and *imagine* it! Yet even he enjoyed the Clarence Day comedy. Movies that year included *Juarez* (Paul Mini); *Dark Victory* (Bette Davis); *Stanley and Livingston; The Ugly Duckling* (Disney); *The Wizard of Oz; The Women; Wuthering Heights; The Old Maid; Broadway Melody of 1940*. The theatre gave us *The Little Foxes, No Time for Comedy, The Man Who Came to Dinner*, Saroyan's *The Time of Your life*. Menotti's *Old Maid and the Thief* had its operatic premiere.

And gloom and darkness settled over the land.

CHAPTER TWELVE: 1940-1941

Roads to Hell

ONE BENEFIT of the Works Progress Administration was free art classes at the Brooklyn Museum. The life drawing class stimulated coordination of the eye and the hand. Rendering three dimensions in two was a fascinating discipline that might have a refining effect on future choreography. Our instructor, a pale young man with the *Daily Worker* in his pocket, looked over my shoulder the first day, scornfully observed, "You're just drawing *naturally*," and went on his way.

My real teachers were the others in the class, whose work and methods I studied during rest periods. There seemed to be an endless variety of approaches, tools, ways of seeing, drawing, accenting. The day the model for drawing failed to appear, I wandered over to the sculpture studio and was permitted to fashion a head in clay, without a model. The blind feeling for form in the fingers seemed to be instinctive, something you could just as well do with eyes shut. I preferred the limitations of line drawing and progressed to making two lithographs. "One More Spring," à la Daumier, was a sketch of the coachmen, horses and carriages opposite the Plaza Hotel as seen huddled under their blankets one snowy March day.

Nikolaides's book, *The Natural Way to Draw*, gave me assurance and practice which was like dancing too: alternating quick gesture studies, performed in one motion, with slow sustained contour drawings, never taking your eyes from the model, not looking at the paper, learning to feel the mass and pressure underlying the outline.

This was helpful later when I tried to record what was happening on the stage in Japan, where I couldn't take my eyes from the performer and often sketched in the dark.

Ballet Intime had a final flourish that spring. Margaret Sande replaced Ernestine Day, Katherine Litz replaced Letitia Ide. First we had two weeks at Monte Prosser's Beachcomber nightclub on Broadway. The clientele was not so upper-class as at the Rainbow Room but the backstage Chinese chefs and crew were always cheerful and friendly. The second two weeks we went to the Boston Beachcomber. The pleasant part was the boat trip to Boston; both Katey and I practiced drawing everything we saw. The South American band, whose musicians were mostly German, reinforced the pro-German feelings around us.

Ballet Intime's last stand turned out to be in vaudeville—and the best. At last we could dance in a real theatre on a real stage four times a day, with an orchestra in the pit. The Fox Theatre in Washington, D.C., a big movie house from the twenties period, was one of the last to offer vaudeville as well as the feature film. It was a stimulating, wonderful discipline to meet audiences four times a day, audiences who were there not for drinks and food but for seeing the performances on the stage. I lapped it up. What professionalism it took! We followed a boy-and-girl team of tap dancers whose dance-as-if-your-life-depends-upon-it intensity made our performances seem pale. Their shoddy material was lifted to an extraordinary level of give-and-take with the audience.

Our professionalism was sorely taxed the second week, when the feature film changed and the timing of the show altered. Somehow none of us noticed the new time bulletin in the elevator, which carried us five flights above the stage to our dressing rooms, completely sealed off from what was below. The only communication was by electric buzzer which gave fifteen, ten and two minute warnings. Sande and I were making up as the first buzzer sounded. "Come on, we must hurry, that's the first bell." We scrambled into our clothes. The second warning, two minutes to go. We rushed to the elevator, passing Fe, calmly swinging her legs. "Hurry, Fe, that was the second bell." Fe continued to swing her legs. "What do they think this is? I'm not warmed up yet." "Fe, this isn't the concert hall where audiences wait. This is *vaudeville*." Sande pushed me into the elevator, we stepped out on the stage level in time to hear the announcer finishing: "Direct from one year at the Rainbow Room—Jack Cole's Ballet Intime!"

As the orchestra began the *Bolero* introduction, Sande whispered,

"I'll go back and get the others, you fill in." Usually I was the third entrée; I filled in first, second, third and fourth entrees, interminably circling the stage, beating myself over and over, looking in vain in the wings for the others. When the music passed the change-of-key climax accelerating to the close, three white-faced dancers sallied out in time for the ending. The audience must have been mystified by this inexplicable solo which ended for no reason as a quartet. If it had been any but the repetitious *Bolero* piece, they might have known when to come in sooner.

A Summer Vaudeville Revue of the Starlight Theatre in Pawling, New York, asked me to perform the *American Folk Suite* every night in their barn theatre from July 22 to 27. This was an amusing experience in the country, living in a barn with all the actors. In the daytime, sketch book in hand, I wandered over the Berkshire farm with its enormous dairy barns, where several hundred head of cattle were milked to Musak twice a day. One morning I ventured into the barn during the process, to be greeted by hundreds of bawling, protesting cows, an unnerving experience. Cows, it seems, particularly object to women.

In the fall, I taught classes at the Westchester County Center in White Plains, composing a dance about bells for the children's classes. Curt Sachs, whom I consulted at the Music Room in the 42nd Street Library, suggested two thirteenth century stantipes for a *Juggler's Dance*. Trudy Goth, Elfrid Ide (Letitia's sister), Betty Colman, and Katey O'Brien helped with some demonstration performances there when we did excerpts from the *Ode to Freedom*.

The shock and horror of war in Europe left me with a feeling of hopelessness, of incapacity to create anything. Then I heard a recording of Hindemith's *Mathis der Maler*, which inspired me. It would be possible to dance even in wartime if one danced about some positive good in life. To the Angel Concert and Kreuzigung sections I made a pair of solos titled *Characters of the Annunication*, seeing Gabriel as a cool, impersonal, airy messenger of good tidings; Mary, earthy, startled, overwhelmed.

When Anna Austin of the Denishawn company came to claim some costume trunks stored at the Theatre Dance Company studio, she kindly presented me with a pair of long circular white net skirts from Denishawn's *The Lamp* production. One of these I dyed chartreuse for Gabriel, and edged the skirt with gilt brocade ribbon outside, a red ribbon underlining. The metallic border created incredible folds in action when I jumped in the air. Betty gave me her old made-in-London dressing gown, a red satin-backed silk crepe, which, with the insertion of a triangular piece in front, banded down the center in blue velvet ribbon, became a perfect materntiy dress for Mary. The first *Characters* performance was on December 22, on the Christmas Festival program in White Plains. Gradually, I realized I could do a whole solo program by adding to the Hindemith contrasting themes of good and evil. The winter of 1940-1941 was prolific. I composed a silent mime—*A Saint and a Devil; The Roads to Hell* suite: Pride, Sloth, Envy, Wrath; and, to end with, a lyrical sitting-lying-on-a-bench dance to Bach's chorale *Rejoice, Beloved Christians.*

Roads to Hell absorbed me for months; I read "Piers Plowman" Chaucer, the Catholic medieval conception of the sins and virtues, Dante's *Inferno.* Essaying all the seven deadly sins, I soon eliminated gluttony as indelicate, covetousness as too similar to envy, and lust as too trite. John Colman, excited about the idea, asked to do the score. "Please, don't let anyone else do it. *I* want to do it."

As soon as Pride, the first sin, was sketched, John came and improvised in what seemed to be a Mozartian vein. He was hoping to make the suite solve his composition problem at Juilliard. Pride, full of starts and stops, of pomposity, blows her own trumpet, beats drums and cymbals for attention, gets trapped in the end in her long medieval robe, making a stiff-necked, defiant ending.

With Sloth a negative bundle of emptiness, the music had to suggest the crises in the world. Sloth, reluctant to wake up, yawns and closes her eyes and ears, too indolent to make up her mind which crisis on the right or left side to answer, evades all responsibility by turning her back and going to sleep again. The struggle of political choice then going on—run to the aid of Britain, France, Belgium, the Netherlands, all in extremis—these were the real crises.

Envy's shape, the pursuit of what one doesn't have, mocking at others, wounding oneself, a catch-the-brass-ring merry-go-round, spiraling in on itself, spitting and hissing, ends in a perverse backward acceleration to the point of exhaustion.

Wrath, starting from the Chinese Sick Heart character, from the center of the body, erupts snakelike, spewing venom like a volcano, destroying only itself, the form disintegrative, the body rising and falling over continually beating knees moving in and out like flames.

By March the sketches were finished. John's music wasn't written down. "I can't get the climate of this one," he would say, at the piano. "Do it over again."

Sachs, invited to a rehearsal, commented, "She will never be mad. She has too much control." I was shaking myself to pieces in Wrath.

Eleanor King in Envy from Roads to Hell. *Photo by Thomas Bouchard.*

He postured on one leg, and asked, "Could you stay like this? It is how they rest in Africa."

The delightful old man was full of wisdom, if of the pedantic German school. His *World History of the Dance* contained declarative sentences such as "All dances beginning on the left foot denote matriarchal society." Fundamentally a mystic, he wrote about dance as the art "which is and gives ecstasy."

I determined to have two programs at the new Humphrey-Weidman Studio on West 16th Street, which, with 144 old Metropolitan Opera House seats on raised levels, and a good wide dance floor, was also a theatre. Transformed by Doris and Charles, the studio, which had formerly belonged to Arnold Weiss, the illustrator, was to serve for a decade or more as a modern dance theatre for them and occasionally for others. On April 27, with Grant Code as commentator and John Colman at the piano, we presented an introductory program on "The American Dance."

Two movement studies based on breathing, followed by a falling study—without resistance, with some resistance, with strong resistance, twisting-turning, and suspension; a swing study on three levels; a Bach Bourrée, Gigue and Mattachines (old French dance) demonstrating types of locomotion. Then projection of movement through space elements; rhythmic factors in timing, a study in 4/4 time moving from wholes, to halves, dotted halves, quarters, eights, triplets and sixteenth notes, against a musical background in reverse sequence from the movement, making strong counterpoint. A syncopation study had the audience clapping the steady beat. For characterization, I mimed a realistic action—sewing a glove—then stylized it, to Scarlatti. In costume, I danced *Song of Earth, A Saint and a Devil* and *Hornpipe.* This program we had successfully tried out at Katonah, New York, where I also taught classes.

The second date, May 28, was of prime importance: my first New York solo recital. Three weeks before, John phoned to say he would not after all be able to complete the score for *Roads to Hell* on which we had been working all winter. I remembered how Genevieve Pitot rescued *Candide* under similar circumstances and fortunately, Pitot was available. She came, took notes, went away, and returned ten days later with completed scores for all but the last dance. Again she took notes, went away and in a few days completed the extraordinary music which stunningly fit the concept. (In 1973, she arranged the score for symphony.) In performance she was a tower of strength at the piano. Grant Code supervised the lighting. New water color sketches of *Roads to Hell,* and photographs by Robert McAfee and Edward Moeller decorated the lobby.

Of course, it was the tag end of the season. I think both Doris and Charles were on vacation; José was in California or the army. At the same time Ernestine was scheduling an evening of her own dramatic and comic dances at the Theatre Studio at 15 West 67th Street, where she assisted her husband-director, Theodore Kommisarjevsky, in teaching movement to drama students. George Bockman was simultaneously appearing with his students at Adelphi College. Though it was the season's end, I had a full and an enthusiastic audience.

The only review, Martin's two-column Sunday article in the *Times* three weeks later, was worth waiting for:

. . . seven [of the eight dances] were of exceptional stature as creative works, and the performance they received was of a piece with their inherent quality. In these seven dances Miss King proved herself an exemplar of the modern dance who had actually got down to the substance of the art. Her years as a pupil of Doris Humphrey and a member of the latter's concert group were evident in her approach to movement, yet she was quite obviously not leaning on an established technique, but appeared to be drawing on inner experience for every impulse and every phrase. Equally obvious was her lack of concern with merely breaking away from established methods; often the surface of her dances was distorted and strange, but never was there the slightest seeking for the outre. Rarely, indeed, has one seen exemplified more completely or more convincingly the basic precepts of the modern dance concerning the objectification of emotional concepts in terms of self-dictated movement and form. An inward strength and a penetrating perception found for themselves an outwardness of uncompromising beauty in which perforce one believed.

It is too bad that those who are convinced beyond argument that when the modern dancer talks of abstraction he means detached lines and angles suspended in a void could not all have been present to see abstraction as the modernist really practices it—as the reduction of experience to an essence, the universalization of a personal insight into realities of one sort or another. One wonders, indeed, if what Miss King herself has been pursuing, during these several years since she set out on an independent career for the purpose of developing a dramatic theatre-dance, has not actually been the achievement of this genuine abstraction. If her program on this occasion satisfied her, then assuredly it has been. At any rate, what she has found is the heart and the true intent of modern dance.

He criticized costuming of the gunny-sack school and programming which

restricted to ecclesiastical and medieval subject matter (though in most cases what she had to say was without any limitation of period), but a certain

Eleanor King dancing Mary in Characters of the Annunciation.
Photo by Thomas Bouchard.

Eleanor King dancing Gabriel in Characters of the Annunciation.
Photo by Thomas Bouchard.

monotony and a definitely erroneous notion of the dancer's range of interests were inevitable.

For Miss King the merely pictorial is manifestly, and no doubt rightly, unimportant; eloquence, however, is the very sum and substance of her art.

There were unforgettable phrases in her Annunication characters of Gabriel and Mary. "A Saint and a Devil" proved to be an admirable dance without music, full of perception and comment rooted in a true humor. What one remembers best, however, after several weeks, are the dances of "Sloth" and "Envy" in the "Roads to Hell." Here too is the same quality of humor, that is not always provocative of laughter, indeed, but is consistently warm and understanding even when tinged with venom. All these dances were notable for their inventiveness, their relation to living emotion and their strong individuality.

In all of these [group compositions] as well as the earlier ones such as "Mother of Sorrows" and "Peace, An Allegory" there was a sense of authority and an originality that were not to be overlooked. Traces of the same feeling for movement, the same comedy turn, the same unorthodoxy were to be found in the compositions last month, but with them was a new maturity. It is difficult in the light of these works to go on any longer thinking of Miss King as merely a promising dancer and choreographer—she has definitely come of age as an artist. She should most certainly be dancing frequently, with an ensemble to support her and experts in costuming and presentation to assist her.

A late starter, a late bloomer. I was thirty-five years old.

The same gray woolen cloth pleated at the back of the neck and falling to the floor, which gave just the right amount of swank for Pride, was also the ideal blanket for lazy Sloth. With a medieval hood of the same wool, it also worked beautifully for the *Saint and a Devil*. A red crepe evening dress with cowl neckline, color removed, dyed gray, made an elegantly slinky dress for both Envy and Wrath. I bought it for two dollars at a benefit. But Martin was right about the heavy opaqueness of the costume for the Bach, designed and made by someone else.

The School of American Theatre, yet another drama school, employed me that summer to teach movement to students in Maplewood, New Jersey, which had a successful summer theatre. One of the youngsters, hired to play the "Buttons" bellboy role in *Her Cardboard Lover*, made enthusiastic noises over Tallulah Bankhead's professionalism. Every night after the show when the curtain came down, she continued to go over bits of business trying to improve the performance of the play, which was a piece of claptrap unworthy of her gifts. Maplewood was extremely hot and, except for the weekly shows, unstimulating.

Then came a mystifying note from John Martin. He wished to talk to me before I signed myself up for the next season. "Big doings are in the air which are and must be secret."

John Colman had brought Fritz Cohen, musical director of the Jooss Company, to the Gertrude Hoffmann Studio on West 56th Street where I rehearsed, and I had performed *Roads to Hell* for Fritz. It seemed that Elsa Kahl (Mrs. Cohen) was about to retire from leading roles with the company, and they were considering me for her parts—among others, the dramatic role of the Mother in *The Green Table.*

A more explicit note from Martin kept my mind in a whirl. He had broken the rules to mention "the secret plan," but a letter from Fritz Cohen in which he mentioned that he wanted me to join the Jooss company made him do it.

The plan is a great American dance company with everybody in it and me directing, and half the money is already raised. Until the other half is raised, however, I will not play. The chances look pretty good and I would not be surprised if by the fall I should be able to talk to you definitely. Meanwhile I wanted you to know that there was something in the air. It is vague where the Jooss proposition is definite, but that is up to you to decide about.

I would like to have you both as dancer and choreographer, and have already got a scenario in mind for you to do. Martha and Doris and Charles and Tamiris and Junger and all the others who are significant are to be in it, and these particular ones have been talked to and are enthusiastic. Oh, yes, Hanya, too, of course.

On a Thursday when John Martin came in from Old Mystic, Connecticut, to make up his Sunday *Times* column, we lunched together. Nothing more was revealed about the great American dance company, but he put me on guard about signing a Jooss contract; the prospects did not seem very good. The Shubert's were offering to take them coast-to-coast on a national tour. As it happened, John was right. The Shubert offer collapsed; the Jooss company disbanded, scattering its members to the four winds. Jooss and Ernst Uthoff left for Chile, and Martin's "something in the air" remained, alas, also in the air.

December 7, 1941. The shock of Pearl Harbor. America went to war with Japan on December 8 and with Germany and Italy on December 11, as the Axis powers declared war on us. A pall of darkness descended on the country, on everyone, on everything. Stunned, I watched Father put up black window blinds as blackout precautions. The practice warning sirens became a weekly nuisance. The great seven-year disruption began: people in uniforms, people moving from one part of the country to another, rationing, scrimping, hoarding for some, and a fever of work at defense jobs in plants which operated in three shifts around the clock. As one Englishman said, "America wages war not as a science or an art, but as a business." Stores were thronged with women workers in fur coats over blue jeans who spent large paychecks as fast as they made them. In Los Angeles, Ruth St. Denis joined the work force to become another "Rosie the Riveter." In New York, I remember a meeting chaired by Louis Horst at the Humphrey-Weidman Studio, where dancers, eager to share and be actively contributing, discussed what they could do in the war effort. Of course, they could always be counted on to perform as entertainers. How to reach the army camps, how to be effective, were the questions. Erick Hawkins spoke wisely and well at that moment.

Life went on, but with an electric undercurrent. Who would, who would not, be drafted? For many women the war was an opening wedge. Soon many of them were in uniform too; and, thanks to that, a college opening would give me an opportunity to leave New York and start on my way west, out of the bleakness, harshness and severity of wartime New York.

The YMHA initiated another series of programs to feature young dancers on January 18, 1942. Twenty dances in one afternoon made up the concert in the familiar, and to modern dance indispensable, Kaufmann Auditorium. Neomi Aleh-Leaf performed Yemenite dances, *Yom Shabat (Sabbath Day)* and *Betrothal Celebration*, excerpts from the 52nd Chapter of Isaiah; and to Arabian melodies, *Flower Vendor* and *Street Dancer*. Nelle Fischer danced *Sarabande, Mad Maid's Lament, Mountain Song,* and *Soubrette '49 Suite:* Banjo, Jig, Hornpipe, Ballad. Elizabeth Waters danced *This Believing World; Try, Try Again* and, with a group, a Mexican ballet. Nina Fonaroff's *Four Dances in Five* consisted of Harlequin Naive (1600) to music of Shostakovitch; Queen of the Amazons (1750); Cafe Chantant 5 a.m. (1890) to Larmanjat; and Hoofer on a Fiver (1900) to Tcherepnine.

Yankee Doodle Greets Columbus, 1492, to music of Louis Horst, was danced by Nina Fonaroff, Jane Becker, Maureen Blum, Jeanette Friedman, Iris Mabry, Minna Morrison and Evelyn Shaw.

Welland Lathrop, the only man dancer, gave his *Three Characters for a Passion Play* (Béla Bartók) and *Harlequin,* a restoration of the commedia dell' arte character of the fourteenth and fifteenth centuries.

My dances were the Bach *Song for Heaven,* Sloth and Wrath from *Roads to Hell* and the premiere of *Novella* to music of Purcell and Scarlatti. Partly a mime-dance, a young girl stitches up a glove, reads a letter, dances for joy. The costume, an ochre-colored dress with circular skirt and sleeves and a velvet girdle, was romantic. John Martin, who had to introduce the program, wrote afterward that the program was overgenerous in length, breadth and thickness. Perhaps it was the last time he reviewed anything so far from Broadway.

My feeling about fascism was given another exercise. Betty Colman recommended me to one of the Group Theatre directors to mime the role of Italia while Arturo Giovanitti's poem of that name was recited at Madison Square Garden. This was a benefit program on February 1, presented by the Italian-American Labor Council, which was anxious to prove its devotion to the United States. After the Philharmonic played and the Metropolitan Opera stars sang, a $20,000 check for the Red Cross was presented to New York's much loved "Little Flower," Mayor Fiorello La Guardia. He said, "Fascism can't produce beautiful music. All fascism has given the world is bombast, bluster, blood, discord, murder, war and defeat. Right there in Madison Square Garden is the real spirit of the liberty-loving people of Italy. America's victory is Italy's freedom."

The lights went out. Dressed in black, with ropes around my arms, I was led to a high narrow platform in the center of the arena. A spotlight from Eighth Avenue pinpointed downward as an invisible Italian speaker read Giovanitti's eighteen verses. Kneeling, I mimed the tragic fate of Italy, at the climax tearing off the drab rags, throwing the cords away, standing up liberated from the bonds of fascism, in a classic white robe, shoulder grided with the Italian colors. The emotional Italians were crying and shouting. As a stage hand guided me on trembling legs through the ropes and cables to the exit he informed me, "You really knocked 'em dead. No kidding. A man in the balcony just died from a heart attack."

The Correro D'America described the close of the poem:

Con un ponderoso gesto la donna, L'Italia, rompe le catena che il brutale facismo le aveva posto ali bracchia, getta il miserabile mantello della schiavitu e, devanti ogli occhi dei 25 mila spectatori appare la donna coperta dai tre color naxionali. La liberta risplended mouvamente su Roma, la Citta Eterna. Il monologo suscita un delirio di applausi fra i presenti.

With a weighty gesture . . . she broke the chains . . . on her arms; threw off the miserable mantle of slavery, and before the eyes of 25 thousand spectators, appeared resplendent Liberty in a robe with the three national colors. The monologue received a delirium of applause from the audience.

Noel Coward's In Which We Serve, Greer Garson in Mrs. Miniver, Tracy and Hepburn in Woman of the Year and James Cagney in Yankee

Eleanor King in the Bouchard-Howorth film Modern Dance —a Technical Approach.

Eleanor King representing "Italy in the bonds of facism."
Photo: Herald Tribune / Rice.

Doodle Dandy were films which fed our patriotism or our need for relaxation. Gershwin's *Porgy and Bess* was the triumphant opera of the year. Thornton Wilder's *Skin of Our Teeth,* with its humorous-frightening second act on the boardwalk at Atlantic City, red signal lights heralding the end of the world, was the paradigm of our times.

Now the Japanese were in Manila; the Philippines had been lost at Corregidor. In the States all Japanese-Americans were rounded up and placed behind barbed wire in concentration camps. The WPA ended; rationing of food, clothing and gasoline regimented the scarcities. Under Eisenhower, the allied armies in North Africa were attempting to drive out the German army under Rommel; the Air Force, based in Naples, was bombing Italian cities. The twenty-six nations now at war with the Axis powers were in effect the nucleus of the United Nations.

That spring in New York some Bennington students worked with me on Bach's *Brandenburg Concerto No. 3* for five dancers and the *Beasts and Saints* fable, for eight. Dora Richman composed a piano and tenor setting, oratorio style, to my adaptation of Helen Waddell's superb Latin translations of early Christian fathers. With Emily Winthrop Miles's hundred dollar check, we were able to costume both works. Carolyn Gerber designed aqua/mulberry parti-colored short dresses for the Bach, one arm bare, one long-sleeved. Molly Howe designed the abbott's brown burlap hooded robe, stiff Romanesque monk's robes of unbleached sailcloth with round brown collars; a dhoti of yellow terrycloth with turban and scarf striped like Rousseau's "Sleeping Gypsy" for the camel driver; and suitable headdresses, gloves, tails and body suits for the lion and the donkey. The lyrical Bach and the humorous *Beasts* had a preview on June 18 at the Humphrey-Weidman Studio Theatre.

I had vowed that there would be no more camps for me, yet when a "Four Winds Camp" in Michigan offered six weeks of freezing by the waters of Lake Michigan, I had no alternative but to accept. I was without a college degree, non-U. But at the end of the summer, Carleton College, whose dance instructor had joined the WAACs, offered me a post in that small, prestigious liberal arts college in Northfield, Minnesota. Carleton would house me, feed me, and supply dance students—all girls. All the men who were dancers or potential dancers were drafted, enlisted or working in defense. The great dearth, it would be a world without men—except in the "theatres" of mechanized killing—for years more.

On both branches of the family tree, ancestors had fought for the American Revolution; neither grandfather participated in the Civil

War; Dad had been too old for World War I; but now younger brother Robert Emmett, a physicist, would work on secret material for RCA, and John, youngest in the family, drafted, would be mustered out from basic training with a permanent back injury.

Over the years I had become what I wished to be, a dancer. Starting with solos, then duets with José and trios with him and Ernestine and Letitia, I had choreographed for The Little Group, for twenty-one dancers in *Icaro,* for the cooperative Theatre Dance Company and for the Bennington Festival (groups of ten). In the right place, the collective dream of the Theatre Dance Company had come at the wrong time. In today's era of foundation grants for the arts, the concept could easily be realized. Perhaps in another fifty years an American Dance Repertory Theatre will also materialize to preserve and continue to express the qualities of American life.

We had danced gaily, sadly, hopefully, in torment, in despair, in love, in ecstasy—for all the reasons; without any music at all, as well as to folk tunes, early American melodies, Italian verse, and opera choruses, accompanied variously by accordion, piano, trumpet, symphony orchestras and night club bands and in places ranging from studio lofts to a cowbarn, in summer theatres, in college gymnasiums, in Philadelphia's Academy of Music and Robin Hood Dell, and in New York's Lewisohn Stadium, Metropolitan Opera House and Madison Square Garden.

Because of—or perhaps in spite of—the war, when keeping a group together was impossible, I had achieved the expedient form of a solo concert. In New York I had gone as far as I could. I heard the refrain, "Go West, young lady, go West." And so I did.

Appendixes
Notes
and
Index

APPENDIX A

PERKINS HARNLEY, the only living artist represented in the National Gallery of Art in Washington, D.C., is a self-taught artist who recorded Victoriana for the Index of American Design and designed the continuity sketches for the film *The Picture of Dorian Gray.* Two of his pictures are in the Metropolitan Museum, New York. His most recent exhibit was a joint show with Picasso at the Los Angeles Municipal Gallery. In 1973 his one-man show traveled to London, Berlin, Paris and Sidney, Australia.

Perkins Harnley to EK, February 18, 1974.

It was through me that José met Doris and Charles. I met him through Archie Schloker, tray wiper at the Colonial Cafeteria in Los Angeles in 1925. José was in the same class as Robert Young at Lincoln H.S. in L.A. The graduating class presented a play, "Sherwood." Robert was Robin Hood. Archie was King Richard and José was Big John. José and his boyhood buddy, Edgar Jones, went to New York from L.A. by motorcycle. On the way Edgar was bitten by a rattlesnake. José administered first aid and there was no serious result. Don Forbes and I started to take José to meet Ted Shawn. On the way to Van Cortlandt Park we stopped at Doris' and Charles' studio on 16th Street [actually 59th Street] to say hello. Pauline was at the piano. She turned and saw the Mexican beauty. And she said to herself, "I'll have HIM." We never got to Ted Shawn's. Three weeks later José appeared on the stage at the Guild Theatre in the background of one of Charles' numbers.

Doris had difficulty being an extrovert. She was pretty much closed up within herself. Her professionalism was complete. She was one hundred percent dedicated to her art. Her private life was secondary. She was objective. She was personally evasive, cold and undemonstrative sentimentally . . . "When I'm about forty," she confided to me, "I'm going to meet a correct man and have a baby." This she did exactly as planned. [She was thirty-eight.] . . . Doris would not yield to criticism from anyone in regards to the nature of her dancing. . . . She worked like a drudge. The only help she ever received was from the Rockefeller Foundation. They paid for the steel beam which supported the ceiling of the studio-theatre, her own institution. There was no similarity to Doris' work and that of Martha Graham. Doris never went in for tricky sensationalism. She never strove to startle or indulge in the wholly unexpected. Much of her work was sheer lyricism. But the folk element was supreme. She was one of the two queens of flat foot dancing.

Now Pauline is something special, as she used to say, "like a prize cow with bulldog tenacity." Most of the heavy burdens fell upon her patient shoulders. She was the indomitable backbone of the Humphrey-Weidman creative endeavors. After the principals left the Denishawn menage and became independent, Pauline took absolute charge of the management, music, [costumes,] domestic concerns and fund raising miseries. Publicity, travel, ironing out of emotional problems in the family and group fell to her ever-able intelligence. After you left the group and began on your own Pauline had a nice confab with you when you stressed "Theatre." She was impressed by your emphasis of theatre. She held you in very high esteem. Of course a wee bit miffed at the loss of you in the family.

I think that Pauline's greatness came out when she took hold of José after he left Charles and became a lost sheep. She drew upon all of her forces: moral, aesthetic and practical to establish José on a sure footing. There was a chaotic period in his life when his energies were scattered in a lack of self-assurance and sense of direction. He was piddling around in San Francisco getting nowhere. "I'll have him!" she said when first seeing him. Now she took possession. He was too weak to resist. Perhaps unconsciously he used her for selfish purposes. Nevertheless it was inevitable that they work together and love together. She repeated her process of directing his career as she had Doris's. It worked. They did triumph. There was a strong spiritual alignment. They reached an impressive artistic apex and folded up their lives together.

Perkins Harnley to EK, March 18, 1974.

When he was sixteen Charles worked for the Lincoln, Nebraska Telephone Company. His salary was about twelve or fourteen dollars a week. He went to school full time, his job on the side. In school he took art and on the side dancing lessons from Eleanor Frampton. He was in the chorus of Madame de Vilmar's opera class at the University. He made his own costumes and batique lamp shades for his friends. A busy boy!

Always he carried a briefcase stuffed with clippings of famous opera stars, movie stars, stage actors and dancers. He painted stage scenery for Madame de Vilmar's productions. In art class the other students did nothing but look at his collection of famous people in his briefcase. In that class Charles did nothing either. It was the only place which he was at leisure. One of our teachers was the sister of Willa Cather, the famous writer. The latter did novels of early Nebraska settlers. Richard Barthelmess was Charles' favorite actor.

His father was twice married. His second wife was named Carrie. Charles' mother was twice married. His sister Lavonne was affectionately close to him.

From earliest memory Charles wanted to own a farm with an antique house full of furniture and bric-a-brac characteristic of early American designs. His father's house was crammed full of heavy carved teak wood furniture which he had purchased in the Panama Canal Zone when he was Fire Chief there during the construction of the Canal. When Charles had the dance parts of "As Thousands Cheer" he made alot of money and his dreams of a farm came true in a big way. He realized all of his cherished dreams of early American architecture and artifacts.

When Doris married Leo Woodford it affected Charles. However, by that time the family had become so integrated domestically that they took one another for granted, Platonically.

The family lived gracefully regardless of periodic financial difficulties when their close friend and patron Adele Brandwen came to the rescue with money. The family had a natural appreciation for festive occasions. They made much of birthdays and season's holidays. There was a high spirit of camaraderie at dinner time, each meal was a picnic put away with decorum. Even in their very busy days this mood persisted.

[His] sense of satire was immense. As a child in Lincoln he and some neighbor kids put on shows in a barn. Ralph Bowers and Varney Ferris were co-producers. They did fairy tales and ballets. Their costumes were made from tinted cheesecloth and Christmas tree tinsel. This primitive attempt at theatricality matured until Charles' name appeared in lights at the old Madison Square Garden . . . the occasion made triumphant by its sponsors, a left wing union of some sort.

Bill Matons has ended up selling "Free Press" papers and Socialistic literature. He wears a uniform covered with medals and an officer's cap spouting a cardboard rocket; he dances on the street and exudes his childish charm unbecoming to his age and appearance.

APPENDIX B

HELEN SAVERY graduated from Barnard in 1929; danced in *Lysistrata* that year, and was with the Humphrey-Weidman group from then until 1934.

Helen Savery to EK, December 12, 1972.

What really happened in my small world, I suppose, was that I had some natural ability as to movement, style (Doris commended this), spirit, etc. But I had no early dance training and only the "natural dance" at college. Therefore, since they needed dancers badly at this time of their break from Denishawn, I was, to a certain extent, usable. It was not long, however, before she realized that I needed lots of technical training in order to do some of the difficult things she was beginning to be interested in. It was unfortunate that they could not have given us daily classes (like ballet co's do) while choreographing. She insisted that I take classes at that uptown studio, or New School for S. R., but I could hardly afford to live, let alone pay for classes. From my viewpoint they were unrealistic in this respect, expecting their group to be financially independent, and somehow miraculously meeting their complicated rehearsal and performing schedules. Of course I was wildly excited about the whole thing in the beginning and would have gladly given my life for them, I suppose, but disillusion took over, and the struggle became altogether too tough and unrewarding. Perhaps I was beginning to realize that I never would achieve in that area, and my departure was a reluctant but a sound decision.

Letter from Helen Savery to EK, no date:

Doris told me once that I should work hard to stretch. "I believe there is no limit to which the human body can be stretched." I marveled at this and, revering her as a goddess, nearly killed myself trying to get stretched. Even went to one of those barbarous professional stretching studios off Broadway. He forced my leg up in back to touch my head (one of those timely acrobatic gestures so necessary to vaudeville performances of the period). It caused a back injury from which I still suffer. I can still see her, rising from her improvised cot back of the studio piano (shortly after the birth of her baby) stretching herself unmercifully in preparation for rehearsal with us for that Lewisohn Stadium concert of a Spanish number [Sarabande, from the *Roussel Suite*].

Another time, I took a taxi with her from one of the classes she was teaching uptown (the beginning of Juilliard?—near Riverside and 80th?). I mentioned my surprise to have seen a front page story of her marriage in the day's paper. She laughed and said, "You thought I was only interested in Dance?" Somewhere downtown near her apartment we went into a restaurant below street level where we could see only the walking legs of workers scurrying home at the end of the day. She looked up and exclaimed something like this, "Poor creatures, they just have no idea what life is all about, do they?"

There were times when I used to resent the fact (in retrospect) that we were used, not trained, that we were expected to somehow support ourselves in spite of depression rigors and still be on hand at all hours for rehearsals and performances. However, I have to recall that in the very beginning when they plucked me out of a class on 59th street and asked me to join the Understudy Group, she clearly told me there was only hard work and no money—but those enchanting words, "Both Charles and I feel that you have talent and we'd like you to be with us," . . . who could resist? Her voice quality was so beautiful. I remember she always said "side-wise" instead of side-ways. I assumed that a creature so perfect must have been right.

I have a feeling that I may have appeared indifferent at the time, but I don't think that was the case. I revered Doris so much that it was very difficult for me even to talk to her. If I could only have had the ability to do really good work (background training, etc.) and had enough money to give me even a minimal living, I would have been happy to follow her to the end of my days or hers, at least.

One time, at a dinner given for us on the road I remember sitting next to her and commenting, "You really should start writing your autobiography and the history of your Dance Family." She laughed and said, "The history of this family is something that will never be written." She must have had a keen sense of humor though it rarely showed.

Yes, I was astonished at her background [as revealed in the autobiography]. I had always imagined that it was lovely, luxurious, cultured and somehow perfect. I never dreamed that it involved near-poverty, nor such hard work that was demanded of her at such an early age. She must have had to educate herself and done a lot of independent research for her dances. For all her delicacy she had guts to revolt against her mother's dominance and to find her way to Denishawn.

In many ways it was all the most exciting time of my life, the most baffling, and the wrench I felt when I found I had to leave the group cut so deep that I think I never did recover from it. Perhaps it was simply the realization that my dream of being a dancer was shattered and that I faced the naked truth that I could never really succeed and must try for other goals.

Letter from Helen Savery to EK, November 1973.

Why did I leave the group? Here goes, as best I can remember and who can truly see it all accurately, from this great distance. Backward, turn backward oh time in your flight—Make me a dancer, just for tonight! How I wish I could go backward and interview that girl, Gale Savery, and see if she was able to tell me what truly happened to her then. Too bad dancers are too busy to keep journals. (Probably Agnes de Mille did.)

1. Financial struggle acute during the depression. I was literally alone in NYC, having arrived after graduation with $5 in my pocket. No help from family. No knowledge of theatre—no connections except a tenuous one with Candace Payne who had taught "Natural Dancing (hearts and flowers)" at Barnard. She had a studio over the 55th St. Cinema where I eventually lived in return for scrubbing the studio floor (an acre) and demonstrating for her classes.

2. Low achievement level. Others in the group seemed better established, had better technique, and seemed to have closer relationship to D. and C. I always felt like an outsider.

3. Eventually, I *think*, the struggle to survive in every way eroded my pure love for and excitement about Dance.

Re: technique—Doris' development of "distortions" (remember?) seemed strange and terribly difficult to me. I could not understand what she was doing, and I found them physically harmful.

Re: her choreography and creative approach—I loved the Shakers best for I could release something emotionally. Perhaps I was more oriented towards acting but hadn't then discovered it. Her intellectually design-oriented dance rather puzzled me and left me cold at times. Being used as a component of a group finally became uninteresting to me, and yet I did not have the courage, ability? or *foundation* to become anything else.

APPENDIX C

ADA KORVIN-KROUKOVSKY to EK, September 23, 1972.

Now I'll tell you what I think about Doris Humphrey. Once a member of her group spoke to her about "compromises." Doris said, "There were no compromises in my life," and I think this is the most important truth about her. The other characteristics: she was always remote, always distant; she was never angry, never irritable. Subconsciously I felt sometimes her mood. For a while she wanted to have more contact with members of her group. She was beginning to work at her new dance "Atavisms." The last third part was called "Bargain Counter" and I danced in it. [*Atavisms* was Charles Weidman's choreography.] The second was (I think) about Sports. Only men were dancing in it. The first one I do not remember. Doris spoke to the group and asked if they had suggestions, but nobody had anything to say. I had the feeling that it made her quite unhappy.

Another time she asked us at what time we would like our daily rehearsal. Everyone wanted it at a different time, so finally Doris said, "If you want to be a member of my group, you must come for the rehearsal at 9 o'clock every morning." Probably for the first time she realized that she had to give us orders and that only orders would keep us together. The happy moment in her life, I feel, was when with the same quiet face she told us, "I shall not be able to do the solo in this dance, as I intended to. I am expecting a baby."

I do not know anything about Doris' childhood and about her family, and I don't think anybody does. She certainly did not have any money—I remember our rehearsals and lessons in the cold, unheated studio. I always thought that she was the most talented dancer and choreographer. Her "Water Study," "Shakers," "New Dance," were real masterpieces—much better than anything created by Martha Graham. Once I was greatly surprised by her judgment and completely disagreed with it. It was her dance "The Life of the Bee," based, I think, on Maeterlinck's story. We just moved up and down the stage, pretending that our arms were the wings of bees. At that particular time she got an offer to appear with her group in a night club. She accepted it, and her choice of the dance for the night club was "Life of the Bee." Fortunately it was cancelled very quickly. It was the time of unions, but Doris did not wish to belong to a union, and therefore, when we danced in various musicals, we were paid much less than the other members of the cast.

I just looked in my Columbia Encyclopedia. Ruth St. Denis is mentioned there. Everybody who is interested in the dance knows Martha Graham, Charles Weidman and José Limón. Only Doris is completely forgotten and probably she was the most talented of them all.

Ada Korvin-Kroukovsky to EK, October 3, 1973.

The picture on your note looked as if it was choreographed by Charles Weidman. No. I haven't read "An Artist First" but I have this book and I shall read it as soon as I finish the one with which I am involved (Biography of Dostoevsky by his wife). Then I shall write to you what I think about it.

All this time I have been working on my diary, which I started when I was

14 years old; I wrote practically every day, so that the tragic events (war, revolution etc.) are described not in the past, but as they were approaching, when nobody as yet knew that they would be so tragic. One copy of my diary is at the Herbert Hoover Archive Institution and the other I shall send to Poland. Quite unexpectedly I received a letter from Gdansk, Poland, asking me to send them my diary. They probably heard about it from my Polish relatives who visited us in July. It is 66 pages long (typewritten) and some of the words became quite illegible, so I have to retype them.

APPENDIX D

H Y L A R U B I N S A M R O C K , to EK, January 15, 1974.

My recollection, like others you mention, is also fragmented . . . as this is going back 40 years and I was with the group between the ages of 13 and 17 . . . during which time adolescent growing pains must have obscured and colored real events.

I enjoyed the new book "Doris Humphrey: An Artist First," by Selma Jeanne Cohen. The first section, a memoir by Doris herself and all too brief, was particularly interesting. José's obituary (Dec. 3, 1972, N. Y. Times) was a fine tribute to both José and Doris. His development in later years was phenomenal, and this thought, of his, particularly impressed me. After seeing a performance of H. Kreutzberg and Y. Georgi, he remarked, "A man could, with dignity and a towering majesty, dance. Not mince, cavort, do 'fancy dancing' or show-off steps. No: dance as Michelangelo's visions dance and as the music of Bach dances." In a sense this sums up (at least for me) what it was all about then.

Recently I attended two revivals. "Water Study" by the Ballet Company of Kennedy Center, Washington, D.C. Their ballet technique was insufficient for this work. Imagine, they couldn't do successions! Secondly, I saw the "Shakers" done by Juilliard students. The fervor, intensity, and basic meaning were gone. "Day on Earth" fared much better . . . but did not compare to the performances of Letitia and José.

I remember Doris climbing the three flights of rickety narrow stairs, to the top floor studio on 18th Street, one month after the baby was born. She looked pale and wan, but within a few hours, with deft choreographic strokes she straightened out the mess of the "Roussel Suite" . . . with which we had been struggling for weeks before. I remember her dancing the "Sarabande," several weeks after this . . . at the Lewisohn stadium still pale and wan, in order to honor the contract for these concerts, which stated that she must appear, no matter how briefly. I remember her clear explanations of "Pleasures of Counterpoint," "Dionysiaques," and "La Valse," and the thrill of being part of the creation of those works.

I remember painful things too. Doris demanded the most from her "girls," expected it was all right for them to starve for their art. Unless you had an outside job (which you were expected to relinquish anytime out of town engagements or tours came along), or you had someone rich to house and feed you . . . you could not survive the rigors of the dance field. I can't remember the Group Fund or José's operation. There was a feeble attempt at organizing, and someone suggesting (possibly me, fresh kid that I was) that all finances be shared equally, and that if they, D. and C., expected us to starve in garrets, why then they should be prepared to do likewise (a highly impractical idea).

The other painful part was Doris' change of style and technique. Whereas the above-mentioned period was naturalistic and lyric . . . she then began to experiment with distortions . . . which may have contributed to the eventual break-up of the early group.

APPENDIX E

G EORGE B OCKMAN to EK, November 18, 1973.

How and when did I join the H.W. Group? I had seen a performance at the old Guild, been to a rehearsal up at Denishawn and was not only fascinated but bitten with a determination to try.

At Denishawn they were rehearsing a marvellous recreation of Miss Ruth's Angkor Vat legend that came to life from her composition of the frieze sculptures. Of course I knew about that because I had been an art student at Pratt where we were exposed to many cultures at the same time we were involved in general design studies, and later in interior design and architecture. I recall Miss Ruth as the snake goddess, the marvellous costumes and headdresses, and one young man who stood out in his dance presence. I could not understand why he danced with his eyes cast down to the floor, but later on in H.W. discovered he was none other than old Jack Cole! . . .

Of the H.W. concert I recall the Water Study (which Louise and I saw ten days ago performed by the National Ballet) the Counterpoint (me-you-you-me-me-you-me-you-you etc.!) I seem to recall Charles in Kinetic Pantomime and I think the Life of the Bee.

Of course we graduated from art school with the depression in full swing and when I was unemployed I was lucky to have gravitated into a social group that loved opera, theatre, etc. . . . I met Irene McBride (at Fe Alf's studio) who was a student and was also dancing in As Thousands Cheer for Charles. She said I was foolish not to try out for a show, but I had no experience and was scared to boot! Irene took me to the Music Box one evening before half-hour and introduced me to Charles. He was most cordial and said I should come down to their studio and meet Miss Humphrey. That I did . . . and just watched spellbound at the group rehearsing. This was much overwhelming to me since I had only seen a group performance on stage, and to be in the same room with all that dynamic movement and powerful personalities was an experience I shall never get over. Doris was also very kind and encouraging, inviting me to return (with practice clothes) and work along with the group. What ever possessed me to do it I cannot tell you. But I did and it all worked out since I did not seem to get in anybody's way nor was I annihilated by the almost uncontrolled energies put forth by José and Bill Matons! I learned some of the repertory that spring and during the summer we began to hear of the School for Husbands.

That was my real initiation into the world of dance and theatre and still a high-light of the whole experience. I shall always remember Osgood Perkins, whom I could never watch enough from the wings. Also fascinating was the magician and his silver ball that flew up to June Walker's balcony! I loved the whole thing, including the two Egyptiennes, my having to rehearse on Saturdays inside of Marcus' bear suit, and all the enchantingly wonderful actors and actresses! Every time I think of all that plumed regalia I must chuckle.

APPENDIX F

KATHERINE MANNING to EK, November 17, 1972.

Doris and I would be together often with neither of us speaking. The only thing I can remember is excusing herself from Leo, Humphrey and me one day at Fire Island with, "Mommy has to go away and think now."

APPENDIX G

LETITIA IDE RATNER telephone comment, December 31, 1972.

Doris was a figure like your own mother filling your life.

APPENDIX H

GERTRUDE PROKOSCH KURATH pioneered the Dance Section of the Society for Ethnomusicology as dance editor for many years, and has contributed an enormous literature on dance, principally related to Amerindian culture.

Gertrude Prokosch to EK, December 20, 1972.

You know that I wasn't in Doris' group. It would have been a privilege but it didn't work out. But I haunted her studio in the spring of 1929. She encouraged the use of her studio for experimentation. Cleo and José and Jerome Andrews and Phoebe Guthrie were there. Weren't you? Nothing came of it as performance but it was fun. I'm sure that Doris' inspiration led to my Earth Mother, which I composed in the summer of 1930 (when Hans and I were in New York and I took lessons from Hans and Doris in all that ghastly heat). I think I showed the dance in her studio in the summer of 1931, when we were also in New York, also the Kyrie Eleison. Today those dances would seem dated. Yet I doubt whether anything inspired by Doris would ever be dated.

She was one of my idols. The other was Curt Sachs. She was not only a great dance pioneer, but a warm and human person, absolutely generous. Her son came into the world a year before my daughter Ellen. She sent me some of her son's baby clothes! How I prized them!

When I think of Doris I am really speechless. Her wonder, and then her dreadful suffering. Also, I think of José, her dance son, who died with similar suffering.

APPENDIX I

LEON ARKUS, director of the Museum of Art, Carnegie Institute, and, prior to World War II, a concert manager in the modern dance field, to EK, 1973.

You wanted to know about Martha Graham's performance. Met her again (after all these years) and she remains a dynamic and fascinating person.

I find I must differ with general acclaim afforded the Graham group. The performance without Graham herself appeared static, flat, devoid of emotion. How obtuse of me not to have realized how reliant Graham was on a theater as a prop for her dance. Theatre tends to evoke pageantry and what bland fare that is! Think back to Denishawn!

"Appalachian Spring" is dated and the aging process doesn't enhance it. Without Graham it lacks force and the vital focus that her personal projection gave it. I can't help thinking of Humphrey and Weidman. They had the enchantment, the intellect and humor that is so much more universal and long lasting. Even when their group appeared without them, it too had this spontaneity that was Doris Humphrey's. Perhaps Doris Humphrey was the greatest of them all.

APPENDIX J

P AUL L OVE , director of the Kresge Art Center Gallery, Michigan State University, East Lansing, Michigan, to EK, December 26, 1972.

I remember Doris in a full and rich but absolutely incoherent way. I am sure that she is choreographing bands of angels—a Bach Mass in B Minor with movement!

APPENDIX K

M ADELEINE G UTMAN'S impressions of Mikhail Mordkin, November 26, 1973.

I was ten years old in 1934. I have had a life-long "crush" on Mordkin since my mother first brought me to him in 1928. By that time although he still attempted the establishment of companies and tours—his interests had shifted from ballet technique to a more amorphous interest in "art" and theatre—which he expressed variously as "sunshine," "Don't poot face in pocket" in order to convey emotions. He was utterly confused by America, knowing that there was no tradition of classical dance, and that Hollywood "gangsters" and "Wild Indians" had captured the public imagination. Modern dance bewildered him as excruciatingly ugly and the worse insult for any student was to be told, "You want to do dot, you go to Martha Graham," or "You go to the Roxy," which he equated with vulgarity.

The tradition of the Bolshoi and his work in Russian theatre stimulated a great interest in mime and acting, which was also more appropriate to his mature years, although he retained enormous physical stamina and control beyond the capacities of much younger students. He was a great flirt but would have thought the portrayal of any direct real passion on the stage, not translated into 19th century balletic stylization, as unseemly. I have yet to see a film he made (1918)—a harem story à la Scheherezade—which I traced and managed to have the Dance Collection acquire for its archives but I suspect that it is a grandiose epic of frustrated passion replete with all the mannerisms of the silent movies—heaving bosoms, hands to anguished brows, etc.

He must have been terrified when confronted with a group of strange modern dancers, none of whom spoke Russian (I assume), in "Revenge," and his behavior was kind of overcompensation, I suspect.

I have heard that during the depression—when he kept up a killing schedule of teaching in a variety of distant, hard to get to places at pitifully small tuition—he fed, housed and taught many impoverished young dancers, like Bob Alton (who later became a successful Broadway choreographer) without seeing a nickel from them for years at a time. He arranged private studies for his pupils in music, art and drama academies, and many teachers in New York and throughout the U.S. are products of his studio, although most had supplementary training elsewhere.

What he insisted on was "dance" rather than routine performances of exercises, with a respect for the individual qualities of the dancer, and they came in all sizes and shapes in his studio. There was no "Balanchine body" set up as the ideal type.

Letter from Madeleine Gutman to EK, May 1, 1974.

In Russia he had worked with Alexander Tairoff, director of the Kamerny Theatre on several plays where he met Stanislavsky, who invited him to be director of Plastic and Rhythmic Education in the Moscow Art Theatre during World War I and the Revolution.

Mordkin settled in the United States in 1922, and sporadically toured with such artists as Vladimiroff, Volinine, Nemchinova, Sokolova in small companies under his own name.

Revenge with Music might have been Mordkin's first Broadway show, but in addition to staging shows for the Junior League, he did the second half of the Greenwich Village Follies staged by John Murray Anderson at the Winter Garden; in 1932 he was responsible for the dances in the Russian Grand Opera Foundation productions of Khovanchina, Coq d'Or.

[On Mordkin's classes] Not a great variety in Mordkin's classes, limited technique, and at times correction was not only verbal but accompanied by the flick of a wooden baton (used to keep time on a wooden bench) across an offending leg, foot or slumping back. Right from the beginning classes, he sought to elicit and communicate vitality, joy or serious emotion with energy and concentration from his students. Bland passivity was anathema even at the barre. He required great diversity of moods and tempi from the class accompanist at the piano.

[I'm] still dazzled by girlhood recollections of Mordkin, when he was regarded as the Nureyev of his time, as much praised for the virility of his dancing as for his physical beauty and nobility of deportment.

Letter from Madeleine Gutman to EK, May 4, 1974.

Doris' advice to her dancers during "Revenge" raises an issue still important today—that of orthodoxies and a kind of artistic chastity. I deplore the promiscuous transience of dance students moving from studio to studio in the vain hope that each teacher will reveal a magic trick to correct deficiencies and they will be "discovered," but I feel strongly that there are few situations from which a serious artist cannot profit and grow. Mordkin, remarking "You vohnt to do dot you go to Marta Gra-hahm," was guilty as Doris—two stubborn people clinging tenaciously to their illusion of revealed truth. Each should have said, "Here is an opportunity to learn from another master."

NOTES

CHAPTER ONE
1. (Page 17) Letters from Perkins Harnley to Eleanor King. See Appendix A.

CHAPTER TWO
2. (Page 35) Lawrence Langner, *The Magic Curtain* (New York: Dutton, 1951), pp. 224-227.
3. (Page 50) Letter addressed to Letitia, Doris Humphrey Collection, 1930. This and other Humphrey letters, unless otherwise specified, are from the Doris Humphrey collection, Library and Museum of the Performing Arts, Lincoln Center, New York.

CHAPTER THREE
4. (Page 66) DH to her parents, Julia Ellen Wells and Horace Buckingham Humphrey, hereafter indicated by the initials HBHs. January 1, 1931.
5. (Page 66) DH to EK, n.d., EK collection.
6. (Page 70) DH to HBHs, July 23, 1930.
7. (Page 73) DH to EK, n.d., EK collection.
8. (Page 73) DH to HBHs, op. cit.
9. (Page 73) DH to HBHs, ibid.

CHAPTER FOUR
10. (Page 81) Fokine's article, "Pathetic Art," is reprinted in its entirety in Winthrop Palmer , *Theatrical Dancing in America* , the development of the ballet from 1900 (New York : Bernard Ackerman, Inc., 1945), pp. 52-57.
11. (Page 83) DH to HBHs, February 22, 1931.
12. (Page 84) DH to HBHs, November 12, 1931.
13. (Page 90) DH to HBHs, n.d.
14. (Page 92) DH to HBHs, May 2, 1931.
15. (Page 97) DH to HBHs, ibid.
16. (Page 97) Helen Savery Hungerford to EK, December 12, 1972.
17. (Page 98) DH to HBHs, July 25, 1931.
18. (Page 99) EK collection, n.d.
19. (Page 113) DH to her husband, Charles Francis Woodford, n.d.

CHAPTER FIVE
20. (Page 114) DH to HBHs, November 8, 1931.
21. (Page 123) DH to her mother, Julia Wells Humphrey, May 17, 1932.
22. (Page 134) DH to EK, n.d.
23. (Page 135) Pauline Lawrence to EK, n.d.
24. (Page 135) DH to EK, n.d.
25. (Page 135) DH to HBHs, November 8, 1931.
26. (Page 135) DH to HBHs, January 1, 1931.
27. (Page 135) DH to HBHs, November 6, 1932.

CHAPTER SIX
28. (Page 142) DH to HBHs, March 28, 1932.
29. (Page 143) PL to DH, March 1, 1933.
30. (Page 143) DH to HBHs, January 2, 1933.
31. (Page 146) DH to herself, n.d.
32. (Page 146) "Those nude studies from her hoop dance show a body
        sculpted like a greyhound."—Tom Borek, book review of
        Selma Jeanne Cohen's *Doris Humphrey: An Artist First, Dance
        Scope,* Spring/Summer 1973, p. 45.
33. (Page 146) Helen Savery Hungerford to EK, January 12, 1972.
34. (Page 154) DH to HBHs, June 25, 1933.
35. (Page 154) Ibid.
36. (Page 154) Ibid.
37. (Page 156) Ibid.
38. (Page 158) Arthur Guiterman and Lawrence Langner, *The School for Hus-
        bands,* adapted in rhyme from Molière's comedy *L'école des
        Maris* (London: Samuel French Ltd., 1933).
39. (Page 161) See Appendix C.

CHAPTER SEVEN
40. (Page 181) DH to JWH, May 13, 1934.
41. (Page 186) DH to JWH, August 25, 1934.
42. (Page 186) DH to JWH, September 4, 1934.
43. (Page 188) Madeleine Gutman to EK, November 14, 1973. See Appendix
        K.
44. (Page 188) Ibid.
45. (Page 189) DH to EK, n.d.
46. (Page 190) DH to JWH, November 4, 1934.
47. (Page 190) DH to JWH, November 12, 1934.
48. (Page 190) DH to JWH, November 27, 1934.
49. (Page 190) DH to JWH, December 10, 1934.
50. (Page 192) John Houseman, *Run-Through,* a memoir (New York: Simon &
        Schuster, 1972).

CHAPTER EIGHT

51. (Page 200) DH to her husband, Charles Francis Woodford, January 21, 1935.
52. (Page 200) DH to CFW, January 14, 1935.
53. (Page 201) DH to JWH, February 3, 1935.
54. (Page 207) DH to JWH, February 23, 1935.
55. (Page 208) DH to JWH, March 27, 1935.
56. (Page 209) Margaret Lloyd, *The Borzoi Book of Modern Dance* (New York: Alfred A. Knopf, 1949).
57. (Page 210) Ibid.
58. (Page 211) DH to JWH, April 14, 1935.
59. (Page 211) DH to JWH, April 23, 1935.
60. (Page 212) Frankie Reed and Hyla Rubin to DH, March 19, 1935.
61. (Page 212) HR to EK, January 15, 1974.
62. (Page 213) DH to CFW, April 1935.
63. (Page 216) DH to JWH, May 30, 1935.
64. (Page 222) EK to EH, May 2, 1936.

CHAPTER NINE

65. (Page 228) Lauro de Bosis, *Icaro,* Translated from the Italian by Ruth Draper (New York: Oxford University Press, 1933).
66. (Page 228) Lauro de Bosis, *The Story of My Death,* Original text in French and a Biographical Note by Ruth Draper (New York: Oxford University Press, 1933).

INDEX

Numbers appearing in italics refer to illustrations.